MEMOIRS
of the
Erie County
Pennsylvania

BENCH AND BAR

Judge Emory A. Walling
OF THE ERIE BAR

HERITAGE BOOKS
2011

HERITAGE BOOKS
AN IMPRINT OF HERITAGE BOOKS, INC.

Books, CDs, and more—Worldwide

For our listing of thousands of titles see our website
at
www.HeritageBooks.com

A Facsimile Reprint
Published 2011 by
HERITAGE BOOKS, INC.
Publishing Division
100 Railroad Ave. #104
Westminster, Maryland 21157

Originally published:
Press of The Erie Printing Company
1928

— Publisher's Notice —
In reprints such as this, it is often not possible to remove blemishes from the original. We feel the contents of this book warrant its reissue despite these blemishes and hope you will agree and read it with pleasure.

International Standard Book Numbers
Paperbound: 978-0-7884-2668-1
Clothbound: 978-0-7884-8649-4

Emory A. Walling

TO THE MEMORY OF OUR DECEASED BROTHERS,
OF THE
ERIE COUNTY BENCH AND BAR,
THE AFTERGLOW OF WHOSE LIVES STILL LIGHTS US
ON OUR WAY,
THIS VOLUME IS RESPECTFULLY DEDICATED

Foreword

A reading of Albert H. Bell's very interesting "Memoirs of the Westmoreland County Bench and Bar" induced me to undertake the writing of this volume. The sketches are of course imperfect and in many cases inadequate, for which I crave indulgence. I have not attempted to mention all who appear on our roll: many were non-residents and others never entered upon the practice, at least in this county, and I have been unable to get any data as to some who probably did practice here in an early day. It is a relief to know that any errors or omissions can be corrected in a second volume, for which our committee is gathering information. The inability of securing photographs in some cases, and the greatly added expense, have discouraged any attempt at illustration. In addition, the group portraits of 1900 and 1920, in possession of many members of the bar, contain photographs of a majority of those about whom I have written.

I am under obligation to the committee of the Bar Association and many others, including the various county histories for help. With some exceptions, as in the case of father and son, or members of well known legal firms, I have inserted the sketches substantially in the order of admission to the Erie Bar. It may be assumed that those admitted to our bar were in due time admitted to the appellate and local U. S. courts, although such facts may not be mentioned.

EMORY A. WALLING.

Erie, Pa., September, 1928.

Hon. Thomas Hale Sill

Thomas H. Sill, son of Captain Richard Sill, was born at Windsor, Connecticut, October 11, 1783. His scholastic education was completed by his graduation from Brown University, R. I., in 1804, with the "B. A." degree. He studied law with Hon. Jacob Brunet at Cincinnati and was admitted to the Ohio bar and began practice at Lebanon in that state in 1809. In 1813 he removed to Erie, Pa., was admitted to our bar as the only resident attorney, was soon admitted to the state supreme court and practiced his profession in Pennsylvania until his death. His record has come down to us as one of the most skillful attorneys who ever practiced at our bar. He was a master of conversational oratory and had great influence with juries. Mr. White, for many years our court crier, told me Mr. Sill would stand with his foot on the rung of a chair and talk with the jury rather than at them, that he was a powerful reasoner and very effective.

Mr. Sill enjoyed in a marked degree the confidence of the public; was Deputy U. S. Marshall 1816-1818; Deputy Attorney General (similar to the present district attorney) 1819; was in Congress 1826, and reelected in 1828, being the only anti-Jackson candidate elected that year in Pennsylvania; was a member of the state constitutional convention in 1838; was a Whig and as presidential elector in 1848 voted for Zachariah Taylor for president and Millard Filmore for vice-president. He was a minute man in the war of 1812 and a member on the staff of General Wallace 1837-1838. Mr. Sill was also trustee of the Erie Academy, a member of the school board and in addition postmaster at Erie, and a member of the First Presbyterian Church. In addition to his practice and official duties Mr. Sill dealt in real estate. In 1816 he was united in marriage with Joanna Botleston Chase of Litchfield, Connecticut. They had five children, Richard, Joanna, Sarah Hale, Joseph and James. Mr. Thomas H. Sill, while of distinguished appearance, was not large or robust. His death on February 7, 1856, in his seventy-third year, closed one of the most prominent careers in the history of our county. He was buried in the Erie cemetery. The long and honorable legal career of Mr. Sill will ever stand prominent in the early history of the Erie Bar.

Hon. James Sill

James Sill, son of Hon. Thomas H. and Joanna Boyleston (Chase) Sill, was born in Erie in 1827. He was of very distinguished New England lineage; a sketch of his father and mention of his grandfather, Captain Sill, appear above, and his mother's father was an eminent divine. James, after a full course at the Erie Academy, entered the New York State and National Law School, where he graduated and, after study in his father's law office, was admitted to the Erie Bar, October 29, 1852, and at once entered upon his profession. In 1857 he was elected district attorney and served with distinction for three years. In 1863 President Lincoln tendered him the appointment of Provost Marshall for the Nineteenth district, which he declined. He was, however, City Solicitor of Erie City during the years 1871-'72. Although engaged in many activities, he never retired from legal practice, but in his later years, rarely appeared in the trial of causes.

In 1870 he secured a charter for and helped organize a bank called the "Peoples Savings Institution" at North East. He helped organize and was largely interested in a bank at Union City, of which his brother, Joseph Sill, was cashier. He also secured a charter for and for many years was a director of the Humboldt Savings Bank, of Erie. He was active and interested in the Union & Titusville Railroad and other projects. He was ever active in politics. Starting out as a Whig, he joined the Republican party in 1856, when in its infancy, and ever after gave it loyal support. He was a natural political leader and perhaps at one time the most potent factor in Erie County politics. Many influential men sought his counsel and followed his leadership. His help, always quietly given, changed the tide of battle in many a primary contest. He was also in close touch with General Simon Cameron and other state leaders. He was six times sent as delegate to state conventions, served twice as chairman of the Republican County Committee and twice as chairman of the Republican City Committee, was also several times a member of the Republican State Committee. In 1868 he was a presidential elector and as such voted for Grant and Colfax. He was elected State Senator in 1880 and, during his four years' term, took a prominent part in state legislation, introducing and carrying through several reforms. He introduced the bill transferring the Marine Hospital at Erie to the State for a Soldiers and Sailors Home, which it is and has been for over forty years. In the memorable contest for United States Senator in 1881, Senator Sill stood resolutely by the instructions of his constituents and voted for Hon. Galusha A. Grow, until finally, Hon. John I. Mitchell, of Tioga County, was elected as a compromise candidate. It was, as I believe, correctly stated at the time that Senator Sill would then have been elected United States Senator had he not refused absolutely to violate his instructions. After the close of that session of the legislature, the senator's Erie friends tendered him a banquet, in commemoration of his loyalty to his constituents.

The failure of the Union City bank about 1882, in which he was largely interested, crippled him financially, but he retained much of his real estate, the management of which occupied a part of his time in later years. He was always interested in civic affairs and in his younger days served as member of the city council. He was not a candidate for reelection to the Senate and thereafter took a less prominent part in politics. He was of medium height, but of rather slight build, had a smooth shaven face, and in his prime, was fine looking. He was never married and ever continued to reside at the Sill homestead, Sixth and Holland streets, with his mother until her death, and thereafter, I believe, practically alone. As a local historian, Senator Sill was in a class by himself. He knew practically every prominent family in the city and county, their parents and their children, who they married and all about the collateral relatives. His memory as to such matters was phenomenal. He could have written a worth while history of the early members of our bar, but unfortunately never did. He also was entirely familiar with the history of Pennsylvania. He was author of the first history of Erie City and sometimes wrote on local historic subjects for the press. Like many another old man he lived to be surrounded by a new generation with whom he was not in step. He inherited to a large extent his father's felicity of diction and could express himself well, for which reason he was frequently selected to draft resolutions or otherwise give expression to the thought of the bar. When the members of the bar made their first annual call at our home (January 1, 1900), he was their spokesman, and as usual, his remarks were happy and appropriate. That was the beginning of a custom which has continued for nearly thirty years. As a speaker, whether in campaigns or otherwise, the senator spoke fluently and delivered his message with energy and in a high pitched voice. James Sill died in January, 1903, at the age of seventy-six years and was buried in the Erie Cemetery.

General Charles Manning Reed

General Charles M. Reed, son of Rufus Seth and Nancy Agnes Reed, was born at Erie April 3, 1803. After completing a course at Washington and Jefferson College, he studied law with Hon. Horace Binney, of Philadelphia, and was admitted to the bar there in 1824. He was a life long resident of Erie and for many years was its foremost citizen. He served in Congress, also in the legislature, and held other positions of distinction, but so far as I have been able to learn, never engaged in legal practice and the records fail to show that he was ever admitted to the Erie County Bar. His portrait appears among the group of Erie County lawyers published in 1900, and he possibly was admitted here before the records were destroyed by fire in 1823. Whitman's History of Erie County states that he was admitted to the bar in 1821. His remarkable career, however, was in commerce and business and, as it is outlined in the various county histories, need not be repeated here. In 1836 he was united in marriage with Miss Harriet W. Gilson. General Reed died December 15, 1871, and was buried in the family lot in the Erie Cemetery. Among the surviving members of his family were his widow, his sons, Hon. Charles M. Reed, Jr., and Lloyd G. Reed and a daughter, the wife of Hon. Henry Rawle. In his day, General Reed was the wealthiest man in Erie and left an estate of several million dollars, and his home, now that of the Erie Club, at Sixth and Peach streets, stands as a monument to his memory.

Hon. John H. Walker

John H. Walker was born in Cumberland County, near Harrisburg, February 9, 1800, of Scotch-Irish ancestry. He graduated from Washington (Pa.) College in 1821 and studied law with his uncle, Judge Jonathan Wallace at Pittsburgh. Upon admission to the bar there he located in Erie and was admitted to our bar in 1824, where he practiced law continuously for over fifty years. He soon acquired a position of leadership which ended only with his death. He was six feet four inches tall, had a tremendously strong, clean shaven face and commanding presence. He practiced in all the local courts, in the supreme court of the state and elsewhere. He acquired an extensive knowledge of law, was the owner of the largest law library in the city and was a powerful advocate. He was thoroughly honest, never resorted to trickery or sharp practice and fought his cases openly and with the strength of a giant. The profession can never cease to admire a man of that type. In the selection of the battle ground, the preparation for trial, the development of the facts, by examination and cross examination of the witnesses, the discussion of law to the court and of facts to the jury, and in the appellate court, John H. Walker was a hundred percent lawyer. William Benson, himself a great lawyer and not lavish in praise of others, said Walker was one of the best lawyers in the state. S. A. Davenport, who would not flatter Jove for his thunder, said the ablest address he ever heard in the court house was made by Walker in a case where he (Davenport) was opposing counsel. James W. Allison, Esq.,* now of Cleveland, describes Walker as

*Note—Mr. Allison died July 25, 1927.

saying on one occasion in his later years, when he arose to address a jury, that he had long since quit attempting anything like oratory, but that he did want to talk to them about the facts of the case, then proceeded to a masterly and unanswerable discussion of the evidence.

This opinion of his contemporaries as well as my own memory of his unrivaled reputation when an old man, and the traditions still remaining of his forensic power, mark him for nearly fifty years as the real leader of our bar. He hammered at the controlling questions and paid little attention to trifles. D. R. Cushman, Esq., of North East, when a young lawyer, sought Walker's advice in a certiorari from a justice's court, where he (Cushman) had filed fifteen exceptions, Walker said, in effect, "You have scattered too much; there is generally one controlling question in a case and rarely more than two or three. Then why file so many exceptions?" The suggestion was good and indicated the experience of a great lawyer. When nearly seventy years of age Walker was retained to defend certain railroad passenger conductors, charged with embezzling company money. The cases were so important that the railroad company brought in eminent counsel from away to assist in the prosecution. Col. Thompson, who was with them, told me Walker's defense was so masterly as not only to acquit his clients, but to fill such eminent counsel with amazement and admiration. They freely said they had never seen a case better defended.

Mr. Walker was a Whig and later a Republican. From 1832 to 1835 he was in the assembly at Harrisburg and the last year was speaker of that body. For the years 1849, 1850 and 1851, he was State senator and the last year was president pro tem of the senate. He was a member of the constitutional convention of 1873 and on the death of Hon. William M. Meredith became president of that body, composed of some of Pennsylvania's most able men. There as elsewhere, he acquitted himself with signal ability. That was his last and perhaps greatest public service. Mr. Meredith became sick soon after the opening of the convention and he designated Mr. Walker to act in his place, and after the former's death the convention unanimously chose the latter as president and at the close of the convention gave him a unanimous vote of thanks for the dignified and impartial manner he had performed his duty. He was generally right, a good judge of human motives and outspoken.

Mr. Walker was public-spirited and ever willing to undertake whatever might benefit the community. This led him to project and be instrumental in building the plank roads, extending from Erie to Edinboro, also from Erie to Waterford and from Erie to Wattsburg, which toll roads, while not a financial success, were a great help to the city and county, until abandoned some fifteen to twenty years later. Concrete has now accomplished what John H. Walker sought to do by plank roads over eighty years ago. He was for many years the ablest local man his party had on the stump and active in every important campaign. Intensely patriotic, when the civil war came, his voice was first and foremost in awakening the people to the danger which threatened the country. Too old to go to the front he sent his sons, one of whom, Thomas M., became a famous general and one of the state's foremost soldiers. After the war, General Walker served as sheriff of this county and also as postmaster at Erie. Later the general engaged in wheat growing in the northwest, spending his winters in Erie where it was my good fortune to know him as a most charming gentleman.

In 1831, Catherine Dudley Kelley, a native of New Hampshire, was united in marriage with John H. Walker. They had nine children, viz: John W., Thomas M., James, Kate (now the widow of Hon. Samuel A. Davenport), George K., Quincy Adams, Isabella M. (who became Mrs. Armstrong), Mary (who became Mrs. Beemer), and Harry. Mr. Walker established his home on West Seventh street, in a large brick house, later the home of the Erie Club and now that of the Y. W. C. A. On the same lot east of the residence was his office, a two story brick building, for many years the residence of Major John W. Walker and now (1927) the home of his widow. Mr. Walker had a large garden in the care of which he found much recreation. The strenuous labors of the constitutional convention overtaxed his strength. His son Major Walker expressed the opinion that it shortened his life. Thereafter he gradually declined and passed away January 25, 1875, as he was nearing the end of his seventy-fifth year. His faithful wife predeceased him and they sleep in the Erie cemetery. That during the formative period of the Erie Bar it had as a leader for half a century a lawyer of such sterling character and great ability as John H. Walker, was indeed a blessing. We are stronger and better today because of his life and work. "Next to the radiance which flows from the Almighty's throne is the light of a noble and beautiful life, shining in benediction upon the destinies of men and finding its home in the bosom of the everlasting God."

Major John William Walker

John W. Walker, eldest son of Hon. John H. and Catherine (Kelly) Walker, was born at Erie, April 19, 1832, and educated at the Erie schools and Princeton College, where he gratuated in the class of 1854. He studied law with his father and was admitted to the Erie Bar the same year. He practiced here for two years, then removed to St. Louis where he practiced until he returned to Erie in 1860, and again took up the practice here. This was interrupted by the civil war for, imbued with a patriotism like that of his father, he raised Company K of the One Hundred and Forty-fifth Regiment, Pennsylvania Volunteers, of which he was captain in the field until after the battle of Fredericksburg. Then he was appointed paymaster in the United States Army with the rank of "Major" and served in that capacity until the close of the war when he was retired with the rank of Lieutenant Colonel; but he was always known as Major Walker. Owing to ill health he never resumed the practice of law, but gave his attention to banking and other interests. He took a great interest in the Second National Bank of Erie of which he was a director continuously for forty-four years. He was public spirited and very active in establishing the Soldiers and Sailors Home at Erie. Rejecting the political faith of his father he became an ardent Democrat and as such was elected to the state legislature by a two to one vote in 1882, and served as chairman of the committee on municipal corporations. During President Cleveland's first term (1885-1889) Major Walker was appointed treasury agent (akin to collector of internal revenue) and during his second term

(1893-1897) United States Marshall for the Western District of Pennsylvania. He was a member and Past Commander of the W. L. Scott Post Grand Army of the Republic. He was also the first Grand Regent of Pennsylvania for the Royal Arcanum; a Knight of Honor, an Elk, a charter member of the Erie Club and was also a member of St. Paul's Episcopal Church. Major Walker was exceedingly companionable, an excellent story teller and had a host of friends. Personally he was six feet five inches tall, stood erect, had a military carriage, wore a very heavy brown moustache, was most distinguished in appearance and always polite and affable.

On June 18, 1861, he was united in marriage with Anna H. Harrison, the daughter of Hon. Samuel S. Harrison, of Kittanning, who was a member of congress from that district. They had no children. Major Walker died February 13, 1913, in the eighty-first year of his age and was buried in the Erie cemetery. He held many important public positions and filled them with ability and fidelity. The widow, although sixty-seven years have elapsed since her marriage, is yet one of Erie's first ladies, and presides over the family home with the same grace and dignity as in other days.

Hon. Elijah Babbitt

Elijah Babbitt was born at Providence, Rhode Island, July 29, 1795. His father, a sea captain, was for many years engaged in shipping between New York and the West Indies, also served as lieutenant in the continental army during the Revolutionary War. The father later moved with his family to the state of New York, where he died, and Elijah, before reaching his majority, came to Northumberland County, Pennsylvania. Having acquired an academic education, he studied law with Hon. Samuel Hepburn, a leading lawyer of central Pennsylvania, and was admitted to the bar of that county in March 1824, where he practiced successfully for about two years. Believing Erie offered better opportunities he removed here in January 1826, bringing all his worldly goods, including a law library, in a spring wagon, drawn by a team of horses. The trip over mountain roads took nine days. He rented an office at the corner of Fourth and French streets, then the center of the town of about nine hundred inhabitants, and hung out his shingle. He was promptly admitted to all the courts of this district and later to the state supreme court and the federal courts. His coming was the beginning of a legal career at our bar extending over a period of sixty years, distinguished alike by great ability, unflagging industry and strict integrity. In the course of years his practice became large and exacting, but he gave every detail the most scrupulous attention and never overlooked anything that could be honestly done on his client's behalf. In his day he was the best technically read lawyer at our bar and probably won more cases on strictly legal questions than any other. It was rare indeed that Elijah Babbitt took an unsound legal position and still more rare that he overlooked a law point on which his case could be won. He told me a lawyer should not be wrong on the law of his case once in a hundred times. That was his high standard of legal efficiency. When a law student I listened to his trial, as attorney for plaintiff, of the case of Ralph vs. Ottoway, for a breach of covenant in a deed. Ottoway had given Ralph a warranty deed of the farm at Moorheadville, now the summer home of President Burnett of the Erie Railroad, and described the land as containing a certain number of acres within defined boundaries. By actual survey the acreage fell short and Ralph sued for damages. Babbitt took the position that, as Ottoway had covenanted for so much land, he must make it good and he was sustained here and in the supreme court. Later, when Mr. Babbitt was about eighty-four years old, I helped him try the case of Lewis v. Lewis, which he won on the legal ground that a widow's dower interest in land was an estate of which she could not divest herself except by an instrument in writing. When nearly ninety years old, as attorney for plaintiff, he successfully tried the personal injury case of Driscoll v. The City of Erie. With many other members of the bar, I listened to that trial. He displayed an ability there rarely equalled at our bar. I have never heard a physician cross examined more successfully than he cross examined the defendant's doctor, and his summing up to the jury was a classic. Hon. George W. DeCamp, who had practiced with both, thought Babbitt a greater lawyer than John H. Walker; but all things considered, I am inclined to give the latter first place. The early history of our bar was honored by at least three preeminently great lawyers—Walker, Babbitt and Sill, of which Walker was the most forceful, Babbitt the most adroit, and Sill the most eloquent. In adroitness, or skill in managing litigation, Babbitt was unrivalled. For example, when he had a dangerous case to try he would on the last day allowable remove it from the trial list by a rule to arbitrate. He indulged therein so often that the practice became known as "Babbittising." He was ever on the alert to take full advantage of the slightest slip in his adversary's pleadings. He won an ejectment case once because the opposing counsel had erred in the recital of one direction of the survey. On one occasion, he warned the jury to beware of the apparent candor and eloquence of Hon. Thomas H. Sill, by saying, "He is as cunning as a fox and as flippant as a blue jay." Sometime after Mr. Davenport had returned from Harvard Law School, Babbitt warned the jury to beware of him, saying, "The gentleman has been to a school where they teach young men to make the worse appear the better cause and he graduated at the head of his class." Once, on leaving the court room, after he had lost the case, Babbitt remarked, "Any lawyer who thinks he can win a case in this court just because he has all the law and all the facts on his side, must be an old fool."

In addition to his remarkable career as a lawyer, Mr. Babbitt performed many distinguished public services. He was prosecuting attorney of the county for two years, beginning in 1834. He served two terms in the legislature, beginning in 1835. He served a term of three years in the state senate, beginning in 1844. While so in Harrisburg, he was largely instrumental in making Erie the northern terminal of the Pennsylvania State Canal. He arose from a sick bed to present to the commission, as he did with telling effect, the public advantage of such terminal. He served many years as solicitor for the borough and later for the city of Erie and drew the charter under which it became a city. He was long a trustee of the Erie Academy. About 1850 he was a prime mover and advanced money to purchase the site of the present Erie Cemetery. In 1828 he helped to organize and became a charter member of the Episcopal Church, now St. Paul's Cathedral, and in that membership continued steadfast and consistent until his death.

His outstanding public service was as member of congress from 1859 to 1863, the most tense period in the nation's history. It was his privilege to be the friend and supporter of President Lincoln, of whom he gave me some interesting facts, among others that the President had very large hands. Mr. Babbitt made an excellent record in congress, standing steadfast in support of the war and advocating on the floor of the House and elsewhere the immediate freedom of the slaves, that they might assist therein. He was succeeded in congress by Judge Glenni W. Schofield, of Warren, who served ten years and became a national figure. It is remarkable how Mr. Babbitt, while performing so many notable public services, ever maintained his position as a leader of the bar. He was a wholesome looking man of medium size, clean shaven, ever genial and approachable, but there was little in his outward appearance to indicate his most remarkable ability. On November 28, 1827, he was united in marriage with Caroline Elizabeth Kelso, daughter of General John Kelso, one of Erie county's pioneer citizens.

Mr. and Mrs. Babbitt both lived to a great age and were survived by seven children. A number of their more remote descendants now reside in Erie and are highly respected citizens. Mr. Babbitt's residence and office, at the time of his death and for very many years prior thereto, was on Peach street, opposite the southwest corner of Perry Square and adjoining Mrs. C. H. Strong's home property. Mr. Babbitt died during the winter of 1887, in the ninety-second year of his age. He was buried in the Erie Cemetery. He was an ornament to our bar for over sixty years and honored every public trust to which he was called.

James C. Marshall, Esq.

James C. Marshall was born July 27, 1799, in Franklin county, Penna., and when he was six years of age, removed with his parents to Trumbull county, Ohio, where he grew to manhood. He attended country and select schools and when seventeen years old went to Virginia where he engaged in teaching for three or four years, then returned to Warren, Ohio, where he studied four years in the Academy. In 1824 he began the study of law with Hon. Thomas D. Weber of Trumbull county, where he was admitted to the bar in 1826 and formed a partnership with Hon. Rufus P. Spalding, later a judge of the supreme court of Ohio. Mr. Marshall practiced in the four counties of that district until May, 1828, when he and Don Carlos Barrett located in Erie and for one year practiced law in partnership. Thereafter Mr. Marshall continued practice alone, but in 1830 became a member of a business firm at Girard, Pa., and located there. He continued in the business for two or three years and thereafter he continued in his profession with offices at Girard. During this time he served a term as postmaster of Girard. In 1839 he was appointed prothonotary of Erie County and served for three years. In 1844 he moved back to Erie City and soon formed a law partnership with Hon. James Thompson, later Chief Justice. This partnership was mutually dissolved because of Judge Thompson's congressional duties. In 1848 Mr. Marshall was appointed Revenue Commissioner for Erie, Crawford and Warren counties and served one term. In 1849 he and Hon. John P. Vincent formed a law partnership which continued five years. In 1861 he formed a law partnership with his son, F. F. Marshall, Esq., as Marshall & Marshall, which continued until the former's retirement in 1882, and was recognized as a remarkably strong firm.

James C. Marshall was an intense worker and, notwithstanding his many other activities, had a legal career placing him among the leaders of our bar. He attained this eminence through many years of constant toil and strict integrity. Without any special gift of oratory, he acquired the abilty of clear and forceful statement, rarely equalled. His arguments seemed, like the speeches of John C. Calhoun, to be "logic on fire." His growth as a lawyer possibly continued to a later period in life than that of any of his compeers. He retained his strength to a marked degree. I am satisfied he was a better lawyer at seventy years of age than he was at fifty. It was refreshing to see with what mental alertness and physical vigor he would put across his propositions when nearly eighty years old. He was intensely earnest in the trial of cases and never trifled. He never surrendered his legal position. If the trial court ruled against him he would often appeal and probably took a greater percentage of his cases to the state supreme court than any other lawyer of his day, with perhaps one exception. He would, as he said, "Let the supreme court have the last guess."

His standing as a lawyer appears by the fact that he had undoubtedly the best line of practice in the county, as he was for years counsel for many large financial interests, including those of Hon. William L. Scott and General Charles M. Reed. My recollection is he drew the latter's will, disposing of an estate valued at seven million dollars. He was also counsel for the Marine National Bank, of Erie, of which he was president for nearly twenty years. He was also president of the Erie County Mutual Insurance Company for about twenty-five years and for nine years trustee of the Erie Academy.

Personally he was about six feet tall, well built, but never heavy; stood erect, even in age, had a large, well shapen head, covered with an abundance of hair and with side whiskers, both becoming gray as the years passed. He also had a very strong face and looked, as in fact he was, a man of great force of character. Although his forbears came early to America, it is certain he was of Scotch-Irish lineage. He was a life long Democrat, but never sought popular office. In November, 1829, he was united in marriage with Eliza Weatherbee of Warren, Ohio, a niece of Judge Freeman of that city. They had four children, viz: James, a fruit grower in California; Mary W., intermarried with Commander James W. Shirk, U. S. Navy; Francis F., the well known Erie attorney, and Laura O., intermarried with S. E. Norris, of Philadelphia. Mr. and Mrs. Marshall were Presbyterians and for many years regular attendants of the First Presbyterian Church.

For many years Mr. Marshall's home was the brick residence on the south side of West Fifth street, adjoining the First Presbyterian Church, where he died, at the age of 92 years, and was buried in the Erie Cemetery. During a long and busy life, James C. Marshall performed all his tasks with a high degree of fidelity and ability.

Francis F. Marshall, Esq.

F. F. Marshall (called Frank Marshall), son of James C. and Eliza (Weatherbee) Marshall, was born in Girard, this county, May 21, 1835, was educated at the Erie Academy and at Yale College, being in the class of 1856. Having studied law with his father, he was admitted to the Erie Bar October 28, 1857. The examining board at the time of his admission was composed of Chief Justice James Thompson, Judge John Galbraith, Hon. Elijah Babbitt and Hon. John H. Walker. Mr. Marshall at once entered upon the practice of law at Erie which continued without interruption for approximately forty years. On January 1, 1861, the partnership was formed with his father, as Marshall & Marshall, which continued for over twenty years and was of the highest standing. Frank Marshall was an exceedingly painstaking, methodical man, wrote a beautiful hand and gave strict attention to the business end of the firm. He and Geo. P. Griffith were considered the two best office lawyers in the city. While deferring largely to his eminent father in the trial of causes, he usually took an active part therein, and they were a strong combination. Frank tried some cases by himself during the continuance of the firm and more at a later period. While he never practiced in the criminal courts and did not try as many cases as some of his compeers, he was a good trial lawyer and uniformly acquitted himself well in court. In speaking, his delivery was fluent and forceful and his voice would have added fame to any baritone singer.

After his father's retirement he continued the business until his own death, having the same select class of clients, including General Reed's Estate, William L. Scott and later, his estate, the Marine Bank and other large financial interests. His professional income during those years was probably equal to that of any member of our bar. In addition to being a fine lawyer he had exceptionally good business judgment. Personally, Frank Marshall was a large fine looking gentleman, not as tall as his father, but of much stouter build. He was smooth shaven, except a moustache, always appropriately dressed and might have been taken for an American banker or financier. He was a man of distinction and looked the part. He was a thorough gentleman, ever genial and of most agreeable manners. His home for many years was at 162 West Sixth street, where he resided, first in a frame house and later in the beautiful brick residence which he erected and now the home of Mr. and Mrs. T. R. Palmer.

In 1862 he was united in marriage with Miss Fannie Camp, daughter of the well known civil engineer and Erie City Engineer, Colonel Irving Camp. They had three daughters, viz: Florence C., Laura and Mary.

Mr. Marshall was a Democrat, but never sought public office, although he was appointed United States Commissioner by President Lincoln in 1861 and held the position for many years. He was a regular attendant of St. Paul's Episcopal Church, of which his wife was a devoted member. He was a long time member and staunch supporter of the Erie Club and among its members none stood higher. He died in February, 1897, in the sixty-second year of his age and was buried in the Erie Cemetery.

Judge John Gailbraith

John Galbraith was born at Butler, Pa., August 2, 1784, the son of John and Ann (White) Galbraith. He was of Scotch-Irish ancestry, but little is known as to his early education. He studied law, however, in the office of General William Ayres at Butler where he was admitted to the bar in 1818 and located at Franklin, Pa., where he practiced his profession and rose to distinction. While residing there he served in the state legislature and also two terms in congress. In 1837 he removed to Erie where he was a prominent and succesful practitioner until 1850 when he became judge of the district. While practicing here he had many students who became prominent at the bar. I feel somewhat touched by the spirit of John Galbraith as I studied law with one of his students (William Benson) and for five years occupied his old office on West Sixth street, opposite the court house. His judicial services were marked by all that goes to make a great judge. He must have been a fine jurist for when I first came to mingle with our bar, more than fifteen years after his death, those old enough to remember, always spoke of him in terms of praise and affection. He must have had remarkable qualities of head and heart, so I feel safe in saying that no more worthy or popular judge ever occupied the Erie county bench. He did not believe in capital punishment, but replied to a voter who objected to his candidacy for judge on that ground that when his (the voter's) case came up he would waive his objections.

In 1824 John Galbraith married Amy Ayres, the daughter of General Ayres, with whom he studied law, and named his son after that distinguished citizen. They had two children, a daughter Elizabeth, who became the wife of William S. Lane, Esq., and a son, Hon. William Ayres Galbraith. John Galbraith resided in a home adjoining his office, both of which have long since disappeared to make way for the magnificent residence of Mrs. Charles H. Strong. The judge was fond of music and indulged in singing and playing upon the violin. He had a slight hesitancy in his speech, which however, detracted nothing from his ability to sing, or to perform his official duties. He was of fine appearance, and I believe a tall man, probably not as large as his son. While enroute to Warren, in the performance of his official duties, he became sick and died June 15, 1860. He was buried in the Erie cemetery. He was a Democrat in politics and a Universalist in religion and ever a real man.

Judge William Ayres Galbraith

Judge Wm. A. Galbraith was born at Franklin, Pa., May 9, 1823, the son of John and Amy Ayres Galbraith, and, when about fifteen years of age, removed with them to Erie. He was well born, being the son of an able lawyer and a distinguished jurist. He received for that period a very liberal education, being a graduate of Allegheny College, also of the Dane School of Law at Harvard, where he received the degree of L. L. D. In addition he studied law in his fathers' office. When twenty-one years of age he was admitted to the Erie bar and began the practice of law with a zeal and industry which never left him. He was endowed with an agreeable personality and commanding presence. In 1846 he was appointed and served a term in the office now designated district attorney. In his early years at the bar a visitor at court on seeing him pitted against older lawyers, felt a sympathy for him but soon discovered he needed none, for even as a young man William A. Galbraith could hold his own with the best of them. He had a fluency of speech not surpassed by any of his contemporaries, and soon acquired, for the time and place, a large practice numbering among his clients some of the most important local interests. When forty years old he was in the front rank of his profession, but, being a man of great sagacity and financially ambitious, he was lured from the active ranks of the profession into successful ventures which were far more remunerative. He helped build the Hoosic Tunnel, was interested in manufacturing business, dealt in real estate, etc. He helped establish what is now the Erie Trust Co. and was its president until his death.

In 1864 he was a delegate to the Democratic National Convention at Chicago and while there bought a piece of real estate for $16,000, paying $1000 down. This initial investment, with various changes, developed into his Chicago holdings, which included a valuable business block and other property.

From the time he was forty William A. Galbraith was for some years the most prominent democrat in this immediate part of the state and, being an accomplished orator, his services on the stump were in frequent demand. While making a political speech in his old home town of Franklin he injured his voice so as to prevent his public speaking for many months. Meantime he and Mrs. Galbraith traveled abroad. He was in good voice again, however, before 1872 and that year took an active part in support of Horace Greeley for President. During that campaign he addressed a remarkably large audience at North East, speaking from a platform erected in front of the Brawley House. It was there I saw him for the first time. He was then in his very prime, forty-nine years old, fully six feet in height, straight as an arrow, in perfect proportion, with face smooth shaven and by far the finest looking man I had ever seen. His speech was one of the best examples of campaign oratory I have ever heard and created great enthusiasm. Our professor in rhetoric made it the subject of a lecture to his class the following week in the course of which he characterized it the greatest speech he had ever heard. Despite of which President Grant won in the locality. In 1876 the Republicans, after a strenuous contest, nominated William Benson for President Judge. He was one of the ablest lawyers at the bar, but his nomination caused some dissatisfaction and resulted in the independent candidacy of William A. Galbraith, who was also supported by the Democrats. After a most remarkable campaign (to which we will refer in writing of Mr. Benson), Galbraith won by a hundred and forty-three majority. The selection of Galbraith to make the fight against Benson was remarkably wise. He had no animosities at the bar, having been out of practice for some twelve years, was a master of politics with ample means to conduct a vigorous campaign, was universally conceded an able lawyer eminently fitted to adorn the bench and the very name "Galbraith" was a tower of strength. While I voted for Benson because he was the regular Republican candidate and because I was registered as a law student in his office, I had great admiration for Galbraith. The latter had kept abreast of the law, gave undivided attention to his judicial duties and for ten years presided over the local courts with great dignity and ability. He frequently had decided views as to the merits of the case and was seldom disappointed by the jury; in other words he was a verdict getting judge. While he was well liked by some members of the bar, he was not by others. There developed an unfortunate estrangement between the judge and certain prominent democratic lawyers who had helped to elect him. They seemed to think he stood so straight he leaned backward and he thought they were expecting undue favors. Both were probably wrong but it caused ill feeling. Some of the younger members of the bar did not seem to hit it up very well with the Judge, but I was district attorney during his term and he uniformly treated me well. In fact, a friendship grew up between us which continued until his death. We had but one disagreement and that was as to county detective. I named Clark M. Cole and the Judge declined to confirm him, but later we agreed upon Capt. John P. Sullivan, who filled the office with great satisfaction for many years. Judge Galbraith presided at the trial of many important cases and was seldom reversed by the supreme court. One of the most notable cases was Rosenzweig v. The Lake Shore and Michigan Southern Railway Company, where a verdict of nearly $50,000 was recovered and sustained (113 Pa.) He could state both law and facts with great clearness and force. He voluntarily left the bench at the end of his term and resumed the practice of law. I believe he did so because of his natural industry, because he loved the law and to assist his sons who had chosen that profession. He continued in active practice for over ten years and until prevented by failing health. During this time he represented important interests including the Lake Shore and Michigan Southern Railway Company. He was painstaking in the preparation of his cases and tried them well, but added nothing to the reputation he had acquired as a trial lawyer in his younger days.

The judge had very strong human traits and a saving sense of humor and would relate a good joke even at his own expense. About the time he quitted the bench, bicycles came in vogue and when in Chicago he entered a riding academy and had the instructor give him a lesson. He mounted the wheel and started around the ring, the instructor holding on to the seat and walking behind. He made several laps, acquiring such speed as compelled the instructor to release his hold, when for some unexplained reason the judge took a header, skinned his nose, blacked his eye and broke his glasses. That ended his attempt to become a bicyclist. It would have been a rare sight to have witnessed the dignified judge take that header. He concluded relating of the incident by saying, "No more, no more for me."

While hunting one day in Venango county, when a boy, the judge became very hungry and seeing a cabin, approached and asked the woman for food and she gave him warm biscuits and maple syrup, which, more than fifty years afterwards he declared was the best meal he ever ate. He was a polished gentleman and among his accomplishments was the ability to converse with a German in his own language. He was a member and regular attendant of the Central Presbyterian church. The late Benj. Whitman also a leading Democrat said William A. Galbraith could always make votes on the stump and that he was the best man he knew to make individual friendships by meeting and talking to men. I think, however, the judge was perhaps too much given to flattery. For example, he said to Tom Crowley, our local chief of police, "Chief you are wasting your time in Erie, you should be chief of police of a great city like Chicago." When I was about thirty and had no thought of ever being judge, I was walking along the street with him when he stopped and said, "Walling, I would like to see you succeed me on this bench." Fortunately I was equal to the occasion and replied, "Judge, that is impossible, for no boy can succeed you on that bench." That the judge however, was partial to me he indicated by recommending me for his successor as local counsel for the Lake Shore and Michigan Southern Railway, by employing me as his personal counsel and, when ill by asking me to try for him the important case of Kies v. Erie City (169 Pa., 598).

In 1846 he married Fanny Davenport, who survived him. They had three children, Fanny, who married Dr. Gilmore of Chicago, and who predeceased her father, and two sons, John W. and Davenport, who survived him, but are now deceased.

For approximately the last thirty years of his life the judge occupied his palatial residence on West Sixth street, where, surrounded by his family, on January 3, 1898, his death closed one of the most remarkable careers in the history of our county. He was buried in the family plot in Erie Cemetery.

John William Galbraith, Esq.

John W. Galbraith was born in Erie, June 12, 1860, the son of William A. and Fanny Davenport Galbraith. He received a liberal education at Erie High School, the Hopkins Grammar School of New Haven, Conn., Yale University, where he graduated in the class of 1883 with the degree of B. A. and at the Pennsylvania University Law School where he graduated with the degree of L. L. B. He also was instructed in law in the office of his uncle, Hon. William S. Lane, in Philadelphia. He began practice in Erie in 1885 and continued until his death. He was retiring, never sought leadership at the bar, seldom appeared in the trial of causes, but served his clients well and ever enjoyed the full confidence of the court and of his professional brethren.

He was always a thorough gentleman and had many friends. He greatly enjoyed music, was himself an accomplished musician and a member of the American Federation of Musicians, Erie Local 17.

On April 25, 1888, he was married to Miss Mary Henning of Evansville, Ind. They had two sons, William A. Jr., now a banker in Pittsburgh, and John Bertram.

John W. Galbraith was of slight build, and in physical appearance but little resembled his father or brother. He died suddenly, in April, 1926, as the result of paralysis. He is survived by his two sons and two grandchildren, his wife having predeceased him. He was buried in the Erie Cemetery. Thus is closed an honorable career, but less distinguished in the public eye than that of his eminent father and grandfather.

Davenport Galbraith, Esq.

Davenport Galbraith was born at Erie, April 8, 1862, a son of William A. and Fanny Davenport Galbraith. He was afforded the best educational advantages, being a graduate of Erie High School, also of Yale (Sheffield S. S.) University, where he won prizes in English literature and graduated second in his class and was given the degree of S. S. S. He also graduated at the University of Pennsylvania Law School with the degree of L. L. B. In addition he studied in the law office of his uncle, William S. Lane, at Philadelphia. He was admitted to the Pennsylvania Bar in 1888 and entered upon the practice at Erie. He was a brilliant young lawyer but soon drifted from the active ranks of the profession, became a banker and for many years was an executive officer of the Erie Trust Company. He was large, of excellent appearance and a princely gentleman, whom it was a pleasure to know. He had fine social qualities, was popular wherever known and was a member of the Erie, Kahkwa and other clubs. He indulged in hunting, fishing, yachting, golf and other recreations.

June 18, 1885, he married Winifred, the youngest daughter of Hon. J. F. Downing, and for many years they occupied their beautiful home (now the Woman's Club) at 6th and Myrtle streets, Erie. They also spent much time at the Galbraith summer home on the shore of Lake Erie. No one in my acquaintance seemed to get more rational enjoyment out of life than Mr. Galbraith, and his sudden death, Sept. 10, 1914, when but fifty-two years of age, was a shock to the community. He was politically independent and never sought public office. He was buried in the Erie Cemetery. They had no children. He was survived by his widow, who is a well known resident of Erie. In the midst of a useful life he was suddenly cut down, so inscrutable are the ways of providence.

William C. Kelso, Esq.

William C. Kelso, son of Genl. John and Sarah Willis (Carson) Kelso, was born in Erie about 1812. His father, a native of Cumberland county, came here as a land agent in 1798 and became an outstanding pioneer settler, occupying many important public positions, including that of associate judge. He was a general in the war of 1812. William, the youngest of seven children, after studying law with his brother-in-law, Hon. Elijah Babbitt, was admitted to the Erie County Bar May 10, 1839 and formed a partnership with his preceptor, which continued many years. He was a painstaking, industrious lawyer of sound judgment, but so extremely modest and retiring that he never became known as an advocate. In 1862 he was appointed an assistant United States Assessor for the nineteenth collection district of Pennsylvania and with marked efficiency performed the important duties of that office.

For half a century he was a devout member of St. Paul's Episcopal church. He was warden, vestryman and secretary therein and as regular in his attendance as the rector. During his later years he was the oldest surviving member of that congregation. He was a medium sized, clean shaven, fine appearing gentleman of the old school, very quiet but of engaging manners, and held in the highest esteem by all who had the pleasure of his acquaintance. He died unmarried in April 1892, in the eightieth year of his age and was buried in the Erie Cemetery.

Hon. Chas. W. Kelso

Charles W. Kelso, son of Joseph and Elizabeth Kelso, was born in Harrisburg, May 17, 1809. He became an accomplished gentleman of fine education and, locating at Erie, was admitted to our bar May 10, 1839, where for thirty-five years he was engaged in active practice and took high rank, in fact, was regarded as one of the best lawyers in the county. He served two terms in the state legislature and, by appointment in 1856, as district attorney. He was the father of Joseph K. Kelso, Esq., who was an alderman in the Fourth ward some fifty years ago and was admitted to the Erie Bar in 1876, but never engaged in practice here. Charles W. Kelso died November 26, 1874, at the age of sixty-five years and was buried in the Erie Cemetery. The favor and frequency with which his name was mentioned by the older members of the bar, during the early years of my practice, convince me that he was not only an eminent lawyer but one of the highest character. He was a cousin of William C. Kelso.

Colonel Carlton B. Curtis

Carlton B. Curtis, son of John Curtis, was born in Madison county, New York, December 17, 1811. After receiving an academic education, he went to Chautauqua county, New York, where he read law with Judge Mullet, who was a famous lawyer and great judge. From there Curtis came to Erie and continued his law studies in the office of D. C. Barrett, Esq. On admission to the bar in 1834 he located at Warren, Pa., where he rose rapidly in his profession, and in some branches of the law became almost without a superior. While he continued to reside in Warren for many years, he practiced on the circuit and was well known in all the nearby counties. He became one of the strongest lawyers in Northwestern Pennsylvania, where he participated in numerous important trials. In 1866 he removed to Erie, where he continued in active practice until his last sickness. He was very popular, especially with the younger members of the bar and frequently assisted them in the trial of causes. He was not an intense worker, but in trial work he was clear, logical and powerful. I recall the pleasure it ever gave me to hear the Colonel argue law questions. He stood in the front rank at our bar and was sometimes referred to as its leader, although in my opinion there were others equally able. Erie has ever had an able bar, but for many years following the death of Hon. John H. Walker in 1875, I doubt if any one stood out above others so as to be justly designated as the leader. Col. Curtis was equally at home in all branches of the law and practiced in both civil and criminal courts. He was a good speaker and frequently appeared on the stump. I only knew him when an old man, even then he had an attractive personality. A fine clean shaven face, tall but not heavy, he looked every inch a man.

He served in the state legislature for three consecutive sessions, beginning in 1836 and in 1850 he was sent to Congress as a Democrat, defeating by a small majority Hon. John H. Walker, Whig candidate. In 1855 Col. Curtis, like many other Democrats, joined the Republican party. In 1872, he won the party's nomination for Congress over Genl. McCreary and was elected. In 1874 he was again the Republican nominee, but was defeated by Dr. Edgbert of Franklin, the Democratic candidate, by eleven votes. This defeat resulted from the general defection of that year, which it was estimated caused a million Republicans in the United States to temporarily forsake their party. In 1876 he was an unsuccessful candidate for the Republican nomination for judge.

At the breaking out of the Civil War he helped organize the 58th Regiment of Pennsylvania Volunteers and became its Lieutenant Colonel. He later was promoted to Colonel of the regiment and served until ill health compelled his retirement in 1863. He was a member of the Episcopal Church. As an enterprising citizen he helped organize the First National Bank at Erie and was the chief organizer and builder of the Dunkirk and Venango R. R. He was a genial companionable man, a fine story teller, who made and retained a host of friends.

In 1835 he married Miss Ann Sargent, daughter of the late Dr. Henry Sargent, of Warren, who bore the Colonel five children and predeceased him by two years. Col. Curtis, after an illness of nearly a year, died March 17, 1883, in the seventy-second year of his age, and sleeps in his old home town at Warren.

Lysander Sterrett Norton

L. S. Norton, son of Rev. Niram and Anna McKnight (Sterrett) Norton, was born at Forestville, New York, January 26, 1845. His ancestry on his father's side came to this country and settled in Connecticut in 1640. His branch of the family removed to New York State about 1780 and to Pennsylvania in 1830. His mother was a member of the well known and most highly respected Sterrett family, prominent in this county for a century, she being a niece of Judge Joseph M. Sterrett. She died at Meadville in 1870. Rev. Niram Norton was a minister of the Methodist Church, and spent the years of his pastorate in at least ten different churches, in New York, Pennsylvania and Ohio. He was an able minister and most highly regarded wherever he was located. Lysander attended the schools or academies wherever his father happened to be stationed and, entering Allegheny College, graduated therefrom in the class of 1864, at the early age of nineteen. He later took a course at Harvard Law school where he graduated with the L. L. B. degree in 1868. Meantime having been registered as a law student by Hon. A. B. Richmond, the eminent criminal lawyer at Meadville, he was on motion of Judge Derrickson, admitted to the Crawford County Bar in 1868. Locating in Erie he was admitted to our bar on October 12 of that year, where he was a successful and prominent practitioner for approximately twenty years. He had a general practice and was counsel in many important cases. One of his most outstanding victories being that of McFarland v. Dr. A. S. Lovett, in which he represented the plaintiff. Dr. Lovett, a successful young physician at Erie, had set a broken wrist for plaintiff and, the outcome resulting in some deformity, the doctor was sued for malpractice. He was defended by the prominent law firm of Benson & Brainerd and the contest was fierce, the defense being largely that the deformity resulted from plaintiff's disobedience of the doctor's orders by going swimming, etc. The jury after long deliberation found a very substantial verdict for plaintiff, which was sustained. Dr. Lovett soon abandoned the practice of medicine, located in Minnesota where he engaged in the real estate business, made good, and now has a winter residence in Florida. In 1873, Mr. Norton joined in law partnership with Col. C. B. Curtis, under the firm name of Curtis & Norton, which continued some ten years, until the Colonel's death. It was one of the strong firms at our bar. Norton had all the requisites of a successful lawyer, was industrious, had a brilliant intellect, was an excellent speaker, with an inspiring personality, being nearly six feet in height, wore a moustache and flowing side whiskers and always dressed neatly and appropriately. He was a man who would attract attention in any presence.

Politically he was a Republican with justifiable ambitions. In 1882 he was a candidate for congress at the Republican primaries and took into the convention a respectable number of delegates. After a stubborn contest however, Hon. S. M. Brainerd secured the nomination through a combination with Captain Mackay, the candidate from Venango county. Norton, although disappointed, stood by the result and supported the Republican ticket. In 1886 he became a candidate, at the Republican primaries, for president judge of the district, as successor to Hon. William A. Galbraith, and ran second to Hon. Frank Gunnison in a field of five candidates. No one doubted his ability for the place, but Judge Gunnison, being a native son and former chairman of the Republican County Committee, his candidacy made a special appeal to the young men and he was nominated. Norton took this defeat very seriously and soon began to show a nervous trouble, which blighted his career. He went to Dakota and perhaps for a year was associated with Col. Green, I believe, at Fargo. He returned to try the important personal injury case of Smith v. Springfield Township, in which he was attorney for plaintiff while Judge Vincent and I were for the defendant. It was a protracted trial, during which he displayed his usual ability; but in the end, the court directed a verdict for the defendant. In two days, Norton's nervous trouble was again upon him and so rapidly developed that he was soon taken to Kirkbride Hospital, Philadelphia, where he remained for some time. Then deeming his health restored, he secured his release by a writ of habeas corpus, for which he prepared the petition and conducted the hearing. Rejoining his family at or near Elmira, his trouble soon recurred and he was taken to a private asylum at Canandaigua, N.Y., where he expired December 3, 1891, in the forty-seventh year of his age. The nervous collapse of so brilliant a man in the prime of life was a sad tragedy. On June 12, 1873, L. S. Norton was united in marriage with Mattie L. Curtis, youngest daughter of Col. C. B. Curtis. They had one child, a son, Carlton Curtis Norton, now a practicing physician at White Plains, N. Y. Mrs. Norton survived her husband and is now the wife of Mr. Henry S. Munson.

Hon. James Darwin Dunlap

James D. Dunlap, son of Dr. James and Nancy Tuttle Dunlap, was born January 15, 1809, at Kaskaskia, Ill., where his father was a practicing physician and surgeon. His father was of Scotch and his mother of Pilgrim ancestry. The latter was a member of the large and well known Tuttle family, early settlers at and near North East in this county. James D. came to North East when young and there received his early education. Then he was sent to his uncle, Dr. Livingston Dunlap at Indianapolis where his literary education was completed, I believe somewhat under private instructors. He studied law in Iowa where he was admitted to the bar. He also studied with Hon. Elijah Babbitt and was admitted to the Erie Bar, May 10, 1839. Thereafter he practiced law in this county, with many interruptions, because of official duties, until his death. We know little of Mr. Dunlap as a practicing lawyer, but in other lines of activity we know much. Soon after coming to the bar, he was sent to the state legislature where he continued in the assembly and later in the senate for approximately twelve years. While there he became familiarly acquainted and on terms of intimate friendship with the public men of the state. For example, he was so close to Hon. Thaddeus Stevens, one of the state's foremost public men, that he was accustomed to ride the latter's favorite horse. As a law maker, he was sane, progressive and influential. He strongly supported the act of 1842, abolishing imprisonment for debt, one of the most enlightened statutes found upon our books. He also gave untiring efforts in favor of statutes for the establishment of a state common school system.

He assisted in securing a charter for the canal extending from Erie toward Pittsburgh; also for the Baltimore and Ohio railroad and for that of the Erie and Pittsburgh and other railroads. But, with many others, believing it impossible to construct a railroad over the Allegheny mountains, did not favor the projected Sunbury and Erie railroad. When I first traveled over that road, over fifty years ago, it seemed a perilous journey; but it has grown to be an important line of transportation and Mr. Dunlap's objections proved unfounded.

As a correspondent, he was in a class by himself among Erie attorneys. He carefully preserved letters he received and his daughter, Mrs. Davis Rees still has the most wonderful collection of autograph letters, written to her father that I have ever seen. They include letters from James Thompson, Thomas H. Sill, Elijah Babbitt, John H. Walker, John P. Vincent, J. C. Marshall, J. C. Spencer, G. Sanford, P. S. V. Hamot, William C. Curry and other prominent Erie citizens, also from H. L. Richmond and Edgar Huidekoper of Meadville, and from Bishop Kingsley of the M. E. Church who was a personal friend of Mr. Dunlap, as was also General Winfield Scott, with whom the subject of our sketch dined in Washington and from whom he received several letters, as he also did from Thaddeus Stevens. There are also several highly interesting letters from Mr. Dunlap to his mother and his diary, still preserved, is intensely interesting and shows not only his attitude on important legislation at Harrisburg, but his travels and the important personages he met, including John Quincy Adams, Thomas H. Benton, Henry Ward Beecher and others.

In the publication of "Dunlap's Book of Forms", the

first edition of which came out about 1844, he did a remarkable service to the legal profession. It has been through numerous editions and is still the standard and now published in two large volumes, making about twenty-five hundred pages. The legal accuracy of these forms was remarkable; so far as the writer recalls, no one has ever been misled by following Dunlap, while it is safe to say a majority of the papers entered of record in the various court houses and presented to the various courts throughout the commonwealth for the past eighty years have been modeled after his form book. In view of his many other activities, it is surprising how he found time to prepare such a work. Dyer Loomis, the name so often found in the form book, was a most highly respected resident of North East and for over fifty years a justice of the peace.

Mr. Dunlap was a charter member and officer of a society aimed to improve the condition of the colored race; also of an agricultural society and spent much time in geological studies and research. He was president of the first common council when Erie became a city in 1851. He was long a member of the city school board and as its president laid the corner stone and helped erect its first high school. He was an intensely active and influential member of the First Methodist Episcopal Church at Erie and for seventeen years superintendent of its Sunday school. In addition to these myriad activities he found time to exchange calls and visits with an unusually wide circle of friends.

In 1853 he was united in marriage with Marianne Finley Russell, a Scotch-Irish lady whose home was Belfast and who had come to America on a visit. Five years later, on March 28, 1858, James D. Dunlap, after a brief illness, departed this life, leaving a widow, and three small children. He was buried in the Erie cemetery. The widow, being highly educated, supported the family by teaching. She sold the copyright of the form book for $250. Mrs. Dunlap lived to a great age and was ever a regular attendant and communicant of the above mentioned church. One of the children, Mrs. Rees, above mentioned, is a well known and highly esteemed resident of the city and cherishes as one of her choice possessions, the spotless name and merited fame of her honored father.

Hon. George H. Cutler

George H. Cutler, son of Nathan Cutler, was born October 29, 1809, at East Guilford, Vermont. He received a common school education and by home study for many years, acquired a knowledge of higher branches, including geology and astronomy. He came to Erie county when young and in 1837 began the study of law with Judge John Galbraith at Erie and was admitted to our bar November 7, 1840. He then began a professional career in this county which continued for approximately fifty years, all that time having his offices at Girard. He soon acquired and long maintained a very extensive practice. In fact, as the years passed, he had more than he could do and associated with him his son-in-law, Calvin J. Hinds, Esq., under the firm name of Cutler & Hinds, which continued for many years. Both being able lawyers and men of high standing, the firm was strong and prosperous. Cutler, a large, handsome man of commanding appearance and engaging manners, at first did most of the trial work, where he was at his best, being a clear thinker and an unusually ready and effective speaker. Hinds, however, became exceedingly strong in that branch of the practice and participated in many trials. Mr. Cutler was ever glad to assist young men and a number who were students in his office later became prominent at the bar.

Although never a politician he was so popular with both bar and public that his name was frequently mentioned for various offices. On one occasion he made a phenominal run as the Democratic candidate for Congress, and upon the death of Judge John Galbraith in

1860, without suggestion from him, his name was by both bar and public strongly urged upon the Governor for appointment as judge. In 1864 he declined a nomination for Legislature, but was elected State Senator in 1872 and became president pro tem of that body and served as such with distinction during the session of 1875. He never sought other public office, but continued to practice law for many years. To the end of his life he enjoyed public respect and confidence to a marked degree. He died July 26, 1892, in the eighty-third year of his age and was buried in the Girard Cemetery.

On February 20, 1839, he was united in marriage with Louisa Stewart, who predeceased him. They had six children, Mark, Elvira, Mary, Helen, Louise and George A. The latter, and to my best knowledge only survivor, is a lawyer in Grand Rapids, Michigan. The son Mark was admitted to the Erie Bar in 1857, but I believe never was in active practice. He did, however, serve acceptably as Deputy Register and Recorder for a number of years. George H. Cutler was originally a Democrat, but joined the Republican party during its early years and ever after remained steadfast thereto.

Calvin J. Hinds, Esq.

C. J. Hinds, a direct descendant of James Hinds, who came to this country, probably from England and landed at Salem, Massachusetts, as early as 1637, was the son of Perly and Sarah (Lawrence) Hinds and born in Girard township, this county, December 27, 1832. Calvin was an ambitious boy and, without any encouragement from his father, left home when quite young to get an education. He attended the Girard Academy and later the Spencerian Business School at Cleveland, in both instances working his way through. After completing a course of legal study under Hon. George H. Cutler, of Girard, he was admitted to the Erie Bar, May 11, 1860. Hinds disclosed such sterling qualities that Mr. Cutler formed with him the law partnership of Cutler & Hinds, which was very successful and continued until the former retired many years later. Thereafter Mr. Hinds continued in practice by himself until his death. While Calvin J. Hinds spent his life in a small town, he was a large man in many ways, a natural lawyer, the embodiment of robust integrity, very industrious, had an unusually clear practical brain, was a forceful speaker, a strong vigorous reasoner and a dangerous antagonist before court or jury. He looked carefully after the details of his cases and seldom neglected to take full advantage of situations. In other words he was alive and alert and never caught napping. Doubtless he would have had a more noteworthy career in a city, but he loved Girard and its people and never chose to leave them. He was a typical country lawyer and above all a peacemaker. Such a man is a blessing to a community. He never brought a suit unless convinced of its justice and he tried only such as could not be fairly settled. He was a close friend and for probably twenty-five years attorney for Col. Dan Rice, the famous showman, who for many years lived at Girard. He was also local counsel for the Bessemer & Lake Erie Railway, was an organizer of the Girard Building and Loan Association, joined with Col. Rice in locating and plotting Rice Avenue, generally represented the borough and school district of Girard in all litigation and enjoyed a large clientele.

While he was an ardent and active Republican, he never sought office, but was appointed postmaster at Girard by President Lincoln. He ever took a deep interest in the public schools and was a most efficient school director in that borough for about twenty-five years. Mr. Hinds was a life long friend of Denman Thompson, the actor, best known in "The Old Homestead", who, by the way, was a native of Girard township. Hinds was a deep student of and thorough believer in the doctrine of evolution. His only church or fraternity was humanity, whose humblest member he was ever ready to help.

His first wife, Elvira M. Cutler, by whom he had three children, was a daughter of Hon. George H. Cutler and, after her death, Mr. Hinds, on May 27, 1868, married Frances Stewart, of Syracuse, New York, by whom he had six children. One of his nine children was accidently killed and the other eight, including Calvin J. Hinds, Esq., an attorney in Cleveland, are living. It is noteworthy that not one of Mr. Hinds' lineal ancestors, in the paternal line, for seven generations had less than nine children. Calvin J. Hinds was a medium sized man of strong constitution and in his later years wore a full gray beard. He died on February 11, 1911, aged seventy-nine years and was buried at Girard. Thus ended a long and useful life. When a young man, Mr. Hinds was employed for a time in Philadelphia and for two years was clerk of a lumber company at Phillipsburg, Penna.

Judge John Pericles Vincent

Judge John P. Vincent, son of William and Elsie (Nichols) Vincent, was born in Waterford township, December 2, 1817. He was a lineal descendant of Levi Vincent, a French Huguenot who settled in New Jersey, near the close of the seventeenth century. Later, members of the family moved to Northumberland county, Pennsylvania, and still later, as early settlers, to this county. His uncle, Hon. John Vincent was an associate judge of Erie county and the late Bethuel B. Vincent, of Erie, father of General Strong and Bishop Boyd Vincent, was his cousin. He was also a cousin of Bishop John H. Vincent of Chautauqua fame. After being reared on a farm and educated at the Waterford Academy, John P. Vincent became a student in the law office of Hon. Elijah Babbitt of Erie, and was admitted to the Erie Bar in 1841, at once entering upon the practice of law at Erie, which was the beginning of the longest and one of the most honorable legal careers in the history of our county. Including two terms as member of the state legislature, where he was recognized as the most concise speaker and a leading member and the ten years he served as judge of the district, he was in active practice for nearly sixty-five years. Before going upon the bench in 1867 he enjoyed a fine practice and was one of the leaders of the bar. He was regarded as an exceptionally sound lawyer, capable of stating his positions with great clearness, and as an advocate took high rank. His defense of Barber Bill, charged with murder, was a classic. The first trial before Judge Derrickson, of another district, holding special court here, resulted in a first degree verdict and sentence of death. This Vincent induced the state supreme court to set aside as the record failed to show Derrickson held the court by invitation of the local judge. On the second trial Vincent, by a masterly defense, secured a lower degree verdict and saved his client's life. In 1866 he was elected additional judge of the district and later, under the new constitution, became the first president judge of Erie county, designated the sixth judicial district. He had many elements of a great judge, learning, industry, common sense, courage, absolute honesty, an intense love of justice, a wonderful command of the English language, and great personal dignity, but, sad to relate, lacked an even temper, and would occasionally display anger, even on the bench. A quick temper, which he realized as his besetment but never fully mastered, clung to him to the last. This minor infirmity was scarcely noticed by the public and overlooked by the bar, who recognized his sterling worth and he would have been reelected, but judgeships at that time in this part of the state were treated as one term offices. In fact, my reelection in 1906 was the first break of that rule in this district, followed by the reelection of President Judge Rossiter, in 1925. In recent years the one term rule has been set aside in most of the nearby districts, so we may truly say northwestern Pennsylvania has joined with the great majority of the counties of the Commonwealth in awarding faithful judicial service by a continuance in office. He had as a judge the admirable quality of uniformly putting himself squarely on the record, so that when the case came up for review there was never a doubt as to what he had decided.

On resuming practice, Judge Vincent opened offices

in the Scott Block, but later rented the small frame building on Sixth street, opposite the court house, many years before the offices of Hon. John Galbraith, where he remained until the building was removed, when Mrs. Strong's residence was erected at Sixth and Peach streets. Here we were located during the five years (1883-1888) of my partnership with Judge Vincent. On resuming practice, he at once did a good business, representing many important clients and interests, including the Erie Gas Company, The Erie City Passenger Railway Company, the County of Erie, and at times acted as special counsel for the Lake Shore and Michigan Southern Railway Company. His legal ability was so generally recognized that he was frequently called in to assist in the trial of important cases in this and sometimes in other counties. He had a profound knowledge of the law and could state the question at issue as clearly and concisely as any lawyer I have ever heard dicsuss legal questions. He often appeared before the state supreme court where he was given marked attention. In fact, I heard Hon. Silas M. Clark, when a member of that court, say that no lawyer in the state presented better printed briefs than Judge Vincent, of Erie. During our partnership we tried many cases together, he usually argued the law and I the facts. He was one of the fairest lawyers I ever heard present a proposition and never once sought to warp the law to fit the facts or the facts to fit the law. His object was as much to vindicate the law as to win the case. I have seen more tactful advocates, but rarely a lawyer of more strength. He was a true lawyer in that he never refused a cause because of its unpopularity, or the poverty of the client. Justice to him was ever important, no matter how small the amount involved.

Judge Vincent was public spirited and always took a deep interest in the city's welfare. He drew the bill for the creation of the Erie City Water Department, and as judge, appointed its first commissioners. He was active in securing the location of the Soldiers' and Sailors' Home at Erie. He was a forceful and an able speaker and often called upon on occasions of public interest. A loyal Republican, ever ready to advance its cause by pen and voice; was a member of St. Paul's Episcopal Church. Until disqualified by age he was an ardent sportsman, very fond of hunting and fishing. It is said that when the bar desired to get rid of the June term of civil court, Col. Thompson would step up to the bench and inform the judge that the trout were biting, and then by general consent the whole list would be passed.

In early life Judge Vincent married Harriet Scott Shattuck, who bore him two daughters, Harriet, the wife and later widow of Captain Charles V. Gridley, who commanded the flag ship at the battle of Manila, and Kate, who became the wife of William T. Swinburne, now Rear Admiral United States Navy, retired. The judge was very fond of his family and especially delighted in his grandson, John Vincent Gridley, who lost his life by an explosion while an officer in the marine or naval service. The judge resided for very many years in his home on West Sixth street, the table of which was always supplied with the best in the market. He personally did much of the marketing and was an excellent judge of good food. The judge left only a small estate, but he lived like a prince.

The judge had the fine personal appearance characteristic of the Vincent family. He was of medium size, exceedingly well and strongly built, with a large, finely shaped head, covered with an abundance of dark hair, which turned gray as the years passed and which he allowed to come down in the back with a square cut, a style I tried so successfully to imitate that it became known as the "Judge Walling hair cut." Aside from a clean shaven upper lip, he wore a full beard, properly trimmed. His features were exceptionally strong and well formed. He would be at once pointed out in any company as a man of distinction. Judge Vincent was a wonderful conversationalist and during our five years together I found him a most charming companion, and we never had an unpleasant word.

In his seventieth year, Judge Vincent suffered an irreparable loss in the death of his faithful and greatly beloved wife. From this staggering blow he rallied and kept at his work for many years thereafter; the daughter, Mrs. Gridley, one of Erie's first ladies, kept his home and lent comfort to his declining years.

Judge Vincent was for over twenty years the nestor of the Erie Bar and a prime favorite. On his eightieth birthday, the bar assembled in the court room and Senator Sill read a series of resolutions eulogistic of the judge, while Col. Thompson on behalf of the bar presented him with a beautiful engraved silver loving cup. The judge fittingly responded and the occasion was a memorable one. The president of the bar association had appointed Senator Sill, Col. Thompson and myself as the committee on resolutions. The Colonel and I delegated the Senator as a sub committee and the resolutions as printed below are as prepared by him, with the deletion of some extravagant expressions, which the Colonel and I feared would not be acceptable to the judge.

"Whereas, Hon. John P. Vincent, late president Judge of the Sixth judicial district, has reached the close of his 80th year of a life, comprising nearly 57 years of professional and judicial service; the Erie Bar Association deem it due to Judge Vincent and becoming the occasion, to manifest their estimate of his character as a man; his attainments as a lawyer, his successful labors as a legislator, and his able administration as judge. Whereupon

"Resolved, That the Erie Bar Association extend their felicitations to their respected associate; so long revered as the Nestor of the bar; and unite in expressing profound respect for the talents, character, bearing and ability with which his long career has been adorned, and the members of the association claim their privilege as his associates in a profession so highly honored in the Judge's career to thus note this epoch of his long and eventful life; and to record their estimate of his character; and admiration of his abilities; especially as illustrated in his extended and faithful service as legislator and judge; during a momentous period of our country's history.

"Resolved, That as a memento of this occasion, the association presents to Judge Vincent a souvenir with such inscription as shall with an engrossed copy of these resolutions, indicate the regard and respect of his associates at the bar, and successors upon the bench—of the county which cherished Judge Vincent as her son; and the inheritor of a name associated with the first settlement as well as with many of the brightest pages of the county's history."

Judge Vincent died in December 1908, after passing his ninety-first birthday and is buried in Lake Side Cemetery. He retained his faculties in a wonderful degree to the last. No lawyer of higher professional ideals or more strict personal integrity than John P. Vincent honors the roster of our bar.

General Strong Vincent

Strong Vincent, son of Bethuel B. and Sarah Ann (Strong) Vincent, was born at Waterford, June 17, 1837. On the father's side he was the grandson of Hon. John Vincent, who settled at Waterford in 1797, coming from Northumberland county. Hon. John Vincent was a pioneer settler in Erie county and one of its foremost citizens, serving as associate judge of the county for more than thirty years, beginning in 1805. Soon after coming to the county he had a controversy with a neighbor over a strip of land and, the laws at the time affording no adequate means of adjustment, they agreed to and did settle the question by wager of battle. Vincent, a man of great physical strength won, and the defeated litigant moving to a western state, later became its governor. The only case of wager of battle found in the history of this county, if not in the state. Judge John Vincent died at his home in Waterford in 1860, at the age of eighty-eight years.

Strong Vincent's maternal grandfather, Captain Martin Strong was born in Connecticut in 1770, settled in Summit township in 1795 and was the founder of a family second to none in Erie County. He was noted for his sound judgment, common sense and strict integrity. He died on the old farm in 1858, aged eighty-seven years. Bethuel B. Vincent, a prominent resident of Erie for many years, was head of the firm of Vincent, Himrod & Co., in the foundry and machine business, also was head of the banking house of Vincent, Bailey & Co., which in 1866 became the Marine National Bank and he its first president. In the same year he joined in building the

National Elevator in Chicago, destroyed five years later by the great fire, but rebuilt the following year. He died in 1876.

Strong Vincent, the subject of this sketch, removed with the family to Erie when a small boy and attended the Erie Academy. In 1854 he entered Trinity College at Hartford, Conn., and in two years was transferred to Harvard College, from which he graduated in 1859. Entering the law office of W. S. Lane at Erie he was admitted to our bar in Dec. 1860, and joined in practice with Mr. Lane. On the first call for volunteers in 1861 he joined as a private, was elected second lieutenant, being appointed adjutant and served three months, at the end of which he reinlisted in the 83rd Regiment Pa. Volunteers, and was made major with John C. McLane as colonel. The 83rd was one of the famous fighting regiments of the Union Army and Strong Vincent fought with it through all the battles. He soon became Lieutenant Colonel and on the death of Col. McLane, killed at the awful battle of Gaine's Mills, Vincent became Colonel of the Regiment. As such he participated in the battles of Antietam, Fredericksburg and Chancellorsville. As Colonel commanding a Brigade under General Mead he entered the battle of Gettysburg, where on July 2, 1863, during the second day's fight, he dismounted and led his brigade against the enemy at the foot of Little Round Top. He faced superior numbers, the fighting was terrific. The ground must be held to prevent the flanking of our left wing and possible loss of the battle. He told his comrades that here Pennsylvanians must defend their own soil to the last man. He was as firm as the rock whereon he stood. He saw where bullets from sharpshooters were hitting the dust nearer and nearer to him; he knew and was warned of his peril but never flinched. The place was held, the day was won, but ere its close the sharpshooter's bullet had found its mark and Strong Vincent fell mortally wounded. The effort to break Mead's right wing also failed. So the only hope left Lee was to break through the center which he attempted the following day by Pickett's brave but fatal charge. Much depended upon Strong Vincent that day, and disregarding personal danger, he met the occasion like a true soldier. Had he faltered, the battle might not have ended in a decisive victory for the Union. His blood was not shed in vain. He was carried to a farm house where he died in five days, but lived long enough to learn the result of the battle, and also to receive a commission as Brigadier General from President Lincoln, sent at the telegraphed request of General Mead.

In going over that battlefield twenty-two years later, I was shown the spot where Strong Vincent fell and the house in which he died. There I met a young man, born soon after the battle who was christened "Strong Vincent." I never saw Strong Vincent, but judging from his photograph there was not a finer looking man in the Union Army. In honor of his memory the Grand Army Post here was christened for him and still bears his name. In my opinion, Erie county's greatest single individual loss in that awful war was General Strong Vincent. On the eve of entering the service, in April 1861, he was married to Miss Elizabeth Carter, of Newark, New Jersey, by whom he had one child, a daughter, who died in infancy. Among his surviving relatives is Bishop Boyd Vincent, of Cincinnati, now eighty-two years of age, whose remarkable book of the Vincent family has greatly lightened my labors in writing this sketch and that of Judge John P. Vincent. It is a coincidence that I have written this sketch on July 2, 1927, the sixty-fourth anniversary of the day Strong Vincent fell at Gettysburg.

In the life of Strong Vincent, the patriotism of the American lawyer appears at its best.

Hon. John Barnette Johnson

J. B. Johnson, of Irish lineage, was born in Crawford county, Pa., Dec. 6, 1817. He graduated at Allegheny College in 1840. There he was one of a group of brilliant young men, embracing Bishop Calvin Kingsley, who died at Beyrout while making an official tour around the world; Hon. Darwin A. Finney, who became one of Pennsylvania's leading men, and died in 1868, while a member of congress from Meadville district; Hon. H. L. Richmond, who also served in congress, and others. During his college days he helped defray his expenses by working as a civil engineer. While there he overtaxed his eyes and temporarily lost his sight. On leaving college Mr. Johnson taught school at Fairview, Erie county, and, having pursued his law studies, was admitted to the Erie Bar April 5, 1842, where he entered upon the practice of law. He was then twenty-five years of age, had a pleasing personality, a keen intellect, a remarkable memory, tireless energy, open, absolute honesty, great courage, an unusual power of expression and, in an incredibly short time, stood in the front rank at the local bar. As the years passed he numbered among his clients many important interests, including the Cleveland and Erie Railroad, in the construction of which he took an important part. He was also solicitor for the county commissioners when the court house was erected (1853-1855) and gave unremitting attention to that important work.

In politics he was a Whig and took the stump for General Harrison in the memorable "Log Cabin and Hard Cider campaign of 1840." His personal popularity and exceptional oratorical ability brought him in great demand in later campaigns. He was twice elected to the state legislature and once to the senate; when chosen to the latter in 1846 he was the youngest man ever sent from Erie county to that body. I was but a year older when elected in 1884. He made a fine record at Harrisburg. In the House he served both sessions as chairman of the committee on corporations and in the Senate as chairman of the General Judiciary Committee. He headed other committees and, in 1848, one to examine the practice of the Court of Common Pleas of Philadelphia, where he made a masterly report. He took an active part in the discussion of important measures and was recognized as one of the ablest debators in either body. During his service in the senate he had the satisfaction of seeing his personal friend and relative, Hon. James Cooper of Adams county, elected United States Senator, being the first Whig elected to that office from Pennsylvania. Mr. Johnson was an ardent supporter of Abraham Lincoln and attended his inauguration in 1861. He was a friend of the President and received from him a photograph, which is highly treasured by Miss T. E. Lebling, Mr. Johnson's granddaughter.

When what is now the New York Central Railroad was constructed through Erie it had troubles. A large majority of the citizens were determined that the railroad coming from Buffalo should end at Parade street and that the railroad going to Cleveland should begin at Sassafras street, making a gap of over half a mile so that passengers and freight must be transferred from one to the other by hacks and drays, and the passengers remain over for meals or lodging. This fantastical scheme, as it now appears, was of course fought by the railroads and finally defeated in the courts. In spite of which the popular opposition continued and for a time forcibly prevented building the railroad through the city going so far as to destroy the bridge erected over State street. The answer to the arguments for the railroad was violence. John R. Cochran, a very prominent citizen, assaulted John H. Walker in front of the court house, but was beaten up in retaliation by the latter's son, John W., at the first opportunity. Mob violence was supreme and it became widely known as the Erie Railroad War. Mr. Johnson had a newspaper office in connection with his law office, where he edited and published a weekly paper called "The Constitution." He not only defended the railroad in the courts, but asserted its rights with unanswerable force through the columns of his paper. This so incensed the opposition that a mob collected and burned both his newspaper and law office, destroying much property, including his law library and valuable papers. The governor of the state sought to end the trouble, and, after its acute stage had long past, sent Hon. Alex. K. McClure here to, if possible, end the strife. After a careful survey McClure decided to call to his room in the Reed House two of the leading belligerents on each side and canvass the situation. How he succeeded is told in his own language in "Old Time Notes of Pennsylvania, vol. 2, page 231, as follows: "(Walker and Courtright being favorable to the railroad and Thompson and Skinner opposed): "The first to appear was Judge Thompson, who was a most delightful gentleman, and whom I did not fear as likely to provoke a disturbance, but who would be probably ready for a battle on any visible provocation. While we were standing at the sideboard taking the first sample of the whisky, there was a knock at the door and John H. Walker entered. He was a fighter of fighters, and the one I most feared. He stopped inside the door, evidently startled at seeing Judge Thompson, and I immediately walked up to him, shook him by the hand, and told him that I had invited him to meet Judge Thompson, as two of the most respected citizens of the city, as my guests for the evening, and asked him to join us in a glass. He hesitated for some moments, and I very much feared that he would respond explosively, but he finally joined me and walked up to Judge Thompson and reached out his hand, and all took a glass together. I felt then that the battle was won, for with John H. Walker, the most implacable of all the belligerents, on terms with Judge Thompson I had nothing to apprehend from Skinner, who was amiable, and from Courtright, who had great interests at stake. They came in a few minutes later, and seeing Thompson and Walker in social intercourse logically fell in, and we at once sat down to a stakeless game of euchre. I had a fine supper for the party about midnight, and the game of cards continued until the sun was purpling the east, with the promise of another day, when they all shook hands in the most friendly way and went to their homes. That settled the Erie riots."

To Johnson, the wanton destruction of his property had been a body blow, but he fought on and lived to see his position completely vindicated. The bitterness engendered by the Railroad War was, however, for many years a drawback to the city.

In May, 1845, he was united in marriage with a daughter of John Caughey, of Fairview, and sister of

Miles W. and William M. Caughey. Among their children were two daughters, Mrs. Lebling and Miss Lizzie Johnson, the teacher, who were prominent in Erie for many years. Mr. Johnson resided during his later years in the home and office he built on West Eighth street, later the residence and office of Dr. H. A. Spencer and his family, now the property of the Y. W. C. A. and adorned by a fine brick structure. Mr. Johnson was an active Presbyterian and helped erect the Park Church, but he was broadminded and acted as a trustee in the erection of the building for the First M. E. Church at Erie. He was an intense man and his most striking characteristic probably was his outspoken love of truth and hatred of shams. He doubtless worked beyond his strength and the destruction of his property and turmoil of the Railroad War, as above stated, tended to shorten his life. He died February 4, 1863, aged forty-five years, and was buried in the Erie Cemetery. Few members of our bar have made a more lasting impression upon the profession or the public than John B. Johnson. The influence of such a life never dies. When his portrait was hung in the court room in 1901, Hon. James Sill wrote for the Daily Times an excellent memorial of Mr. Johnson, which has greatly facilitated my labors in preparing this sketch.

William S. Lane, Esq.

William S. Lane, son of Samuel A. Lane, was born in Mifflin county, Pa., April 8, 1818. After graduating at Jefferson College with the B. A. degree, he studied law in the office of Hon. Samuel A. Purviance, at Butler, and coming to Erie was admitted to our bar July 22, 1844, where he engaged in practice until 1864. Removing to Philadelphia, he continued to practice in that city until his death in 1901. He was considered a good lawyer, both here and in Philadelphia; as to the details of his practice, I am not well informed. When I first came to the bar Mr. Lane was frequently and favorably spoken of by the older lawyers. I remember seeing him when he came here on a visit. He was a tall, spare, dark complexioned, fine looking gentleman, with elegant manners.

August 21, 1845, he married Elizabeth A. Galbraith, only daughter of Judge John Galbraith. They had five children. Mr. Lane was accustomed to hunt and fish and was engaged in private banking. I have an impression he also engaged at one time in truck farming in New Jersey. He was a Mason; also a member of the Union League of Philadelphia. When in Erie he belonged to St. Paul's Episcopal Church and later to Protestant Episcopal Epiphany Church in Philadelphia. He was a Republican but never sought office. He died in Philadelphia, December 20, 1901, in the eighty-fourth year of his age, and was buried in that city. He was a man of high ideals and an honor to the profession.

Chief Justice James Thompson

James Thompson, son of William and Mary Thompson, was born in Butler county, Penna., October 1, 1805. His ancestors were Scotch-Irish and first settled at Carlisle, but later located in Butler county. James learned the trade of a printer, but at the early age of nineteen began the study of law with John Gilmore, of Butler, and later studied with Thomas Blair at Kittanning. He was admitted to the Butler County Bar April 9, 1828, and located at Franklin, Venango County, where he began practice. In 1845 he began practice in Erie and for some years occupied a brick residence on the east side of State street, where the Marine Bank Building now stands. From that time until 1857 he was in active practice here, interrupted by public services, to which we will refer. We know by history and tradition that James Thompson was a remarkable lawyer, one of the most able in the state. During his practice he tried important cases in many counties, with great ability. He successfully defended a criminal case in Mercer County, with an ability probably never surpassed in that county. While eminent as a civil lawyer he did not spurn the criminal courts and was at his best in the defense of homicide cases. His charming and magnetic personality, his quick and strong mental grasp, his industry and phenomenal memory, his knowledge of law and fine oratorical powers, his deep knowledge of human nature and broad sympathies, with his manifest integrity and high character, rendered him the ideal advocate.

Those and other qualities also made him so immensely popular, wherever known, that he was chosen to so many public positions as to seriously interfere with his work as a practicing lawyer. In 1832 he was sent to the legislature from Venango County and by successive re-elections continued there for several years. During that service he attained the high position of Speaker of the House. In 1839 a special judicial district, including Erie County, was created for the term of six years and he was appointed the judge thereof and served with distinction during that term. This brought him to Erie where he entered upon the practice of law, as above stated, in 1845. At the end of his judicial term, however, he was elected to congress where by successive re-elections he remained for six years and took high rank. He took an active part on the popular side in the railroad war, to which we refer in speaking of Hon. J. B. Johnson, and to serve that cause accepted an election to the legislature in 1854 and remained there until 1857, when he was elected a member of the supreme court of Pennsylvania for the then term of fifteen years, the last five years of which he served as Chief Justice. By his work in that court he is best known and will be longest remembered. That he made a great judge and a great Chief Justice is to the legal profession a matter of common knowledge. His opinions appear in forty volumes of the state reports, ending with 72 Pa. One of his distinguishing characteristics as a judge was strong common sense, another was his desire to reach the merits of the case, in spite of legal quibbles, or technicalities, and another was his loyalty to the ancient landmarks of the law as previously laid down by the court in which he sat. He rarely joined in the reversal of a decision rendered by his predecessors; and it may be truly said his decisions have rarely been reversed by his successors. His opinions were written in plain, unadorned, but vigorous English and left no doubt as to the meaning. He decided the case before him, giving his reasons and references, but seldom, and only when necessary, did he indulge in extended discussions. In general it may be said he wrote sound law in language easily understood and helpful alike to the profession and the public. His manner upon the bench was in every respect most admirable. Considering the high positions he held and the able manner in which he discharged the duties thereof, Chief Justice James Thompson must be awarded first place among the members of our bar who have held judicial office.

Soon after locating in Franklin he was joined in marriage with Miss Mary Parker Gustine Snowden. They had six children, Sarah Gustine (who became the wife of Samuel Robb, Esq.), Col. J. Ross, Snowden, Samuel Gustine (who served twice as justice of the state supreme court by appointment), Miss Clara and William Eldred, all now deceased; of whom two, Hon. Samuel Gustine, of Philadelphia, and Col. J. Ross, of Erie, became eminent in the father's profession. After his election to the supreme court, Judge Thompson removed to Philadelphia, where he purchased a residence at 1632 Spruce street, which became the home of the Thompson family for some sixty years. There the judge kept open house, as he had ever done, and dispensed a most charming hospitality. As a gracious entertainer and generous host he was not second to any member of our bar. He was ever genial and most considerate in his intercourse with others, and probably had as wide a circle of warm friends as ever fell to the lot of a member of the supreme court of

Pennsylvania. He was a consistent Democrat and received many honors at the hands of his party, but, whenever a candidate for popular office, he was supported by those who knew him, regardless of party. He was a consistent member of the Presbyterian Church. Ever an industrious lawyer who loved his profession, when his term of office in the supreme court expired, January 1873, he entered upon the practice of law in Philadelphia. One year later, January 28, 1874, while arguing a case before the supreme court, where he had so long presided, he was stricken and died in the room where so much of his life's work had been done. He literally died in the harness. The court at once adjourned out of respect to his memory and the following morning suitable resolutions by both bench and bar were adopted and appropriate eulogies delivered. This is reported in 72 Pa., page 1. I am told it is the only occasion when the death of one not then a member of the court has been so honored. He was buried in Woodlawn Cemetery, Philadelphia. Personally, James Thompson looked every inch a judge, slightly above medium height, compactly built, with a large head and a wonderfully strong, yet kindly face, smooth shaven except a border of whiskers extending around under the chin, after the Horace Greeley pattern, a style of facial adornment formerly much in vogue.

James Thompson's widow, who lived in the family home until she was ninety-one years of age, now sleeps by his side.

Colonel James Ross Thompson

J. Ross Thompson, son of Chief Justice James and Mary Parker Gustine (Snowden) Thompson, was born at Franklin, Penna., December 6, 1832, of Scotch-Irish ancestry. He was educated at the Erie Academy and Princeton College, graduating from the latter in the class of 1854. Entering his father's law office as a student he was admitted to the Erie Bar, May 3, 1856. He immediately entered upon a legal practice which covered a period of fifty-four years, and extended into the state appellate and federal courts and into many counties of the state. In his day he was perhaps the most widely known member of our bar. He was attorney for the Pennsylvania Railroad Company, and all its affiliated branches in this part of the state for fifty years. He soon became prominent as a trial lawyer and often appeared as counsel in both civil and criminal courts in this and other counties. All told he probably participated in the trial of more causes than any other member in the history of our bar. He acted upon the theory of the late John G. Johnson, of Philadelphia, in his prime the leader of the American Bar, that every litigant was entitled to an advocate. So Col. Thompson never refused a retainer, however desperate the cause might be. His exceptionally fine appearance, thorough knowledge of elementary law, great natural ability, phenomenal memory, mental alertness at all times, with an ever ready wit and exceptionally fine gift of oratory, gave him prestige as an advocate. When forty years of age he was regarded the best criminal lawyer in Erie. For a period of years, beginning about 1875, the three most prominent criminal lawyers at our bar were Col. J. Ross Thompson, Hon. George A. Allen and Hon. S. M. Brainerd. Of these, Brainerd, who had served as district attorney, was stronger for the Commonwealth than for the defense; Allen was stronger for the defense than for the Commonwealth; while Thompson was equally strong on whichever side he might be engaged. He fought equally well, regardless of causes or clients and greatly enjoyed trial work, although not over diligent in preparation. Like many other brilliant lawyers he depended possibly too often on his genius. He was wonderfully strong when associated with some lawyer who would attend to the preliminary details. His advocacy of a case he had fully mastered was remarkable. When I was district attorney he assisted me in the prosecution of Dr. French, charged with the commission of an abortion and his final summing up of that case to the jury was masterly in the highest degree. We were associated in the defense of the Brown murder case, where his advocacy, especially on the second trial, was memorable. He was ever a good associate and a dangerous adversary. One element of his strength was an intense earnestness in presenting the case to the court or jury. But no matter how earnest, he was always a gentleman and in addressing the court employed legal expressions as fluently and accurately as any member of the bar. While his knowledge of law covered all branches, he was especially expert on questions of negligence and all matters pertaining to railroads. He loved the common law, of which he was master, and resented the code practice act of 1887, as he would that of 1915 had he lived. The truth is Col. Thompson had every element, but one, of being a commanding figure at the Pennsylvania Bar; he lacked industry and sometimes tried cases more on general principles than on the exact law and facts of the particular case. As it was he did well, but with hard work, he might have done better.

Col. Thompson was of medium height, of massive build, had a very large head and strong, attractive features. In his later years he was smooth shaven, except for a moustache. He was uniformly well dressed; it might be said expertly dressed. His clothes were ever in fashion and the best that metropolitan tailors could make. He often wore spats, striped trousers, a figured waistcoat and dark coat, with a rose or rosette attached and, while such head gear was common, a silk hat and usually carried a light cane. His appearance and demeanor were always those of a man of distinction, and there was never anything of the commonplace about him. He was very genial, but never at the expense of his personal dignity. In private conversation he used perfect diction and had but few equals. He was a most delightful companion, possessing a wonderful fund of information and enjoyed discussing matters of moment. When my office was in the court house, he was accustomed to drop in occasionally and would talk in a most charming manner for perhaps half an hour. When he could come no more, I missed him sadly.

Col. Thompson was ever a consistent Democrat, and in great demand as a campaign speaker. In 1876 he was a delegate to the National Democratic Convention which nominated Samuel J. Tilden for President, and in 1880 he was named as a Democratic presidential elector. In 1887 he was the Democratic nominee for judge of the state supreme court and declined a like nomination for the same office in 1888. The death of one of the judges during that summer made two vacancies and had he accepted that nomination he would have been elected for a twenty-one year term, as was Hon. J. Brewster McCollum, who did accept such nomination. That was how near Col. Thompson came to obtaining the office formerly held by his father.

He was popular with his brothers at the bar, for no matter how sharp the contest his blows left no scars. When he had completed his fifty years at the bar, the Erie attorneys tendered him a most remarkable banquet, largely attended by local lawyers and by some from away, and letters of regret were received from others. Numerous toasts were responded to and it was a memorable occasion. A part of my remarks was a little doggerel, substantially as follows, viz:

"Of our profession it has been found
The best like potatoes are under the ground;
For of a lawyer, whatever is said,
He's always a good fellow as soon as he is dead;
And live as he may, whenever he dies,
The court doth in his honor rise.
But here tonight we are quite willing
To pay a tribute to the living,
And of our honored guest declare
We are full glad his joy to share.
For years we have traveled on together,
Through sunshine and through stormy weather,
And found him ever wise and kind,
A hand to help, a soul refined.
As a lawyer he hits from the shoulder;
No one strikes harder, younger or older.

But though he deliver welt upon welt,
He never was known to strike under the belt.
So on this occasion let us be fair
And admit the Colonel is on the square.
Though his race is largely run
We wish it were but just begun;
This we know can never be,
For tonight is his golden jubilee.
But though his sun be in the west,
We trust his future may all be blessed,
And when comes his twilight and evening star,
That kind angels may pilot him over the bar."

The above was my first and properly my last attempt at rhyming and is only inserted here as somewhat indicating the sentiment prevalent on that happy occasion. A loving cup was presented the Colonel as symbolizing the affection of his professional brethren.

He served on the staff of Governor Packer, under the rank of Lieutenant Colonel and later was Colonel of the Sixteenth Regiment Penna. Militia. In 1858 Colonel Thompson was united in marriage with Miss Josephine Mayer, daughter of the late Martin Mayer of this city and a sister of the late Henry Mayer, in his day one of Erie's most successful and progressive citizens. Mrs. Thompson died in 1877, leaving a family of seven children viz: Sarah Gustine, Samuel Gustine, Elizabeth, James, William L. Scott, Clara and Robert M., of whom only Elizabeth (Mrs. Neide), James and Robert M. are now living. Colonel Thompson never remarried, but kept up the family home at Twelfth and Holland streets, some of the children ever remaining with him. There he died June 23, 1910, in the seventy- eighth year of his age. His mortal remains sleep in a beautiful mausoleum in the Erie Cemetery. While a Presbyterian by birth, he was for many years a seat holder and regular attendant of the First Methodist Church. A fine portrait of Colonel Thompson and also of his father may be found in Miller's History of Erie County, vol. 2, pages 33, 34.

The Thompson family life was ideal. After the death of the Chief Justice, his widow kept open house for all the children who wished to remain, as some did, and to which others, including the Colonel, were frequent visitors. The family for more than half a century maintained a summer home at the sea shore, first at Cape May, N. J., then at Spring Lake, N. J., and last at Narragansett Pier, R. I., at which the Colonel ever spent his summer vacations. He was fond of sea bathing, also often seen at races, ball games, etc. He indulged for very many years in his favorite sports of hunting and fishing. In fact, he never gave up the latter so long as he was able to walk the banks of a trout stream.

William L. Scott Thompson, Esq.

Scott Thompson (commonly so called), son of Colonel J. Ross and Josephine (Mayer) Thompson, was born in Erie, October 11, 1867. His father was of Scotch-Irish and his mother of German lineage; both being members of prominent families. Scott received his education at the Erie Academy and Massachusetts School of Technology, at Boston. He studied law in his father's office and was admitted to the Erie Bar, December 11, 1895, and became associated with his father in practice as J. Ross Thompson & Son. During the early years of his practice Scott tried a few cases by himself and showed ability, but the father being an exceedingly able trial lawyer, Scott had little need of forensic ability and soon confined his attention to office and business practice and the preparation of cases for trial. He, however, usually sat in at the trial of important cases and by his more intimate knowledge of the facts, made many valuable suggestions. Some years later, Hon. Uriah P. Rossiter, now President Judge of the district, joined the Thompson firm and, as he was a past master in advocacy, Scott still had no need to develop ability in that direction. The result was Scott Thompson never became a trial lawyer, although he continued actively in the profession and as one of the representatives of the Pennsylvania Railroad interests until his death. In the summer of 1916 he became the victim of a malignant attack, which ended in his death on December 6 of that year, at the age of forty-nine years. He was buried in the Erie Cemetery. I well remember Scott when, as a robust boy of ten, dressed in short pants, he used to come into court with his father.

He grew to be a strong young man of good build and medium size, always affable and well dressed, with every prospect of long life, but, in his prime he was stricken.

He was a prominent member of the Erie Club, where he could often be found in company with his fellow members. He inherited to a great extent the fine social qualities so prominent in his grandfather and father, but he was never married and ever remained at home, as one of the family, where he was the embodiment of thoughtful kindness. He was the last lawyer in the Thompson family, and by the way, he and his brothers and sisters were the only grandchildren of the late Chief Justice Thompson, and, as none of them so far have any children, it looks as though the race of that truly great man might become extinct. In religion, Scott was a Presbyterian and in politics a Democrat, but he never sought public office, although it is my recollection that at one time he was a deputy United States Marshal.

Colonel Benjamin Grant

Benjamin Grant, the son of Joseph Perkins and Clarissa Loomis Grant, was born April 22, 1822, on a farm in Wayne township, Erie County. He was educated at the common schools and Waterford Academy. Coming to Erie he studied law in the offices of Galbraith and Graham and was admitted to the Erie Bar in October, 1845, and practiced law at Erie continuously from that date until his death. He was highly regarded by the public, by his brother lawyers and especially by those who had been students in his office. He had a fondness for legal research, which caused him to publish as side reports, three volumes of decisions of the state supreme court. In this he did a notable service to the profession, for his well selected cases have ever been and still are often cited by court and counsel.

In 1847 Benjamin Grant married Miss Sarah Franklin of Erie, who died in 1849 and in 1851 he married Miss Maria Elizabeth Wilder, a native of Vermont.. They had a family of four children, Clara J., who became the wife of Col. Charles M. Lynch, Emma S., the widow of W. H. Nicholson, Frank W. Grant, Esq., of Erie and Ada Grant. Mrs. Nicholson and Frank W. live in Erie. Colonel Grant was a member of the Democratic party, and of St. Paul's Episcopal Church. At the breaking out of the Civil War in 1861, he helped recruit a regiment of which he became Lieutenant Colonel. He died November 24, 1877, at the age of fifty-five years and is buried in the Erie Cemetery. Thus ended, all too soon, the life of an industrious, capable lawyer and good citizen.

There was a well known colored wag in Erie named

Jim Stewart, who swept Col. Grant's office and one day a woman came in while Jim was alone in the office and asked if he was the lawyer to which he gave an affirmative reply and seated himself in Col. Grant's chair. The woman stated her case and Jim with due solemnity advised her as to her legal rights, for which he charged and received two dollars. It is also related of Jim that he stole Senator Morrow B. Lowrey's chickens and then sold them back to him as those of a superior breed.

Frank Wilder Grant, Esq.

Frank Grant, son of Col. Benjamin and Maria Elizabeth (Wilder) Grant, was born in Erie, May 25, 1852. It might be said he was born to the law, for his father was one of our leading members. After attending the Erie Academy and Dr. Taylor's private school at New Brighton, Pa., Frank entered Washington and Jefferson College, from which he graduated in 1870, with the A. B. degree. Among his classmates was Hon. George B. Orlady, for over thirty years a member of the Pennsylvania Superior Court and for very many years its president judge. On more than one occasion that eminent jurist asked the writer about Frank Grant and expressed great friendship for him. Following his college graduation Frank entered his father's office as a student at law and, on March 12, 1874, was admitted to the Erie Bar. Three years later on the death of his father, with whom he was at first associated, he formed a law partnership with Capt. Charles L. Pierce, under the name of Grant & Pierce, which continued until the latter's death in January, 1880. The firm seemed to do a fairly good business, and after its dissolution, Mr. Grant continued practice for some years and whatever he undertook he did well. But for some reason when he was approximately thirty-five years of age he abandoned active practice. Later he accepted and for quite a good many years held a position in the Erie office of the Pennsylvania Gas Company. Soon after coming to the bar he was appointed a United States Commissioner, a position he held for over fifty years, and the duties of which he ever performed with scrupulous care, fidelity and ability. Frank Grant was a high type of man of excellent ability and doubtless might have had a distinguished legal career; but his inclinations did not seem to point in that direction.

He was a medium sized, smooth shaven, fine appearing gentleman, and, while undemonstrative, was uniformly affable, courteous and well liked by all with whom he came in contact. That he made an excellent and remarkably efficient United States Commissioner is a matter of common knowledge. He was a member of the Erie, the Kahkwa and the Erie Yacht clubs for many years. He was a Democrat, but not usually very active in politics and never sought public office. Frank Grant, who never married, died September 10, 1927, and was buried in the Erie Cemetery. He lived his entire life of seventy-five years and died in the home where he was born, at 132 East Fifth street, which is also the home of his sister, Mrs. William H. Nicholson, now the only surviving member of Col. Grant's family. Mrs. Nicholson is quite an extensive traveler and her brother, Frank, accompanied her on different occasions. He was a lover of the out-of-doors and as long as he was able greatly enjoyed golf and other recreations.

Hon. Samuel Ebenezer Woodruff

S. E. Woodruff, son of Rev. Ephraim Treadwell and Sally (Alden) Woodruff, was born at Coventry, Connecticut, in 1817. His father, a nephew of Gov. Treadwell, graduated at Yale College in the class of 1797 and was a prominent Presbyterian minister and teacher for approximately fifty years, beginning in New England and ending in Ohio. His mother was a lineal descendant of the Pilgrim Alden of Plymouth Rock. S. E. Woodruff graduated at Hamilton College and then studied law at Cincinnati where he was admitted to the bar in 1841. Hon. Salmon P. Chase, afterward Chief Justice of the United States Supreme Court, being one of the board of examiners. He located at Rock Island, Ill., where he practiced law for a few years and then removed to Girard in this county and was admitted to our bar in 1846, where he practiced law continuously until his death. He was a diligent student and a painstaking, hard working lawyer. No business committed to his care was neglected. Gradually he acquired a large clientage and worked his way up in the profession until he became an exceedingly sound and able lawyer. Every case entrusted to him was carefully prepared and well tried. Few members of our bar have developed better as lawyers than did he.

In 1853 he became district attorney of Erie County, and in 1867, on the recommendation of his college classmate, Hon. Glenni W. Schofield, then in congress from this district, and on approval of Chief Justice Chase, Mr. Woodruff was appointed Register in Bankruptcy for this district. In 1872 he took up his residence in Erie, where he and his family thereafter resided, and where he continued to practice his profession. He gave careful attention to his official duties and his services therein gave great satisfaction, until the Bankrupt Statute was repealed in 1877.

He won many victories at the bar, one of the most notable being that of Turner v. Scott, 57 Pa. 126, and Scott v. Scott, 70 Pa. 244, where he contended for and established the rule that a deed to take effect at the death of the grantor was in effect a will and as such revocable. Another important case he had was that of Com. v. Hoskinson, indicted for maintaining a brick yard in South Erie, which neighbors sought to abate as a public nuisance and employed Mr. Woodruff to assist the district attorney; this he did with signal ability. It was one of the most stubbornly contested cases ever tried in Erie county. S. A. Davenport put up a masterly defense and the jury, after forty hours deliberation, rendered a verdict of "Not guilty, but pay the costs." Soon after my admission to the bar, I consulted Mr. Woodruff about a contested case in the orphans' court, where his clients and mine had like interests. He took down a volume of the State reports and called my attention to a case which was in point and won ours. That was characteristic of Mr. Woodruff; he found and cited the controlling case or principle and did not burden the court with irrelevant authorities. In other words he had a discriminating legal mind, and there were few if any better at our bar. He wore dark chin whiskers and moustache, was a large, well built, fine looking gentleman, whose influence was enhanced by his high character and strict integrity. He never harbored a dishonest thought.

On May 12, 1848, he was united in marriage with

Miss Eliza Sterrett, member of a very numerous and high class family. They had three children, a son, T. S. Woodruff, Esq., and two daughters. All lived to old age, but the daughters are now deceased. Mr. Woodruff was a Republican and had Erie county's endorsement for judge in 1870, but was defeated in the district by Hon. L. D. Wetmore, of Warren. A more kind and thoughtful man in his family, or one more useful in the community than Mr. Woodruff would be difficult to find. He was exceedingly popular with the bar. I well remember the feeling expressed at his memorial services. Voices rarely heard on such occasions spoke his praises. We all realized we had lost a true friend. His death was somewhat remarkable. In good health and strength, his kind heart led him to the room of a friend afflicted with erysipelas, where he contracted the dread disease and in a few days was dead. Thus, sadly, ended the career of Samuel E. Woodruff on April 15, 1881, in the sixty-fourth year of his age. He was buried in the family lot at Girard. His widow survived him for many years and died in 1912. In early life he accepted the faith of his father and was ever after a consistent and active member of the Presbyterian Church.

William Benson, Esq.

William Benson, son of James and Rebecca (Van Kirk) Benson, was born in Waterford township, this county, March 7, 1819, and grew to manhood on his father's farm, which he helped to till, also worked in a saw mill on the farm, which was run by water, being on the Le Boeuf creek. William attended the neighborhood schools, also the Waterford Academy and at one time the Erie Academy. He studied law with Hon. John Galbraith and was admitted to the Erie Bar in 1846. Then an amazing thing happened, he took a western trip, which included St. Louis, and returned to his father's farm, where he remained for over ten years, making no use of his legal learning, except to try an occasional suit before some local justice of the peace. The cause of this loss of years has never been satisfactorily explained. He made to me the wholly inadequate excuse of lack of funds. About 1857, when approximately thirty-eight years of age, he found himself, came to Erie and began practice, being for a time in the office of Hon. Geo. W. De Camp. Then something else equally strange happened, within seven years this homespun country man, by his unaided efforts, had reached the front rank of Erie lawyers and many hundreds of people, mostly from the rural districts, were his clients. This sudden rise to eminence has few parallels at our bar. His active practice extended over a period of about thirty-five years, when he was in all the courts and probably tried as many cases, during that time, as any member of the bar, while he frequently appeared in criminal cases he was essentially a civil lawyer. He loved the law and made a deep study of it. No one in this county was more familiar with the common law or the decisions of our state supreme court than he.

While a student in his office he gave me a thorough examination every week and I was amazed at his knowledge of elementary law. From his memory he took me through Blackstone, Kent, Chitty, Parsons, Greenleaf etc., without a skip. I recall but one occasion when he took up the book and that was some question in Parsons on Contracts. He was equally familiar with the general statutes of the state and the decisions of our supreme court. His knowledge of case law was admirable. He told me that when he read a case he did not merely glance at it, but fixed it permanently in his mind. So when a law question came up he was quite apt to recall the relevant authority, if such there were, and give book and page. He prepared his cases with great care on law and facts. It was his rule never to call a witness he had not previously examined, nor an unnecessary witness, nor one who could be discredited. He said an impeached or successfully discredited witness hurt the whole case, for where one part of it was false the whole might be so regarded. His cross examinations were generally brief but comprehensive and so framed as to bring out the weak points in the testimony but not to enable the witness to strengthen it by reiteration. His law arguments were brief but cogent and well condensed. He submitted few requests and none he did not consider sound. His final address to a jury was a full analysis of the facts, so plainly stated as to be understood by the dullest man on the panel. During the trial he was very serious and his talk to the jury was intensely earnest and usually with loud voice. He illustrated what Judge Mehard once said "That a lawyer who believes in his case generally makes some noise." One of his elements of strength was his earnestness. No trifler was ever a good jury lawyer. Another element was his well known honesty. He had the highest possible reputation for integrity and he merited it. There were other lawyers just as honest; but I do believe he made more capital out of his honesty than any other member of the bar. He never doubted his own integrity nor sought to conceal it. As to that virtue he did not hide his light under a bushel. In the course of his address he sometimes resorted to the expedient of informing the jury that he personally knew his client to be a most excellent citizen. In addition, he was in his day the best lawyer we had to select a jury. He had a wide acquaintance among country people, knew their feeling toward him and how they would likely stand on the case in question. With jurors from the rural districts he certainly had great influence. For about twelve years, beginning in 1874, he was in partnership with Hon. S. M. Brainerd, with offices in the Olds Block, at 722 State street, and the firm did a very extensive business, probably as large as any firm in the city. Thereafter Mr. Benson continued alone at the same location. He was very patriotic during the civil war, and when Roger Sherman, a native of Virginia, who had expressed some alleged disloyal sentiments, came up for admission, Benson as chairman of the board of examiners successfully objected on that ground. Sherman was admitted in Crawford county, located at Titusville and became a great lawyer. A few weeks after I became judge here, Mr. Sherman came in court on some business, and on my suggestion, was qualified as a member of the Erie Bar.

In 1876 Mr. Benson reluctantly became a candidate for president judge of the county. At the primaries he was opposed by Judge Vincent and Colonel Curtis, but easily won the Republican nomination. Benson, while a great lawyer, was a poor politician and instead of trying to placate the members of the bar who had opposed his nomination ignored them, as he also did for a like reason, prominent citizens, in different parts of the county. For example, he refused to shake hands with Perry Devore of Springfield township, who had supported Vincent at the primaries. Devore said, "Mr. Benson, this will cost you five hundred votes," and it did cost him at least some. Opposition developed against Benson, a numerously signed call was extended to William A. Galbraith and he became an independent candidate. Then followed probably the most bitterly contested election in our history. Enmities were engendered that took nearly fifty years to heal. Benson's numerous friends rallied to his support; affidavits were made and published charging him with being a slanderer and a hater of women and an infidel. The charges he vigorously denied, especially the former and, contrary to precedent in judicial contests, took the stump in his own behalf. On the Saturday night before the election DeCamp came up from Pittsburgh and, speaking to a multitude in the park, made a vicious attack upon Galbraith's record. During the campaign about one hundred and twenty-five young Republicans in the city formed a marching club and asked Benson to give them one dollar each to purchase uniforms, a legitimate campaign expense. This he peremptorily refused to do and ill naturedly sent them away. Then they went to Galbraith with a similar request which he gladly granted, with the result of changing their votes and with it the result of the election, for he won by only one hundred and forty-three votes. Many reasons were given for the result of the election, but Benson's lack of political sagacity was sufficient. It may be noted that the saloons fought him because he was a pronounced temperance man and the churches fought him because of his lack of faith. It illustrated what Giles Price once said that "the churches and the saloons usually sleep together on election night." While the defeat was galling, I do not think Benson cared deeply about the office. Whether he would have made a satisfactory judge will never be known. He was able, honest and industrious, but whether he could have discarded his strong prejudices is uncertain. I am sure he would have tried. He was temperamentally better fitted for the bar than the bench. His lack of sagacity in that campaign is inexplicable. In the trial of causes there was not a more adroit lawyer at our bar with the possible exception of Elijah Babbitt, and Clark Olds, an intimate friend of Benson, would not make that exception. Benson never took a case in which he lacked faith but once started he was one hundred percent for his client, whose cause to him was always just. He was very successful before the state supreme court, where he won many cases. He was of medium height, very strongly built, with a large head. In later years he never used a razor, nor patronized barbers but kept his face clipped as close as possible with the shears. He was very bald and what little hair he had, was also clipped with the shears. In cold weather he wore a large slouch hat and clothes made of Jamestown Blue, and in warm weather he wore an old-fashioned straw hat and linen clothes. He was very robust and for many years left off his flannels on April first. As to that, W. W. Lyle, one time Commissioner of Erie county, had a safer rule. He never removed his flannels until he ate a cherry pie, made by his wife from fresh cherries picked from their own tree. Benson, who never married, slept in his back office and took his meals for many years with Mrs. A. T. Marsh, who kept a high class boarding house on West Eighth street.

Although doing a very large business he was a modest charger, a poor collector and never had a very large income, but accumulated some property. He was kind-hearted and gave much to the needy, and sometimes made improvident loans. On one occasion he made a loan to me, for which he would not take any note, nor, when I repaid him, some years later, any interest. Speaking at his funeral, Mr. Brainerd said Benson gave away at least one thousand dollars a year. He had many devoted friends, among them Hon. John D. Stranahan, of LeBoeuf township, who shortly after his first wife died visited Benson's office. A more affecting scene I have seldom witnessed; both shed tears, but neither had the serene faith which brings peace to the troubled soul. Lewis W. Olds, for many years a leading citizen of Erie and large property owner, had been in school with Benson and they were life long friends. When Olds built his block on State street, Benson loaned him money and ever after had his office in that building. Olds was a frequent visitor at the office and they were very intimate. They were both what might be called original characters. Benson was attorney for a large Irishman named John Carse in a suit which he won and ever after he and Benson were chums. When one of our banks practically ceased paying depositors, Carse, who had money there, on Benson's advice visited the bank, and by refusing to leave finally got his money and was the last depositor paid, except through a receiver. Benson had not only warm friends but bitter enemies, one of the latter was Hon. A. W. Blaine, in his day North East's first citizen. Finally Mr. Blaine died and on meeting Benson, I said, "Alex. Blaine is dead." He replied, "Well my mind has no difficulty in conforming to that decree of Providence." This was like the case of Senator Summer and Judge Hoar of Massachusetts, who were sworn enemies. On the morning of Summer's funeral, a mutual friend asked Hoar if he would attend the funeral, to which he answered, "No, I am not going, but I am in favor of it." One of Benson's notable victories was the recovery in ejectment of a two-thirds interest in the Presbyterian Church property at North East. He was not a member of any church, and once, while gazing at that magnificent structure known as St. Peter's Cathedral at Erie, he shook his head sadly and remarked, "Too bad, every stone in that building would have bought an astronomy."

His memory failed him on one occasion. He had a red covered book containing stories about lawyers in which I had become interested and which he gave me on my admission to the bar. Some two years later he said to me, "It beats hell how people do steal books. Some thief has carried off that red book of mine." I replied, "No, Mr. Benson, you loaned me that book and I have neglected to return it." He said, "Oh, no hurry; I thought it was stolen." Needless to say I took it back.

He and I had an emergency matter one time before

Judge Galbraith which turned on a legal question. It was argued by us and by the opposing counsel, without preparation, but the next day 1 looked up the law and found a supreme court decision directly against us, which I showed Benson. He looked at it and said, "That is the law, say nothing." A day or two later the judge read from the bench a vigorous opinion in our favor. Benson sitting near me, whispered, "How wise some people can talk about something they don't know anything about."* The opinion stood unchallenged. The error resulted from the fact that the case had to be argued and decided while the judge was in court, without opportunity for examination, which was our good luck.

During the fall of 1890 and early winter Benson was sick, but gradually recovered so as to be out and attend to business and on Decoration Day, 1891, he visited the Waterford Cemetery, where some friend on seeing his improved appearance said, Benson you are good for ten years," to which he replied, "Yes, for twenty years." However, he took cold and on returning to Erie two days later had a severe chill and died in a few hours. Carse, who found him sick in his office, hastened for medical aid, but as Benson had so recently denounced the medical profession because he contended they had improperly treated him during his recent illness, no one would respond. Carse finally got Dr. P. Hall, a druggist and old time friend of Benson, to come and prescribe for him, but while Carse went to the drug store to get the medicine Benson died alone in his office. A special car filled with sorrowing friends, accompanied the remains to Waterford, where after appropriate eulogies by Hon. John P. Vincent and Hon. S. M. Brainerd, he was buried

---

*Note: He forgot that by like talk we had misled the judge.

in the same cemetery where within a week he had said he would live twenty years. Thus ended the career of the most unique character who has appeared at our bar. Benson's will divided his estate among his brothers and sisters, excepting his brother Isaac, who got nothing, the will saying, "Isaac has plenty." He had a large law library which the will gives to such of his nephews as may read law, but never to be sold, rather to be burned. There was some question as to the interpretation of this clause but the supreme court construed it as including those admitted to the bar and those studying at his death. He left a large farm in Green township, also six hundred and forty acres of land in northwestern Iowa, which he had bought some nine years before his death and which proved to be the best part of his estate.

Benson lived alone and lacked human ties. Had he married and raised a family it would have broadened and strengthened his life. He had no church or lodge affiliations, avoided crowds and I do not recall ever having seen him at a public gathering, except at one of Col. Ingersoll's lectures. He hated tobacco and would not permit smoking in his office, except by Hon. Geo. W. Decamp, who had assisted him in getting a start in Erie. I never knew a man who would do more for a friend than Benson. I recall his signing a note for three thousand dollars with a young lawyer (not myself) to enable him to make a favorable purchase of land. The last time Benson signed his name was as endorser for a friend, and he was as apt to give a poor client money as to take a fee from him. He was emphatically the people's lawyer and seldom appeared for corporations, except municipalities.

Judge Paul Allen Benson

Paul A. Benson, son of Hugh Hamilton and Lydia (Doyle) Benson, was born in Venango township, Erie county, Penna., August 26, 1865. Educated at the public schools and Allegheny College, he began the study of law in the office of his uncle, William Benson, Esq., at Erie and upon the latter's death in 1891 continued his legal studies in the office of Clark Olds, Esq., in the same city. He was admitted to the Erie Bar April 3, 1893, and at once began practice at Erie which continued uninterruptedly until his appointment to the Erie County Bench in May 1911, to fill the vacancy caused by the creation of an Additional Law Judge for this county. From about 1898 he practiced in partnership with Hon. John B. Brooks, as Benson & Brooks, and later the firm name became Benson, Brooks and English, Charles H. English, Esq., becoming a member thereof. Soon after his admission Judge Benson acquired a considerable practice which was gradually augmented during his continuance at the bar. He was emphatically a man of the people and was generally found advocating their causes. He had great native ability and his intense earnestness carried conviction. He was a good lawyer, but lacked the industry which characterized his uncle William. He was elected district attorney in 1896, and filled that office ably and with excellent judgment. There and in all his professional work he exhibited strong common sense.

His appointment as judge proved exceedingly popular and was ratified by an overwhelming majority at the ensuing election. In January, 1912, he began a ten year term as my associate, and our relations were uniformly the most cordial. He was a good judge, but ill health overtook him before he fully realized his judicial ambition.

Judge Benson was a 32° Mason and very active in the work of that fraternity, but the Independent Order of Odd Fellows was his ideal. He early became a member of Presque Isle Lodge, I. O. O. F., also of other branches of the fraternity. He thought Odd Fellowship, dreamed Odd Fellowship, worked Odd Fellowship. It was his hobby. Some of its members were his closest friends. His affection for Odd Fellowship was fully reciprocated. He was one of the state's most prominent Odd Fellows and his passing through the state chairs of that fraternity, closing with his term as Grand Master, was one of the crowning achievements of his career. Had he lived, I have no doubt he would have become prominent in the national councils of this great order.

Paul Benson was a distinguished personality, nearly six feet tall and weighing two hundred and fifty pounds, with a smooth, well shaped face and dignified appearance. He could express himself well and forcibly. He was outspoken and never left a doubt as to his position. He made and retained a host of friends. He was an active member of the Park Presbyterian Church.

June 28, 1897, he married Mary Fraser of Buffalo, by whom he had two sons, who are now (1927) well known and highly respected citizens of Erie. He was survived by his widow, who resides in the family residence at 720 West 9th street, Erie. Paul Benson was naturally robust, but he contracted diabetes which ultimately caused his death, July 21, 1915. He was buried in the Erie Cemetery with full honors of the Independent Order of Odd Fellows. Thus ended in its fiftieth year a life that accomplished much and had it been spared doubtless would have reached greater achievements.

Hon. Jonas Gunnison

Jonas Gunnison, son of Benjamin and Clarinda (Parker) Gunnison, was born in Greene township, Erie county, December 25, 1824, and educated at the Erie Academy. He studied law with Hon. John Galbraith, was admitted to the Erie Bar Nov. 9, 1849, and thenceforward until his death practiced law in Erie. He was recognized as a lawyer of fine ability and a public spirited citizen of the very highest character. The confidence reposed in him is attested by the fact that during his practice he probably settled more estates than any other member of the bar. He was entirely worthy of the universal trust reposed in him, for his work was always well done. His practice was largely in his office and in the various offices in the court house. He was an excellent example of the business lawyer. When I came to Erie fifty years ago his memory was fresh in the minds of the attorneys and his name was uniformly mentioned with great respect. He practiced for some years with General D. B. McCreary, a fine advocate, who took a leading part in their trial work.

Mr. Gunnison was elected to the state legislature as a Republican in 1859 and frequently represented this county in Republican state conventions. He served as a member of the Common and also of the Select Council of Erie city and was president of the latter body, and also served many years as trustee of the Erie Academy.

When the civil war came on, not being physically able to go to the front, he sent a man in his place. On May 9, 1847, he was united in marriage with Charlotte A. Spafford. To this union five children were born, three of whom lived to maturity, one, Hon. Frank Gunnison, became prominent at the bar and served ten years as President Judge of the district. The two daughters, Mrs. Clara G. Force and Miss Marion Gunnison, now reside at Pasadena, California. Jonas Gunnison was a member of the Unitarian Church. He was a gentleman of fine appearance, but never robust, gradually lost his health and died July 21, 1871, in the forty-seventh year of his age. He was buried in the Erie Cemetery. His death at such an early age was a public misfortune. His wife survived him in good health and useful activity for approximately forty years. An interesting history and genealogy of the Gunnison family appears beginning on page 901 of Whitman's History of Erie County, published in 1884.

Judge Frank Gunnison

Frank Gunnison, son of Hon. Jonas and Charlotte A. (Spafford) Gunnison, was born in Erie, February 2, 1848. He was educated at the public schools, the Erie Academy and Michigan University. He then attended the Harvard Law School from which he graduated with the degree of L. L. B. He also studied law in his father's office and was admitted to the Erie Bar, February 7, 1870. Gen. McCreary and his father were law partners and on the latter's death in 1871, he continued the partnership with the General until 1875 and then by himself. He was an exemplary young man, attentive to business, and soon became recognized as a sound lawyer with exceptional judgment and practical ability. He retained a large percent of his father's clients and had many new ones. He had a most agreeable personality and uniformly inspired confidence. To know Frank Gunnison was to believe in him. In his early practice, like his father, he preferred his office to the court room. Few if any of the local bar had a better office business. He took an interest in civic affairs and among his activities, served as a member of the select council.

Because of the confidence reposed in him, he was often selected as master or auditor, where he uniformly displayed fine judicial qualities. Although a very modest young man, his sterling qualities and eminent fitness for the bench, directed attention to him as a fit successor to Hon. William A. Galbraith, and, over four competitors, he received the Republican nomination for president judge of Erie county by a decisive majority in 1886 and in the fall won the election over Theodore A. Lamb, Esq., the Democratic candidate. He thus became president judge of the Erie district when less than thirty-nine years of age, and the youngest man to attain that position in the history of the county. The district was one of the largest in the state, having but a single judge, with an immense amount of legal business of every conceivable variety and hundreds of cases awaiting trial. In addition, he was succeeding a judge unsurpassed for learning, dignity and judicial bearing. Under these trying circumstances, Frank Gunnison took the bench, where he presided with quiet dignity for ten years, always at his best and always master of the situation. I saw him in hundreds of perplexing situations, but never once disconcerted or impatient. During that entire time he never uttered an angry or unkind word. He was uniformly fair and unbiased. In legal ability, integrity, patience, industry, efficiency, courage and common sense, he was an ideal judge. During his term he not only kept up with the business, but reduced the number of untried cases, and his decisions were well sustained by the appellate courts. His reelection was generally desired and generally conceded. But in handing down the licenses that spring, he attached an order forbidding the sale of liquor to be carried from the premises. This was counter to the habits of many people in sending to saloons for mugs or pails of beer, etc., was called "The Growler Order" and caused a revolt. The judge, being still a young man and knowing he could do much better financially at the bar, declined the nearly unanimous call of the local attorneys and refused to stand for reelection. About the same time he sent for Col. Sproul and myself to come to his home on a Sunday afternoon and canvass the situation which we did. We had a nice luncheon and a full discussion. The judge said our names had been mentioned and that one of us should become a candidate as his successor. Sproul declined to consider it, giving as one reason the fact that he had planned a trip to Europe with M. W. Shreve (now our Congressman) for that season and was unwilling to give it up. I was loath to undertake it, because of the inadequacy of the judicial salary (then $4000 a year) to meet my financial needs. However, I finally decided to become a candidate, which proved the beginning of my judicial work, now covering a period of thirty-two years.

Judge Gunnison at once resumed practice and soon took high rank at the bar, representing many large and important interests, including the Bessemer & Lake Erie R. R., the Nickel Plate R. R., the Scott Estate, the Second National Bank (of which he also became a director), the United States Steel Corporation, and other large interests. He exhibited this remarkable characteristic, that, while before going on the bench he had not been a trial lawyer, on resuming practice he exhibited great ability in that capacity. He skillfully tried numerous and important cases in this and other counties, and was equally able in the appellate courts, where he often appeared and was listened to with pleasure and marked attention. He was able, efficient, exceedingly industrious and continued in full practice until his death. For some years he headed the law firm of Gunnison, Rilling and Fish and later, until his death, that of Gunnison, Fish, Gifford and Chapin. Out of reverence for his memory, the latter firm still carries his name at its head.

In addition to being a great lawyer and a great judge, he was an exceptionally able business man. He had charge of a large amount of real property, mostly of the M. B. Lowry Estate, of which he was trustee, from which he managed to get excellent returns. John C. Brady told me he considered Judge Gunnison the best man in Erie to get returns from outlying property. Winning or losing, the judge maintained a cheerful attitude and had a smile that would not come off. He was a good story teller, had a keen sense of humor and enjoyed a good joke. On one occasion while a boy in school, Henry Rea, a smaller boy, who later became clerk of courts and a well known citizen, sat near him and on a Friday afternoon as pieces were being spoken, Henry remarked that he had none, when the judge said, "Go out and say, 'I am old and I am tough, and I have spoke enough.'" When called upon, the boy did as suggested, but the master was not to be trifled with and quietly said, "Henry, you may stay after school and we will see how tough you are." Henry got whipped, but whether the joke was on him or the judge is a moral question. When being examined for admission to the bar, J. W. Wetmore, Esq., of the committee, asked the future judge how Greenleaf divided his work on Evidence, to which the latter replied, "Into three volumes," which satisfied the committee on that subject. He was an active Republican and was chairman of the county committee in 1884. He was a traveler, and with Mrs. Gunnison, spent several winters in California, and traveled extensively in Europe. Personally the judge was slightly above medium height, but not heavy or of athletic build. He attended the Unitarian Church and sometimes I believe, went with his wife to the First Presbyterian Church.

On September 5, 1872, Frank Gunnison was united in marriage with Lila Lowry, daughter of Hon. M. B.

Lowry, who in his day served three terms in the state senate and was otherwise a man of remarkable achievements. The judge and Mrs. Gunnison had two sons, one Hugh, who died in infancy and Morrow Benjamin, who had a family and for some years resided at Pasadena, California, but recently spends at least a portion of the year at the family residence at Sixth and Holland streets, in this city. The judge had a theory that it was safe to go to Florida or Southern California and return in the early spring and he did so for several years with impunity. He said it was no greater shock to go from a warm to a cold climate than to go from a warm room into a winter atmosphere. However, he returned from Southern California early one year (1919) and caught a cold, which ended in pneumonia and caused his death, on April 23, 1919, aged seventy-one years; he was buried in the Erie Cemetery. Mrs. Gunnison survived the judge for some years and died recently.

The Gunnisons, of which the judge was one, were a large and noteworthy family. The one to first reach America was Hugh Gunnison, who came from Sweden and landed in Boston as early as 1631. Among his descendants was William Gunnison, the progenitor of the Erie county Gunnisons, who first came here in 1815. For more than a century the Gunnisons have been among our most useful and highly respected citizens. The judge was an ornament to his family, an ornament to the bench, an honor to the profession, and in every walk of life rang true.

Jerome W. Wetmore, Esq.

J. W. Wetmore, son of Lansing and Caroline (Ditmars) Wetmore, was born in Warren county, Pa., May 1, 1820. He was educated at the Warren Academy and at Union College, N. Y. He later became principal of the former and in 1846, removing to this city, taught for two years in the Erie Academy. He was admitted to the Erie Bar August 8, 1848. Having read law with Hon. John H. Walker, he became an office associate with that eminent leader of our bar and so continued until the latter's death in 1875. Mr. Wetmore then acquired Mr. Walker's extensive law library, which he kept up to date and ever continued a close student of law. In his practice he often raised intricate legal questions. On one occasion he was urging upon the local court some nice distinction when the judge said, "Mr. Wetmore, that is a fine point." The latter replied, "Your Honor, the study of law is the study of fine points." He enjoyed a fair practice, but never sought distinction in the forum. He divided his time somewhat between the law and other enterprises. He invented a wagon spring which for some years he successfully manufactured and I believe was otherwise interested in business enterprises. He also owned a farm in Harborcreek township and accumulated considerable property, probably more in business than by his practice or from the farm. He had faith in Erie and erected the brick building at the northwest corner of Seventh and Peach streets, now known as the Fischer Hotel, and on the first floor he had his offices. He was a brother of Hon. Lansing D. Wetmore, of Warren, who in 1870 was elected law judge of this district, after a spirited contest.

J. W. Wetmore was about six feet tall, of slim build, wore a full beard, except for a clean shaven upper lip, stood erect even in age, and was fine apeparing. He was never married and died in 1900, at the age of eighty years, and was buried at Warren, Penna.

Hon. Wilson Laird

Wilson Laird, son of Thomas and Mary Ann (Topsley) Laird, was born in Erie City, January 31, 1825. His father came from Alexandria, Huntingdon county, Pa., and settled in Erie in 1804. He had faith in Erie and bought most of the land between Seventh and Ninth streets, on both sides of State street. He also bought several hundred acres of land in the vicinity of what is now Waldameer Park, including that occupied by Trinity Cemetery. He built a home on the west side of State street between Eighth and Ninth streets, which stood as a land mark until comparatively recent years. There Wilson was born and grew to manhood. He enjoyed the best educational advantages the time afforded not only at the Erie Academy, but at Washington and Jefferson College, where he graduated. He then studied law with Hon. James Thompson, later a judge and Chief Justice of the state supreme court. Wilson was admitted to the Erie Bar, February 8, 1849, and practiced his profession at Erie from that time until his last sickness. However, he was greatly diverted by public office and private business. He was in the oil business, also in general merchandise with Lucien Rust.

In 1852 he was elected alderman of the East Ward and, in that office, was widely known for impartiality and efficiency. Few of our magistrates have left as enviable a record. He served three terms as Mayor of Erie, being first chosen to that office in 1855. So great was his popularity that in 1858 he was elected to the legislature as a Democrat by 256 majority in a county which normally was Republican by over 2000 majority. While in the Assembly his cousin Hon. William A. Wallace, later a United States Senator and a Democrat of national prominence, was a member of the State Senate. Many years later in 1882 Wallace was again elected State Senator and I had the pleasure of serving with him in the session of 1885, and found him a most charming gentleman.

In every position to which he was called by the partiality of his fellow citizens, Wilson Laird distinguished himself by faithful and efficient service. There was then no salary to the office of mayor but those who gaze upon his portrait in the city hall, behold one who gave himself unsparingly to his duties and who never forgot that a public office is a public trust. After retiring to private life, Mr. Laird continued his legal practice but never reached the eminence therein to which his fine ability and high character entitled him and which would have been his had he not devoted the best years of his life to official service. He was a fine speaker, could try a case well and was intensely loyal to his clients.

He was of medium size, wore a full beard and had a most kind and agreeable personality. He was of Scotch-Irish ancestry and in politics a life long Democrat. Mr. Laird was twice married; by his first wife, Jeannette Kennedy, daughter of David Kennedy, he had two children and after her death he married Miss Sloan, sister of B. F. Sloan, for many years secretary of the Erie Water Board, and by her he had eight children. Several of his children and grandchildren are now well known and highly respected citizens of Erie. In addition to his other activities, Mr. Laird wrote and had published a complete History of the Erie Railroad War. The fates were unkind to Wilson Laird, although for nine years he was the only surviving member of his father's family of nine children, yet, in his old age, he suffered from bereavement and ill health. He died October 11, 1893, in the sixty-ninth year of his age. He died as he had lived, an honest, honorable man and was buried in the Erie Cemetery.

General David B. McCreary

David B. McCreary, son of Joseph F. and Lydia (Swan) McCreary, was born on a farm in Mill Creek township, Erie county, Pennsylvania, February 27, 1826. The father, of Scotch-Irish lineage, was born in Lancaster county in 1776, and the mother, a daughter of Captain Richard Swan, was born near the present city of Harrisburg. Both families were pioneers here, the father coming on horseback in 1800 and the mother, then a girl, with her family, by wagon to Pittsburgh, thence up the Allegheny river and its tributaries by flat boat to Waterford in 1802. Captain Swan, coming as agent for the Harrisburg and Presque Isle Land Company, settled near Swanville. So the McCrearys and the Swans have been residents of Erie county for over a century and a quarter, and all this time have been high grade progressive and law abiding citizens; for those desirable qualities no community in the county stands higher than West Mill Creek. David, one of nine children and an exceptionally bright boy, had the usual experiences of farm life of that period, attended district schools, also the spelling schools and debating societies of the neighborhood, in both of which he soon became prominent. In those early debates he developed the faculty of clear thought and forcible expression, for which he was justly noted in after years. Later he was a student at the Erie Academy, to which he daily came from home, a distance of some five miles, on horseback and often on foot. Thereafter for a time he was a student at Washington College. Meantime he taught school and in fact was principal of the first graded school in Erie. He was later principal of the school located on what was afterwards the Judge Galbraith lawn at Sixth and Myrtle streets. A vine covered ruin of the old school house stood there until recent years.

While engaged in teaching, McCreary registered as a law student with Hon. John and Wm. A. Galbraith, each of whom subsequently became president judge of the district, and so diligently did he pursue his law studies that he was admitted to the Erie Bar on August 8, 1851. September 17, of the same year, he was united in marriage with Miss Annette J. Gunnison, daughter of E. D. Gunnison, Esq., and sister of John B. and Charles E. Gunnison, all of whom were citizens of the highest standing and for many years, familiar figures in the business activities of the city. Mrs. McCreary was a highly cultured lady of charming personality. After the wedding they went to Kentucky, where for two years he had charge of a boys' seminary and during the same period his wife taught in a nearby girls' school. While in Kentucky McCreary made a pilgrimage to Ashland to call upon his political idol, Henry Clay, who received him most cordially. He also had the distinction of attending the funeral of that great statesman, where he saw some of America's foremost men. McCreary also while there made the acquaintance of Gen. John C. Breckenridge, later Vice-President and United States Senator. In the district where he taught were two small boys, James B. McCreary and William J. Stone, the former a distant relative of the General, both of whom became men of national prominence. McCreary became Governor of Kentucky and the latter Governor of Missouri and both were United States senators in 1903.

D. B. McCreary had every element of a great teacher,

but the lure of the law brought him back to Erie, where he formed a law partnership with Hon. J. B. Johnson, which, I believe, continued until their office was burned during the railroad war, which we have mentioned in speaking of Mr. Johnson. In any event in 1856, McCreary formed a law partnership with Hon. Jonas Gunnison, which continued until the latter's death in 1871 and then for five years with his son, Hon. Frank Gunnison. Thereafter he continued his professional career by himself, having his offices for very many years at 704 State street. He was a sound lawyer and a fine advocate. He had a delightful personality, was a fluent and forceful speaker and enjoyed the contest of the forum. His practice extended into the federal courts and he often appeared before the state supreme court. He also did a fine office business and ever had a good class of clients, although because of his public activities, to which we will refer, his practice was not as large as it otherwise would have been. He enjoyed the full confidence of the court and bar and was often chosen as master in equity, auditor, referee, etc., where his dignified but kindly bearing, fairness and ability were uniformly recognized. He would have made an able judge but never sought that distinction.

McCreary was a born patriot; preceding the civil war he was a member of the Wayne Guards, under the rigorous discipline of Capt. John C. McLane. When the war came and President Lincoln called for seventy-five thousand volunteers, for the three months service, he was one of the first to respond and joined McLane's regiment. In 1862 he enlisted and was made Lieutenant Colonel of the One Hundred and Forty-Fifth Regiment

Penna. Volunteers, which was rushed to the front in time to get under fire and help bury the dead at Antietem. General Hiram L. Brown went out as Colonel of the regiment. Later in the fall it was in the thickest of the fight in the awful battle of Fredericksburg, where one-half of its numbers fell on the field. Col. Brown was seriously wounded and McCreary was placed in command of the regiment. At Chancellorsville he, and many of his men, were captured and taken to Libby prison, where after a month he was exchanged and rejoined the regiment. As a part of the Army of the Potomac he and his regiment went through many hard fought battles and in 1864 he was again taken prisoner in a charge upon Petersburg, and for nine months suffered in southern prisons, but was able to rejoin the regiment near the close of the war. After marching in review before the President in Washington and some delays, the regiment, or what was left of it, received an honorable discharge, Col. McCreary being discharged with the rank of brevet brigadier general. He also at one time served on the governor's staff with the rank of brigadier general. The regiment returned in a body to Erie, where a public reception was accorded them in the park and after an address of welcome by Hon. Charles W. Kelso, and response by the Colonel, the battle scarred veterans returned to their homes, but to the end of their days Col. McCreary, as they ever called him, was their idol. In fact, the people of the county were so impressed by his military career, that he was elected and reelected to the legislature where he served with distinction during the sessions of 1866-1867. At the close of the latter he had acquired such prominence in the state that Governor Geary appointed him Adjutant General. This office he held for three years, with the rank of brigadier general and, by his constructive ability, greatly strengthened the state's military organization. At the end of this service he was again sent to the legislature where he served during the session of 1870. Thereafter he was strongly urged as a candidate for congress, but the conditions in the district (composed of three counties) were such as to prevent his nomination, and he continued to practice law uninterruptedly until chosen state senator in 1888, to which office he was elected, and reelected in 1892, with practical unanimity. I preceded him in the senate and was one of the first to suggest his name as my successor. He made a fine record there; was twice chosen as chairman of the Judiciary General Committee and once as chairman of the Judiciary Special Committee. He also served on various boards and received many marks of distinction. This service closed his public career.

In 1893 the General suffered a crushing blow in the death of his devoted wife, but he rallied and continued at his profession. He was a strikingly handsome man, slightly above medium height, well built, stood erect, wore a moustache and well cropped chin whiskers, always dressed in good taste and was well groomed, a thorough gentleman on all occasions. He and his family had many friends in Harrisburg, as I discovered from numerous enquiries about them by prominent residents there. Probably no member of our bar had a more extended acquaintance among men of distinction than the General. Socially he was most delightful and had an apparently exhaustless supply of good stories which he related in an inimitable manner. Whatever the surroundings, he was always optimistic and to the end enjoyed good health and was fond of good dinners. His home for many years, on Sixth street between French and Holland streets, was the center of a charming hospitality.

The General was a stalwart Republican, enjoyed politics and as a campaign speaker had few equals. His speeches were clear cut and strong but devoid of personalities. He never, to my knowledge, spoke unkindly of any one. He was ever a devout Presbyterian and one of the founders of the Park Church.

The McCrearys had two children, the eldest, a daughter, born in Kentucky, is now the wife of Judge Henry A. Clark, and with her two children, Annette and Harry, are the only survivors of the family. The son, Wirt McCreary, graduated with honor from the U. S. Naval Academy at Annapolis, became a naval officer and died in 1913.

After a brief illness General McCreary died February 4, 1906, at the age of eighty years, and was buried in the Erie Cemetery.

Mortimer Phelps, Esq.

Mortimer Phelps, a resident of Edinboro, was admitted to the Erie Bar, September 12, 1850. He continued to reside in his home town and practiced his profession in a very quiet manner, and, as I recall, served as justice of the peace. He was a man of good judgment, highly respected by his neighbors, and so far as possible settled difficulties out of court. While he came into court with petitions, etc., I do not recall that he participated in the trial of causes during the last twenty years of his life. He died on or about December 25, 1899, and was buried at Edinboro.

Rev. Andrew Harvey Caughey

A. H. Caughey, son of Andrew and Martha (Canon) Caughey, and a member of the pioneer and prominent Caughey family of Millcreek township, Erie County, Pa., was born on a farm in that township November 1, 1827. His ancestors many years ago came from Scotland. He was educated at the Erie Academy and at Washington College, of which he was a graduate in the class of 1849, studied law in the office of Hon. J. B. Johnson and was admitted to the Erie Bar November 26, 1851. He was all his life a busy man of the highest type but never actively engaged in legal practice. He was principal of the Erie Academy for several years, beginning in 1868, also for some years a professor in Lafayette College and later for a considerable period kept a book store in Erie. At one time he held a position of deputy collector of customs at Erie, but, although an ardent Republican and universally held in the highest esteem, he never sought public office. For some years he was interested in the newspaper business at Erie. He ever took an active interest in the moral uplift of the community. To associate with A. H. Caughey was to become a better man. He was one of the founders and in its early days president of the Young Men's Christian Association of Erie. He collected its first public library and for years had charge of its lecture course which brought many prominent men to the city.

He was the author of several books, including "A Life of Isaac Moorhead"; "A Life of Rev. Eaton" and two small volumes of poetry. Mr. Caughey, after passing middle life, became a Presbyterian clergyman, which calling he followed successfully for many years, being pastor of a church at Belle Valley and later, for years, of one at Kingsville, Ohio, where he closed the active work of his life. On October 9, 1851, Mr. Caughey was united in marriage with Miss Elizabeth A. Reed, a sister of Miss Sarah Reed, of Erie, now active in her nineteenth year and an outstanding example of the highest type of American womanhood. Two children were born to Mr. and Mrs. Caughey, a daughter, who died in infancy, and a son Reed Caughey, who was the father of a large family and a well known and highly respected resident of this city for many years and later of Ann Arbor, Michigan, where he died February 14, 1924.

A. H. Caughey was above medium height but of light build and delightful personality. It was my good fortune to spend some days with him in Maine in the summer of 1904, where I came to know him well and to appreciate him most highly. He was in the best sense a charming companion. He was ever fond of good literature and also fond of recreation in walking, especially in the open country or along the ocean shore. He died at Ann Arbor, Michigan, June 22, 1916, in the eighty-ninth year of his age, and was buried in the Erie Cemtery.

Dr. Henry R. Terry

Dr. Terry was a practicing physician at Edinboro, in this country, and, while practicing as such, studied law and was admitted to the Erie Bar, January 25, 1852. He continued as a practitioner of medicine and attended to such law business as came in his way, mostly an office business. I recall that some fifty years ago he occasionally came into court with petitions and other matters of business. At such times he would drive over from Edinboro in a double carriage. I do not remember that he came in foul weather, but my first trip over that road was by stage in March, 1873, when the road was so nearly impassable that it took a whole day to make the journey, stopping at Middleboro for dinner. Being doctor and lawyer had some advantage, for if the patient failed to respond to the treatment the attending physician was there to prepare his will. Dr. Terry was a gentleman of fine appearance and enjoyed in a marked degree the confidence of the people of his part of the country. The records show he occasionally had a law student, so he must have kept in touch with the profession. He died on or about November 23, 1884, and was buried in the Edinboro Cemetery.

Samuel Selden Spencer

S. S. Spencer, son of William and Deborah (Selden) Spencer, was born at Hadlyme, Connecticut, May 29, 1826, and is a lineal descendant of Gerard Spencer, who came from England and settled in Connecticut in 1630. S. S. Spencer's grandfather, Israel Selden Spencer, served as captain and major in the Revolutionary War, while his father was a sea captain, owning a line of coastwise ships, going from New York to New Orleans. Through his mother he belonged to the Selden family, which with the Spencers, the Marvins and the Griswolds, all interrelated, formed a most remarkable group of people, prominent not only in New England, but here and elsewhere, embracing among their numbers many men of national prominence, among them the late Chief Justice Morrison R. Waite, of the United States Supreme Court. S. S. Spencer received his education at Williston Seminary and Yale College, graduating from the latter in the class of 1848. He chose the legal profession and on February 12, 1853, was admitted to the Erie Bar, of which he was a practicing member for fifty-seven years. The selection of Erie as the place of his life work was likely influenced by the fact that his older brother, Judah Colt Spencer, was the general agent here for the Population Land Company, a position the brother held for many years, as he also did that of the presidency of the First National Bank of Erie. As S. S. Spencer was a young lawyer of fine ability and engaging personality, he soon acquired and for very many years retained a large practice. Being probably the most fluent speaker at our bar he soon became recognized as a jury lawyer and was frequently engaged in the trial of causes and could ably present both the law and the facts. In 1860 he formed a partnership with Judge Selden Marvin under the firm of Spencer and Marvin, which was very prosperous and continued until Judge Marvin became Mayor of Erie in 1877. In addition to other practice the firm did an enormous collection business, a branch of practice later largely absorbed by the banks. Mr. Spencer did most of the firm's trial work. They also did an extensive business in the settlement of estates. After Judge Marvin's retirement Mr. Spencer was for a short time associated in practice with Theodore A. Lamb, Esq.

Personally Mr. Spencer was tall, somewhat athletic, although never heavy, wore a gray beard in his later years, and was a fine looking gentleman of the New England type, with most engaging manners. He was the first lawyer I ever saw as my mother took me to his office when I was nine years old, he being the counsel in settlement of my father's estate. He talked to me in such a friendly, encouraging manner that I never forgot him. Many years later we were accustomed to discuss health problems, and he informed me of his habit of daily taking a cold bath. Inspired, at least in part, by his example, I adopted that practice and have consistently followed it for nearly twenty-five years.

On October 20, 1860, he was united in marriage with Miss Eliza Deborah Palmer, daughter of Mr. and Mrs. D. Lofferts Palmer, of Saratoga Springs, N. Y. They had three children, a son and two daughters. The son, Selden Palmer Spencer, graduated at Yale College, adopted the legal profession, settled in St. Louis, took high rank at the bar, became judge, also President of the State Bar

Association. Later, was twice elected a United States Senator from Missouri and died in Washington, May 1924, while a member of that body. So far as I recall, S. S. Spencer was the only member of our bar whose son became a United States Senator. Amelia, one of the daughters, died unmarried, in 1901; Kate, the other daughter, became and is the wife of Professor Kemper Fullerton, of Oberlin College.

Mr. Spencer, a man of profound religious conviction, was a charter member and for many years Ruling Elder in the Park Presbyterian Church. He was also superintendent of the Sabbath School in that church for nearly twenty years and, when he retired, as a token of affection, the Sunday School presented him a beautiful gold watch and chain. It was said he missed his calling in not being a clergyman. Certainly his deep religious nature, his broad human sympathies, his remarkable geniality and unusual gift of speech would have made him preeminent in that profession.

In early life Mr. Spencer was a Democrat, but later joined the Republican party and was active therein for many years. One evening he and I, after addressing a Republican rally at Lake Pleasant, started to drive home, but the night was so dark and rainy that our team stopped at the foot of a hill and could not be persuaded to go on. In our dilemma we found lodging in a farm house and, after breakfast, drove home in a most charming October morning. Although friends for many years, that was the only night we ever slept in the same bed. He was fond of out-door life and often indulged in walking, fishing and swimming. For very many years the Spencer home was at 155 West Sixth street, now remodeled and the home of Mr. and Mrs. James Thompson. His fondness for the bath continued to the end, for he was fatally stricken while swimming in the sea at his winter home at Daytona Beach, Florida, and died January 8, 1910, in the eighty-fourth year of his age. He was buried in the Erie Cemetery. His faithful and beloved wife survived him and died at Oberlin, Ohio, in May 1914. In domestic life, Samuel Selden Spencer was the personification of devotion, and in the community, he represented a high type of Christian manhood.

Judge Selden Marvin

Selden Marvin, only child of Hon. Dudley and Mary (Whalley) Marvin, was born at Canandaigua, New York, June 9, 1819. His father was one of the leaders of the New York Bar and for eight years a member of congress. The judge's Christian name was that of his parental grandmother, who was a member of the Selden family. He was educated at Canandaigua Academy and at Jefferson College, then located at Cannonsburg, Penna. After spending one year in a printing office in Boston he began the study of law in his father's office in New York City and was admitted to the bar of that state in 1841. The same year he located at Ripley, N. Y., where for five years he engaged in farming and in 1846 began the practice of law at Jamestown, N. Y. The following year (1847) he was united in marriage with Miss Sarah Wilson Dinsmore of Ripley and returned to the farm. Soon thereafter he resumed the practice of law in partnership with Hon. George W. Parker at Westfield, New York. In 1852 he was elected special county judge of Chautauqua County and in 1855 county judge of that county, in which capacity he served with great credit until the expiration of his term, January 1, 1860. Having been admitted to our bar in December, 1859, he located in this city and in June 1860 became a member of the law firm of Spencer and Marvin. The extensive and successful business of which has been mentioned in referring to Mr. Spencer. The partnership continued for seventeen years and was one of the best known law firms in this part of the state. The judge confined his attention largely to the office and business end of the firm while Mr. Spencer, a fluent trial lawyer, did most of the court work. Judge Marvin, however, was a fine lawyer and a good speaker and undoubtedly could try cases well and probably sometimes did. The judge's cousin, William E. Marvin, for many years a prominent citizen at Greenfield and North East, married Mr. Spencer's sister and they were probably otherwise related.

Judge Marvin was a consistent Democrat and very popular wherever known. In 1862 he was nominated for member of Assembly and in 1870 was a candidate for Congress, coming within five hundred votes of election in this strongly Republican district. In 1877 he was elected Mayor of Erie and served with great satisfaction. He met with courage and fidelity the duties devolving upon him as mayor during the great railroad strike of 1877. In the fall of that year he was elected City Recorder under a new statute and held the office, being reelected thereto, for some seven or eight years, until the City Recorder Act was declared unconstitutional. The City Recorder was given jurisdiction in civil cases up to six hundred dollars and also criminal jurisdiction as a magistrate. The court proved highly satisfactory to the profession and of great benefit to the public. Marvin was an ideal judge, industrious, patient, kindly, ever courteous, but dignified and firm in his conclusions. He possessed a wonderful knowledge of the common law and so far as I recall, his legal conclusions were uniformly sustained. If right on the law you were safe in his court. For example, on one occasion a raft of logs coming down the lake was broken up by a storm and some of the logs, washing ashore near North East, were jointly appropriated by two young men. The owner demanded payment therefor and settled with one of the young men, he paying one-half the value of the logs and taking a receipt and release in full. The other young man, who refused to settle was sued before Marvin and I defended him on the legal ground that a release of one joint tort feasor discharged both. The Recorder sustained the defense, because as he said, it was sound in law, although it did not seem to meet the equity of the case. The judge sometimes ruled against me, but he was always fair. Socially he was charming and our occasional chats were ever a delight. I do not recall any man with a more agreeable personality. So far as my memory goes the judge did not reenter active practice after leaving the City Recorder's office.

Judge Marvin was a very large man, six feet in height with broad shoulders and fine build and must have been a powerful man in his younger days. His massive head was covered by an abundance of dark hair and, except being clean shaven about the mouth, he wore a full beard. He had strong features and was of very distinguished appearance. My first acquaintance with the judge was when he came to North East and made a Democratic speech in the campaign of 1872. It was a strong speech, entirely devoid of personalities. He died in 1894, and was buried in the Erie Cemetery. He was survived by three of his five children, to-wit, Charles Dinsmore, a banker in New York; Anna Humphreys, wife of William D. Lewis and by Elizabeth Selden, wife of Robert W. Neff, of Boston. Judge Marvin's home for many years was on the northwest corner of Ninth and Sassafras streets, now the residence of Captain John R. Metcalf.

Hon. Samuel A. Davenport

Samuel A. Davenport, son of Captain William and Phylana (Tracy) Davenport, was born in Schuyler county, New York, near Watkins Glen, January 15, 1834. He was of English and Scotch-Irish ancestry and a lineal descendant of Rev. John Davenport, one of the founders of Yale College. In 1835 Captain Davenport removed with his family to a farm, which he had purchased in Harborcreek township, this county. He lived there about four years and then came to Erie which became their permanent home. Captain Davenport was a soldier in the War of 1812 and also had been a sea faring man and for about twenty years after he came to Erie was captain of various great lakes ships owned by General Reed. Captain Davenport had two sons, William R., the well known manufacturer and foremost in Y. M. C. A. and other good work, and Samuel A., the subject of this sketch, and several daughters, one of whom became Mrs. William A. Galbraith. Samuel was an ambitious youth and after securing the best education attainable in the schools of Erie, studied law with Hon. John Galbraith and was admitted to the Erie Bar when twenty years of age. He then took a course in Harvard Law School, where he graduated with high rank and the L. L. B. degree, in 1855, and at once began practice at Erie. He rapidly won his way to the front, although competing with such great lawyers as Walker, Babbitt, Vincent, William A. Galbraith, Benson, DeCamp, Col. Thompson and others. That young Davenport held his own with the best of them is a matter of history. Strong lawyers make other lawyers strong. Our bar is greater because of what our fathers were. For a century Erie county has been blessed with an able bar. In 1860 he became district attorney and filled that office with distinguished ability, but never afterward practiced in the criminal courts, except in cases of nuisance or the like. He told me he liked to try cases more important than were usually found in the quarter sessions. However, he enjoyed trial practice and kept steadily at it for fifty-six years, trying in my opinion, more important civil cases than any other lawyer ever tried at our bar, and earned more in his profession than any other member of the bar about whom I am writing, not referring to the present bar. Mr. Davenport had great natural ability and he made the most of it. He had wonderful health and was an intense worker. He used excellent judgment in devoting his time to important matters and could not have done better than he did. His cases were uniformly well prepared and in their trial he was exceedingly able. He was an expert mind reader and rarely taken by surprise. His development of the facts of his side of the case was masterly and his cross examinations were searching, although his rule was never to cross examine a woman. He was familiar with the rules of evidence and rarely violated them. The law of the case he had well in hand. He had a large library and found and cited the cases which supported, or which he contended supported his contention. Sometimes he took an extreme view of the law which could not be granted, but he made his position clear. He represented many corporations and in a large majority of cases appeared for the defense, where it was important to make the most of the law, and he did it. In summing up to the jury, he was clear, logical and forceful, spending no time in platitudes or idle declamation; ever a powerful reasoner, driving his points home with the force of a sledge hammer. He never minced matters; if convinced there was perjury in the case he boldly charged it. As he grew older, I thought he was on some occasions, possibly too bitter, but to him a law suit was at all steps a hostile proceeding. It must be said that while intensely earnest, he never showed anger or lost his head. Whatever happened he was the same implacable unrelenting advocate. He never used unprofessional language in court. True, he struck blows that left scars and made enemies. He never tried to avoid making them. In one way he was hard for the court, for although deferential he probably raised more law questions and submitted more border line points, adroitly drawn, than any other member of the bar. It was not easy to correctly answer all of his requests, nor to rule properly upon all the points he raised on the admission of evidence. It was possible, however, in that manner for the record to disclose some error that might upset the verdict, if adverse. Mr. Davenport did not depend altogether on legal points, but also tried the case strongly upon the facts; the legal record he made being merely an achor to windward.

The Nickel Plate railroad was constructed through Erie county, about 1881 and Mr. Davenport was its attorney. Much trouble and litigation resulted over the question of right of way. When settlements could not be effected the cases were fought out in court. Mr. Davenport was then about forty-seven years of age and probably never did better professional work than in the defense of these cases. Almost without exception he secured reasonable verdicts.

While he made some enemies he made warm friends to whom he was intensely loyal. He was a born fighter and possibly enjoyed his enemies. He never lost his fighting spirit; when the verdict was adverse he moved for a new trial; if denied he took his appeal and the fight ended only at the last ditch. He was perhaps the best example at our bar of a bitter ender, that is, he fought as long as he could, but if finally defeated he was not in my opinion a hard loser. I was never a close friend of Mr. Davenport and had tried some stubbornly contested suits against him at the bar, yet he was one of the first to ask me to become a candidate for judge in 1896. He practiced for many years in partnership with Geo. P. Griffith, Esq., and later J. M. Sherwin, Esq., was associated with him. Considering the extensive interest he represented, the amount of business he did and the length of his practice, practically with three generations of lawyers, he must be given a place in the very front rank at our bar. He was sometimes referred to, both here and elsewhere, as the leader of the Erie Bar, but, as I said referring to Col. Curtis, I doubt if we had any one during the years when Mr. Davenport was at his best, who was justly entitled to that distinction. No one kept more faithfully at his work to the very end of his life than he. I recall in June, 1911, he called me on the 'phone and asked to have a case of his postponed until fall when he expected to be able to try it. I cheerfully granted his request, but before fall he had entered into eternal rest. Referring to his ability, Captain W. B. Chapman told me the ablest argument he ever heard at the bar was Mr. Davenport's summing up to the jury in the Hoskinson Brick Yard case. Mr. Davenport was a close personal friend of the late Bishop Mullen and his legal adviser. As such he assisted in locating St. Peter's Cathedral and secured an act of Assembly exempting churches from taxation while in course of construction. This was a great relief as it required several years to build the Cathedral. He was broadminded and a generous but unostentatious giver.

Mr. Davenport was of medium height, well built, with a magnificent head and face that would attract attention anywhere. He dressed in perfect taste and his linen was as clean as the driven snow. In addition to his extensive law practice he was interested in numerous business enterprises, including The Stearns Manufacturing Company, the Erie Car Works, Erie Boot and Shoe Company, Keystone Boot and Shoe Company and the Derrick and Felgemaker Pipe Organ Company. He was also a large owner of outlying real estate, much of which was incumbered, when the great panic of 1873 struck the country; but he worked all the harder, carried his property through the long depression and came out successfully. He owned the property near the Soldiers' Home known as "the sand beach" on which he gave a thirty or sixty day option, pending which another party offered him $20,000 more, but he stood by his option without a whimper.

Mr. Davenport was an active Republican and influential in party councils not only locally, where he was the leader, but throughout the state and was a close friend of Col. Quay, Senator Penrose and other state leaders. He seldom sought office for himself but served the state two terms (1896-1900) as congressman at large. While there, although a good speaker, he took little part in the debates, but was an able representative and especially efficient in securing appropriations for our harbor and protecting other interests in this part of the state. He was a delegate to the Republican National Conventions in 1888 and 1892.

In 1862 he was united in marriage with Miss Kate Walker, daughter of Hon. John H. Walker. To this union one child, a daughter, was born, who grew to womanhood but predeceased her father. Mr. and Mrs. Davenport spent their married lives in their beautiful home at Tenth and Sassafras streets, where Mrs. Davenport still resides. As husband and father he was a model of kindness and all he should have been. He was a charter member of the Central Presbyterian Church. Although he took but little time for recreation, he greatly enjoyed extending happiness to the children of the neighborhood, to whom he was a veritable Santa Claus for the entire year. On the streets he would often stop and give some children of his acquaintance roasted chestnuts and other things equally delectable to the juvenile appetite. In Erie to this day there are many men and women who speak enthusiastically of the favors received at the hands of Mr. Davenport when they were children. This giving happiness to little children was one of the constant delights of his life. He took excellent care of his health, never indulged in tobacco or strong drink, but, soon after passing his seventy-sixth birthday, became afflicted with a malignant disease which despite of all that could be done to relieve his sufferings ended in his death, August 1, 1911, in the seventy-eighth year of his age. He sleeps in the Erie Cemetery.

George Perry Griffith, Esq.

George P. Griffith, son of Stephen and Susan (Perry) Griffith was born at Mayville, Chautauqua county, New York, October 29, 1837. His parents were natives of that county, to which their forebears came as early settlers from New England. The Griffiths were of Welsh extraction. The family settled in North East, Pa., in 1846, where the father, among other activities, engaged in the manufacture of hats, and also in grape culture, and was for nearly forty years one of North East's foremost men. Among local offices held by him was that of Justice of the Peace. He was a leading member of the Methodist Church, and superintendent of its Sunday School. He was a large man with a remarkably keen intellect. He often acted as counsel in trials before magistrates and never to the writer's knowledge suffered in an exchange of wits with lawyers brought in to oppose him. He was a most highly respected citizen and delightful companion. His death in 1883 was generally regretted. His wife who survived him by twelve years, was a member of the large Perry family of whom Commodore Perry was the most illustrious. When a girl she was chosen as one of twenty-four representing the twenty-four states, to welcome General Lafayette on his historic visit to America.

George P., the subject of this sketch was the eldest of four children, all of whom became highly respected citizens. He was educated at the Fredonia, N. Y., Academy, in which village he also learned the newspaper business. While following this occupation at Freeport, Illinois, he reported the famous debate of Lincoln and Douglas held there. Returning to Erie he was for a time employed on the Erie Observer, then engaged in the oil business at Titusville. Again returning to Erie he studied law in the office of Hon. Samuel A. Davenport and was admitted to the bar in 1864. In 1870 he became junior member of the firm of Davenport & Griffith, which continued for nearly a quarter of a century and did a business surpassed by none in this corner of the state. The firm was exceedingly strong, for as business and office lawyer Mr. Griffith never had a superior at our bar, while his partner was second to none in the trial of causes. The firm did an immense business and Mr. Griffith with a perfect system had at his finger's end every paper and document in the office. He continued practice, after the dissolution of the firm and for a time was with Hon. A. B. Osborne. Later he devoted most of his time to the business of the Barber Asphalt Paving Company, with whom he became generally associated. He was ever considerate of his professional brethren and especially of young lawyers, to whom he was ready to give kindly advice. He was an expert penman and for a time acted as clerk for the city council. At one time he was secretary of the Erie School Board and for many years its solicitor. His employment with the Paving Company took him much from home and while in Boston he was taken sick and died on May 19, 1901, in the sixty-fourth year of his age. He is buried in the Erie Cemetery. He was a large, fine looking gentleman, wore a dark moustache and was of the most agreeable manners. The second volume of "Miller's History of Erie County" contains an excellent portrait of Mr. Griffith.

In 1864 he married Miss Ella C. Richards, who at

this writing (1927) is still in good health and one of Erie's most charming ladies. They have two sons, Dr. Richard Griffith, of California, and George P. Griffith, Jr., who for many years has been engaged extensively in contracting at Los Angeles, California.*

The Griffiths were noted for hospitality, and about the end of December, 1886, at the expiration of Judge William A. Galbraith's official term, gave at their home on West Seventh street a most charming banquet in honor of the outgoing and incoming judge. All members of the local bar and others were invited. It was an unusually happy occasion which is fresh in the writer's memory after more than forty years.

---

*Note: George P. Griffith, Jr. died since the above was written.

Rush S. Battles, Esq.

Rush S. Battles, son of Asa Battles, Sr., and Elizabeth Brown Battles, was born at Girard, Pa., in 1833, was educated at Girard Academy, also at Kingsville, Ohio, Academy. He attended the National School of Law at Poughkeepsie, New York, also studied law with Hon. S. E. Woodruff at Girard. He was admitted to the Erie Bar Dec. 12, 1855, and formed a partnership with his preceptor, but soon abandoned the law for other pursuits and spent his long and useful life in banking, manufacturing, farming, fruit growing and in oil business. He was very successful and one of Erie county's most substantial citizens, a man of high ideals who enjoyed the entire confidence of the community. He was tall, wore a beard and was a fine appearing gentleman, dignified, but uniformly kind and courteous. He was a Republican, but never sought office.

In 1861 he was united in marriage with Miss Charlotte M. Webster of Girard. To them three children were born, one of whom, Miss C. Elizabeth Battles, is a well known resident of Girard.

In the days of horses, he was fond of driving, also traveled quite extensively. Mr. Battles died March 27, 1904, and is buried at Girard. This closed a highly honorable and useful career. (See Reed's History of Erie Co., vol. 1).

William Griffith, Esq.

William Griffith, uncle of George P. Griffith, was a native of Chautauqua county, New York, and located at North East about 1845, and was a pioneer in the grape industry of that section; in which he was very successful. He had an unusually keen intellect and was a brilliant speaker. For many years he was put forward by North East to welcome delegations and express the best thought of her people and he always made good. Because of his natural aptitude for the law he took it up as a side line late in life and was admitted to the Erie Bar in 1875, when approximately fifty-seven years of age. He then opened a law office in North East, bought a law library and devoted himself to the practice so far as his delicate health and other activities permitted. He tried many cases before local magistrates and some in court, and always with ability. On my admission to the bar in September, 1878, he handed me the key to his office, which I occupied for over three years, during which time Mr. Griffith died in May, 1881. He had long been in failing health and had on one occasion said he was going to have me draw his will and told what disposition he desired made of his estate. He neglected, however, to do so, but on the day of his death, the attending physician sent his horse and buggy for me and I went to his home and found Mr. Griffith in the throes of death. He said, "Make my will as I told you," which I did and he said, "Sign my name to it." This I also did and he touched the pen and the doctor and I signed as witnesses. Mr. Griffith asked, "Is it done?" I said, "Yes," and he breathed no more. He was buried at North East. Thus ended the career of one, who, had he adopted the law as a profession in youth, might have become eminent. He was of medium height, but of slight build, wore a full beard and bore no resemblance to his brother Stephen, who was large and smooth shaven.

By his first wife, William Griffith had one child, a daughter, who became the wife of Col. John Greer, of the Regular army. Mr. Griffith's second wife was Miss Helen Lester of Fredonia, New York, an accomplished lady of rare charm, who survived him for some years. Their home in a grove on his farm north of the borough, overlooking Lake Erie, was one of Erie County's most beautiful spots.

Hon. Jerome Francis Downing

J. F. Downing, son of James and Roxanna (Forbush) Downing, and the youngest of twelve children, was born in Hampshire county, Mass., March 24, 1827, and grew to manhood on his father's farm. His parents were also born in Massachusetts. This worthy son of New England gratified his ambition for a broader education than could be obtained in the home schools largely by the fruits of his own toil, which enabled him to spend two years in Amherst College. In 1850 he became for two years a journalist, in turn editing a newspaper at Holyoke, Mass., and at Troy, New York. Then for two years, beginning in 1853 he was principal of the Male High School, at Carlisle, Pa., meantime studying law with Hon. William B. Penrose, a leader of the Central Pennsylvania Bar, and relative of the late Senator, Hon. Boies Penrose. After admission to the Cumberland County Bar, Mr. Downing located in Erie and was admitted to our bar in the fall of 1855. Thereafter he continued a progressive and helpful citizen of Erie for nearly sixty years. His professional and personal standing was such that he was elected district attorney in 1863. In this office, as elsewhere, he proved himself able and faithful. During this official service there came a turning point in the life of Mr. Downing which practically removed him forever from the active ranks of the legal profession and enabled him to become one of America's foremost fire insurance underwriters. About 1865 the Insurance Company of North America, located at Philadelphia, tendered him the position as its general western agent. After some hesitation he accepted. It was customary for the western agencies of such companies to be located in Chicago, but he continued temporarily to reside in Erie, so if the venture failed, he could resume the thread of his legal practice. In other words he "kept an anchor to windward." The sequel showed his fears were groundless, for under his superb management the business of his company grew by leaps and bounds in the entire western district. In a few years his commissions were such as to put to the blush the income of the leaders of the bar. His remarkable success was such as to soon attract the attention of other companies, and he was made the general western agent of the Pennsylvania Fire Insurance Company of Philadelphia. Meantime he built up a large local fire insurance business which is still prosperous and extensive after a continuance of some fifty years. To accommodate his vast business, Mr. Downing erected the fine office building at the northwest corner of Ninth and Peach streets, still in use for local business. For many years, Mr. Downing's palatial home on West Ninth street was one of the finest in the city.

For some years he was extensively engaged in wheat growing in the northwest, also became a large real estate owner in and about the city of Erie. Among other investments he erected the six story block at the northeast corner of Ninth and State streets, which when built, was the largest block in the city. For many years it has been the home of the extensive department store of the Trask, Prescott & Richardson Company. He also became interested in local manufacturing enterprises. Among other activities he served upon the school board and as member of the city council. He was in the highest and best sense a public spirited citizen and always willing to contribute liberally to every cause. It was a pleasure to approach him on behalf of any worthy charity for he gave willingly, not grudgingly. It was due to his munificence that we have Glenwood Park, which will remain a blessing and a joy forever. In the closing years of his remarkable career he became generally known as "Erie's Grand Old Man", a token of affection worthily bestowed. He was a leading spirit in whatever tended to promote the general welfare of the city. He was a strikingly handsome man, above medium size, well proportioned, with a full dark beard, which turned to gray as the years passed. Having a good voice and being an orator of note, he was frequently put forward on great occasions to express fitting thoughts and was uniformly equal to the occasion. When James G. Blaine visited Erie as a candidate for President in 1884, Mr. Downing was chosen to meet him on his way, escort him to the city and present him to an admiring multitude and he did it masterfully. Standing on the platform with that Prince of Americans, Mr. Downing suffered naught by comparison. When Erie celebrated her centennial in 1895, he was the orator of the day and as usual acquitted himself with great credit. He joined the Republican party at its birth and was ever potent in the advancement of its cause by voice, pen and means. For many years he was one of the strongest pillars in the First Presbyterian Church.

In early life Mr. Downing was united in marriage with Miss Henrietta Bagg, of South Hadley, Mass. A fit companion for her distinguished husband, this union, continuing unbroken for over fifty years, was blessed by seven children, six of whom survived their parents and are prominent in the business and social life of the city.

Some forty years ago I heard their oldest son, Wellington, make the startling prophecy that he would live to see the time when a man could eat his breakfast in Portland, Maine, his dinner in Omaha, Nebraska, and his supper in Portland, Oregon; and he has. Shortly after their golden wedding anniversary, Mrs. Downing died and some years later Mr. Downing married Miss Lucia Barney, an accomplished New England lady, who comforted his declining years. He died in 1913, at the age of eighty-six years and was buried in the family mausoleum in the Erie Cemetery. Subsequent to his death the western insurance agencies he held were removd to Chicago. While Mr. Downing's taking up the insurance business removed from the active ranks of our profession a member of fine ability and of the highest character, yet he was doubtless thereby enabled to accomplish vastly more for the city and for his family than he could otherwise have done.

Captain David Wells Hutchinson

Captain D. W. Hutchinson, son of Judge Myron and Nancy (Wells) Hutchinson, was born at Girard, Erie County, Pa., June 21, 1830. His father, a native of Madison County, New York, was a pioneer settler of Girard and became a justice of the peace and also an associate judge of Erie County. The judge's father was a soldier in the Revolutionary War, the judge's wife was of distinguished New England lineage, being a blood relative of General Nathaniel Greene of Revolutionary fame. The Hutchinson family was of unusual prominence. One of the judge's daughters became the wife of the late David Olin of Girard, a prominent merchant and one of our county's foremost men. Another daughter became the wife of John Clemens of Erie, in his day, a prominent manufacturer and highly honored citizen. David W. was educated in the schools of Girard and at Kingsville, Ohio, Academy. He studied law with Hon. George H. Cutler and was also a graduate of the National Law School at Poughkeepsie, New York. He was admitted to the New York State Bar May 11, 1853, and on May 11, 1855, to our bar, when he entered upon the practice with offices at Girard.

Captain Hutchinson was a very patriotic citizen and I believe organized a company at the breaking out of the civil war. He was also a distinguished member of the Eighty-Third Regiment Pennsylvania Volunteers and won his title of "Captain" by heroic services. After the war he resumed his practice at Girard. He was a sound lawyer and a thorough gentleman of the highest type. He was tall, of slight build and most agreeable personality. He had the entire confidence of bench and bar, but seldom appeared in the trial of causes, his practice being largely confined to the office where he faithfully served many clients. He looked after the settlement of many estates and when the railroad known as the Nickel Plate was located through Erie County, about 1881, he was employed to secured the right of way. In this capacity he rendered the railroad company highly valuable services, but was also just to the land owners, for in the majority of cases, where litigation resulted, it appeared in the end that the Captain had made fair offers for the property. In 1886, probably at the suggestion of Hon. William L. Scott, he was appointed Receiver of Public Monies, United States Land Office at Bismark, Dakota, and ably discharged the duties of that office for four years. Returning home he again took up the practice of law in this county.

On November 25, 1861, he was united in marriage with Miss Mary T. Kaiser, of Girard. They had six children, three sons and three daughters, two died in infancy and the survivors are Myron Wells, Irene Elizabeth (now Mrs. Adelbert B. Gray, Frank Joseph and James Monroe Hutchinson. Captain Hutchinson, after the example of his father was a Universalist in religion, and a Democrat in politics. He died in Erie January 19, 1894, in the sixty-fourth year of his age, and was buried in the Girard Cemetery. He enjoyed the companionship of his friends, was fond of cards and dancing, but not much given to athletics. Probably no member of our bar ever lived a more upright life or left a more spotless record than David Wells Hutchinson.

William Wallace, Esq.

Sanford's History of Erie County states that, "William Wallace, Esq., a brother of Dr. J. C. Wallace, the first burgess of Erie, was a lawyer of prominence who came to Erie from Harrisburg in 1800, as the attorney for the Pennsylvania Population Company. He married in 1803 Rachel, daughter of Dr. A. Forrest, who died in Erie in 1804. In 1806, he married Eleanor Maclay, of Harrisburg, and returned there to reside in 1810. He resumed his profession, was elected the first president of the old Harrisburg Bank, and was burgess of Harrisburg at the time of his death. He was a polite, urbane man, of slight frame and concise address. His only daughter, Mary Eleanor, married Rev. W. R. De Witt, D. D., long the pastor of the Presbyterian church of Harrisburg. Dr. William M. Wallace, the prominent physician of Erie, and Irwin M. Wallace, Esq., (sons of William Wallace), were among our most valued citizens for over half a century. Miss Julia A. W. DeWitt, a grandchild, is the author of 'How he made his Fortune' and 'Life's Battle Won', and is a frequent and able contributor to church papers. Rev. John De Witt, D. D., a professor of Princeton Theological Seminary, and a gifted preacher, is also a grandson." Mr. Wallace was buried at Harrisburg. By the way, he was the first resident attorney in Erie County and served as deputy attorney general (now district attorney) in 1909.*

His son, Irwin M. Wallace, was admitted to the Erie Bar in 1843. Whitman's History states that he attained high rank as a lawyer. I recall him in 1878 as an old gentleman, but he was then in retirement.

*Note: This sketch was prepared late and is not in its chronological order.

Hon. George W. DeCamp

George W. DeCamp, son of Mr. and Mrs. George DeCamp, was born July 6, 1823, in West Newton, Westmoreland County, Pa., and moved to Waterford township, Erie County, Pa., in 1832. His grandfather, Col. John DeCamp, a Frenchman of prominent family and large means, settled at Winchester, Va., in 1770 and in 1773 married Suesann Gray, a cousin of President James Monroe. The next year, Col. De Camp, his wife and infant son, George, settled in Westmoreland County, where the Colonel died and George remained until coming to Waterford as above stated. George W. DeCamp's educational opportunities were meagre. On leaving the district school he had to go four miles to attend the Waterford Academy; this he did, sometimes on foot and sometimes on horseback. Although of distinguished lineage he was practically a self-made man. So far as I can learn, his school days ended with the Waterford Academy and he then taught school in Mercer county, where he married Miss Nancy Rambo about 1845, and where he practiced law for some years.

Having removed to Erie, DeCamp was admitted to the bar of this county August 7, 1857, as a resident practitioner. In an incredibly short time he acquired a large practice and became a leader of the bar. While he was not above medium height, he was very strongly built, with large chest and broad shoulders, and head covered by an abundance of bushy hair, with unusually heavy eyebrows and, at least in later years, wore a moustache and well cropped chin beard. His features were strong and his whole appearance was that of a man of great force and ability. I have rarely seen a man of more striking personality. He was very industrious and became a thoroughly well read lawyer and a brilliant advocate. His most striking characteristics were intense force and aggressiveness. In those qualities he was never surpassed at our bar. He was an offensive fighter and metaphorically speaking, struck terrific blows. His client's cause was his cause and he knew no such words as "friendly enemies." Such lawyers usually make, as he made, warm friendships and lasting enmities. He was a strong and fluent speaker equally at home before court or jury. When aroused he spoke with tremendous energy. He was not only an able lawyer but had remarkable business sagacity. In the spring of 1868 he bought a very valuable estate on Staten Island, including real and personal property, from which he realized a handsome profit. The management of this property took him temporarily away from home and at its completion, in the fall of that year, he located in Pittsburgh, being then forty-five years of age. He was admitted to the Allegheny County Bar, November 2, 1868, and for the next fifteen years actively practiced his profession with offices in that city. The Pittsburgh Bar was as able as any in America and that he there made good is proof of his legal ability. He was a cosmopolitan lawyer and his practice extended into other counties and often before the federal courts and into other states and before the United States Supreme Court. He told me his income while in Pittsburgh sometimes amounted to fifty thousand dollars a year, a very large sum for those days. This amount may have included his profits on real estate transactions which he frequently had while in Pittsburgh.

DeCamp was ever a believer in real estate; while in Erie he owned several pieces of land, including his home, No. 134 West Ninth street, now the site of the Shannon apartment, and a farm on West Lake road near the Tracy place. When about sixty years old, being in affluent circumstances he decided to retire from practice and spend his declining years in the west. To that end he bought a large tract of land near Emporia, Kansas, on which he located about 1881. He was in Pittsburgh thereafter more or less for a few years to close up some important legal business, including his work as solicitor for William Varnum, Receiver of the German Insurance Company. While so engaged, I became well acquainted with him by meeting him often in Erie and in Harrisburg. At that time he tried with marked ability a number of cases here growing out of the matters of that insurance company and became acquainted with the younger members of our bar. Sometimes when waiting for his cases we would listen to his conversation, which was out of the ordinary and quite remarkable. He had a wealth of knowledge and power of expression not often found.

He was an active Republican and had great fame as a campaign speaker. In 1863 Pennsylvania's war governor, Hon. Andrew G. Curtin was booked for a war speech in New York City and George W. DeCamp was selected as the one to introduce the Governor. This he did in a most notable speech. At one time I asked him how he prepared that speech, and his reply was, "By reading in the Book of Isaiah," which he said he had done that day in his room at the hotel. He also said that in the Bible the English language appeared at its best. The orator was hard to find who could make a better speech than he on such an occasion. In my opinion George W. DeCamp had as much native ability as any member in the history of our bar. In his day he did an immense amount of work and earned the rest he allotted himself in age. He never very actively engaged in practice in Kansas, but probably gained much by the increase in value of his extensive land holdings in that state. There on the boundless prairies his restless spirit found ample room and there in the midst of this great country the mortal remains of this most remarkable man are forever at rest. Early in the year 1905 his health began to break and he died at his home in Emporia, January 4, 1906, in his eighty-third year, and was buried there in the Maple Wood Cemetery. He was a member of the Masonic and I. O. O. F. fraternities. He was survived by three sons and five daughters, who, so far as I am informed, are living in Kansas. One son became interested in politics and was a member of the Kansas legislature. He also has four grandchildren. Mrs. DeCamp, an exemplary Christian woman of delightful personality, survived her husband and died December 14, 1913. DeCamp in his own home was ever kind, affectionate, thoughtful and all he should have been. He loved the beautiful in art and nature, also good books, and was strikingly familiar with the best literature. He was a man of remarkable physical as well as mental strength, as was his father, who lived to the great age of ninety-one years. George W. DeCamp was called "judge" in his later years, but so far as the writer knows he never sought or held judicial office in Pennsylvania.

David W. Rambo, Esq.

David W. Rambo was born in Coolspring township, Mercer county, Penna., September 8, 1835. He was educated in the public schools and at West Minster College, New Wilmington, Pa. He was engaged in teaching before his admission to the bar. He was admitted to the Erie Bar, November 2, 1864, where he practiced his profession for about ten years. My information is that he had been admitted to the Mercer County Bar and practiced there before coming to Erie. In 1875 he was admitted to the Pittsburgh Bar and located in that city. A part of the time while here and all of the time while in Pittsburgh he practiced with his brother-in-law, Hon. George W. DeCamp, a trial lawyer of great ability, who probably did most of the court work. As both were sound lawyers and hard workers, they made a strong team. Mr. Rambo's legal judgment was remarkably good. As I recall him he was a large, fine looking gentleman and wore a beard. In 1879 he moved to Howard, Kansas, and later to Richmond, in the same state, where he continued to practice law.

In 1858 he was united in marriage with Miss Belle Carmon, of New Wilmington. Of their seven children, three sons are living, one, a conductor on the Santa Fe R. R., one, a Y. M. C. A. Secretary in Texas, and the third is a resident of Kansas City, Mo., and one daughter, Mrs. Nannie A. Ross of Xenia, Ohio, whose son, James Merle Ross is a naval officer, now or recently stationed in China. Mr. Rambo died June 12, 1907, in the seventy-second year of his age and was buried at Richmond, Kansas. Mrs. Rambo died the next year and was buried beside him.

David Brice Innis Sterrett, Esq.

Innes Sterrett (commonly so called) was born in McKean township, Erie County, Pa., April 12, 1837. He was the son of David and Mary (Sterrett) Sterrett and the grandson of James and Anna (McKnight) Sterrett, who came from Cumberland county, Pa., in 1807, and bought a large farm at Sterrettania, occupied by them and their descendants to this day. Thomas Sterrett, a brother of Innis, spent his life on this farm and for nearly fifty years was the foremost citizen in that locality. Another brother, Andrew Jackson Sterrett, was for seventeen years Clerk of the Erie County Commissioners and one of the most popular officials in the history of the county, of which county one of his sons, Thomas G., is now sheriff.

Innis Sterrett's great, great grandfather, Robert Sterrett, was born in Scotland, married in Ireland and settled in Pennsylvania in 1719. He was also the great great grandfather of Hon. James P. Sterrett, late Chief Justice of the Pennsylvania Supreme Court, and of Hon. A. B. Richmond, the celebrated criminal lawyer of Meadville. He was also the great great great grandfather of Hon. Sylvester B. Sadler, now a Justice of the State Supreme Court. An excellent sketch of the Sterrett family will be found in Reed's History of Erie County (vol. 1), page 699.

Innis made a brilliant record in Allegheny College, where he graduated in the class of 1857. Among that class were James M. Thoburn, later a famous Bishop of the Methodist Church; Levi Bird Duff, who became a great lawyer in Pittsburgh, and others. In fact seven members of that class, including Mr. Sterrett, were known as "The 7 of '57." Innis studied law in the office of his cousin, Hon. A. B. Richmond, and then for a brief time opened a law office in Kansas, of which state his brother, A. J., was a resident. He then located in Texas where he practiced law and edited a newspaper. The latter expressed such strong abolition sentiments that he and his partner were driven out of the state. Returning home, he was admitted to the Erie Bar May 7, 1861, and began practice in this city. He was at once recognized as a young lawyer of unusual ability, and was soon made city or county solicitor. While rapidly winning his way as a practicing attorney, his health failed and he died September 4, 1863, at the early age of twenty-six years. It is doubtful if any lawyer of the same age in the history of our county ever made a more favorable impression on the bar and public. Hon. John P. Vincent was chairman and Hon. Jonas Gunnison secretary of the bar's committee on resolutions, which gave the deceased such unstinted praise that a copy thereof is still preserved by members of his family, as is also a silver cup won by him in a literary contest while in college.

The untimely death of Innis Sterrett is one of the sad events which I am called upon to record.

Charles Burnham, Esq.

Charles Burnham was for many years a resident of Edinboro and while there studied law and was admitted to the Erie Bar, November 11, 1864. He entered upon the practice and had his office at Edinboro for about ten years, then located in Erie where he continued to practice until his death. He was a fluent speaker and a good trial lawyer. He was tall, of dark complexion and of most genial personality. He was an active Republican, but never aspired to office, except I think he served as justice of peace at Edinboro before coming to the bar. He was twice married, that to his first wife, a widow with four children, proved unhappy and ended in a divorce. Later, he married a Miss Williams of Edinboro, who survived him. He also left one daughter residing in the West. He died about 1880, approximately sixty years of age.

Hon. Charles Ordean Bowman

Charles O. Bowman, son of Godfrey and Susannah J. Bowman, was born March 9, 1825, at Brookfield, Tioga County, Pa. The father, Godfrey Bowman, was a soldier in the war of 1812 and with Perry at the battle of Lake Erie, where, although so severely wounded as to be unable to shoot, he rolled cannon balls and helped supply other ammunition to his comrades. For his heroism he received the thanks of congress and a medal. Charles attended district school and Lima University, New York, then taught school and read law evenings. Soon as practicable he studied law in the office of R. G. White, Esq., at Brookfield and later with A. F. Monroe, Esq., at Knoxville, in Tioga county, and was admitted to the bar of that county in 1852. He then began practice at Knoxville and so continued until his removal to Corry in 1865, where he was soon recognized as the leader of the bar of that city, which position he retained unchallenged until his death. During this time he was retained in a majority of the important litigation emanating from that section of the county. Mr. Bowman had a thorough knowledge of law and was an excellent trial lawyer. As an orator he stood in the front rank at our bar. He had a striking personality, being about six feet tall, well proportioned, with a clear complexion, black hair and moustache and sometimes wore a beard; dignified, but ever kindly and with engaging manners. He was an all round lawyer and tried with ability many cases in the Erie county courts and in adjoining counties, also practiced in the state supreme court. He was generous to a fault, wonderfully kind hearted and probably careless about collecting his fees. He would espouse a just cause regardless of compensation. In Corry he was local counsel for a railroad company and might have represented the Standard Oil Company. His ability would have brought him distinction in a large city, but he enjoyed better living in a small one. The Corry people all knew and all liked Squire Bowman. He secured their city charter about 1869.

When a very young man he had served a term in the legislature from Tioga county and a few years after locating in Corry, Erie County sent him again to the legislature and shortly thereafter (in 1872) sent him as a delegate to the state constitutional convention, his ability as a lawyer and experience as a legislator eminently fitting him for that service. Although composed of many of the state's foremost men, Mr. Bowman took an active part in the extended deliberations of that body and many of the provisions he urged upon the floor of the convention became a part of the constitution; which constitution was overwhelmingly ratified by the people and, with some minor changes, has stood the test of half a century. One of the elements of Bowman's strength was a strong vein of common sense and another was his absolute integrity. He had a keen sense of humor, was a fine story teller, a delightful companion but on all occasions revered sacred things and would never use or permit to be used in his presence any profanity or vulgarity. In other words, he was a clean spoken, high minded gentleman.

Soon after coming to Corry, he formed a law partnership with Hiram A. Baker, Esq., which continued for several years. He was ever glad to assist young lawyers and especially law students, of whom he had many, some of whom, including C. L. Baker and C. George Olmstead, became especially prominent at the bar. Bowman's eloquence was captivating. On one occasion he and I were defending a case before S. L. Gilson, Sr., Esq., legal arbitrator. The trial was held at Corry, and when the plaintiffs rested, we submitted no proof, but asked for a dismissal of the case. Bowman said, "Walling, you open the argument and I will support you," which I did and he followed for about twenty minutes in a speech of surprising eloquence and force. In fact, he convinced the large audience, but unfortunately not the arbitrator, of the righteousness of our cause. We took an appeal and I have always thought the effect of that speech enabled us to secure a favorable settlement.

Bowman was a very strong man on the stump and took an active part in many campaigns. In fact, the papers frequently referred to him as a Republican wheel horse. In 1880 I was local chairman of a Garfield and Arthur Club at North East and Bowman and Olmstead came there to open the campaign. In the course of his speech, Bowman told the story of the pig and the pup, which caused great applause. Some days later in speaking at Cherry Hill, I told Bowman's story with like result. Some weeks later Olmstead in speaking at Cherry Hill repeated the same story, but got little response from the audience. Then just before the election Bowman was sent to Cherry Hill to close the campaign and innocently repeated his story. This third repetition of the same story in the same campaign to the same audience was too much for them; they not only refused to applaud but nearly threw Bowman out the window. An explanation followed at the close of the meeting, when the speaker discovered he was the victim of what might be termed a practical joke, but he took it good naturedly, and we had a hearty laugh over it afterward. He was raised a Methodist, but never joined the church. He was very fond of his family, loved fine horses and was an expert checker player.

In 1850 Mr. Bowman was united in marriage with Miss Jane A. Monroe, of Palmyra, New York, by whom he had one daughter, Eva, now Mrs. Eva Bowman Gill. His first wife died in 1887, and in 1888 he married Miss Lizette Smith, who with four children of that marriage, survived him. Some of the children, at least Mrs. Bessie Bowman Shea, now reside in Corry. Charles O. Bowman died November 20, 1887, and was buried at Corry. His life long desire to avoid giving pain to others was rewarded by his own painless death, which came to him without sickness, while sleeping quietly in his bed.

Alburn J. Foster, Esq.

A. J. Foster was born at Boston, Erie County, New York, September 16, 1832, of Revolutionary stock. He was educated at public schools and the Kingsville, Ohio, Academy. He taught school for a number of years; while so engaged at the Erie Academy, and at grade schools, he studied law with Hon. John P. Vincent and was admitted to the Erie County Bar on March 15, 1865. Thenceforward, he practiced law in Erie until his death. He never acquired a large practice but was an earnest, hard working lawyer and never slighted any business intrusted to him. When I was a law student, I was sitting in the criminal court room when Foster was appointed to defend an impecunious defendant charged with larceny, and I well remember the zeal and earnestness with which he fought that case. When his client was convicted he moved for a new trial and argued the motion with intense earnestness and vigor. Had he received a large fee he could not have worked harder. I confess he created in my mind a doubt as to the defendant's guilt, which has lingered with me for fifty years. It was a striking example of professional duty, regardless of fees. It was characteristic of Foster that whenever he had a case, he devoted himself unsparingly to it. For a number of years he was solicitor for the Board of Directors of the Poor, and that board never had or could wish for a legal adviser who would look with greater care after every detail of its business. When he represented the board there were no funds lost for lack of attention.

Foster was of sandy complexion, generally wore a beard, was large and strongly built. He and Judge Vincent were friends and he often visited our office. He married Mary Hunter, whose father was a very well known citizen of Erie and resided near Sixth and Chestnut streets. Another daughter was the wife of the late James P. Covert.

The Fosters had three children, William S. of Chicago, J. Boyd, of Baltimore, and Mary Adelaide, employed in the Pension Department at Washington. While Mr. Foster never accumulated much he was a good citizen and reared an excellent family. He was a Methodist and a Republican in politics. When about sixty-four years of age his health began to fail and he died November 9, 1898, at the age of sixty-six years. He was buried in the Erie Cemetery.

Hon. Edward Camphausen

Edward Camphausen was born at Cologne, Germany, Feb. 20, 1823. He was well born, had a university and military education in Germany, but because of an active part taken by him in favor of the Revolution for Democracy in 1848, was compelled to flee from Germany. He came to the United States via England, the voyage from Plymouth to this country on a sailing vessel took forty-eight days. After remaining in Erie a few months he became so desperately homesick that he decided to return to Germany and meet whatever fate awaited him. When there, however, he found the revolution still on and at the earnest entreaties of his father and other friends was induced to return to Erie, which became his permanent home.

On April 18, 1853, he was united in marriage with Miss Sophia Catherine Zimmerman, daughter of Frederick Zimmerman, who lived on the Zimmerman Road, and was one of the county's most substantial farmers. The civil ceremony attending the marriage was performed by Judge John Galbraith. Mr. Camphausen soon became well established in Erie where he filled many important offices, including that of justice of the peace, school director, city councilman and was president of the select council in 1871, acting as mayor in the absence of Mayor Wm. L. Scott. Meantime he studied law and was admitted to the Erie Bar March 15, 1865, and for the next twenty years was in active practice and became prominent at the bar. His fine ability, high character, industry and thorough knowledge of the German language, gave him a large and renumerative clientage.

No other case, here or elsewhere, occurs to me where an attorney, coming to the bar so late in life (42 years of age) made a finer record than Mr. Camphausen. He was a very busy lawyer, had an extensive office practice and tried many cases. He became a master of English as well as of his native tongue. When district attorney I prosecuted an Italian named Leonardo for murder. His guilt was clear and seemed to be of the highest degree. Mr. Camphausen was his attorney and seeing the peril of his client probably saved his life by entering a plea of guilty and submitting the degree to the court. Less adroit counsel would have missed the opportunity.

In 1885, through the influence of his friend, Hon. William L. Scott, then in Congress, Mr. Camphausen was appointed U. S. Consul to Naples, Italy, where he and his family resided for five years. His success there was phenomenal. Every American who met him came back sounding his praises, and that of his family. We were probably never better represented at Naples than during his consulship. In fact it is said he was the most popular consul in Europe. Mr. Camphausen and his family had a host of warm friends in Erie. On the occasion of a prior visit to Europe, friends assembled at their residence and left presents and good wishes. There was also a friendly demonstration on their departure from Naples and their return in 1890 was the occasion of a public reception at Maennerchor Hall, which was filled to the doors. My wife and I were among the throng. Many happy speeches were made, that of Michael Liebel, Sr., was to my mind the most notable. After his return, Mr. Camphausen built his beautiful home on West Tenth street, where the daughters now (1927) reside.

He was above medium height, light complexioned, wore a beard, had a military bearing and presented a fine appearance. Few, if any, foreigners coming to our city have made a deeper or more abiding impression upon the community than Edward Camphausen. After his return from Naples he had an office but never resumed active practice. He was a public spirited, loyal American and helpful citizen. He tendered his services to the Government during the civil war, but I believe, saw no active service. He was an incorporator of Hamot Hospital, also an incorporator and financial supporter of the Glenwood Park Association. He was a Mason, a Democrat and a Lutheran, also a member of the Erie and Kahkwa Clubs and of the Board of Trade. He was keenly interested in domestic animals, such as fine horses, cattle and dogs.

He died February 13, 1903, at the age of eighty years, and sleeps in his mausoleum in Erie Cemetery; the influence of his life still abides.

Col. Charles M. Lynch

Col. Charles M. Lynch, son of Charles and Mary Ann (Parmater) Lynch, was born at Erie, April 10, 1842. His father was a descendent of one of the signers of the Declaration of Independence and his maternal grandfather fought in the war of 1812. Col. Lynch was educated in the schools of Erie. In August, 1862, when twenty years of age, he enlisted in Company D, 145th Regiment Pennsylvania Volunteers and became captain of the company. He was a fighting soldier and participated in all the great battles in which that regiment took part, including Antietam, Fredericksburg, etc. On November 13, 1863, he was promoted to Lieutenant-Colonel and in March, 1865, to the rank of Colonel; and was mustered out May 31, of the same year. Although young to hold such high rank, Col. Lynch had a remarkably fine war record. His devotion, courage and skill endeared him to his comrades and earned his promotions. On returning home Col. Lynch resumed his law studies, which the war had interrupted, in the office of Col. Benj. Grant, and was admitted to the Erie Bar, February 6, 1866, when he entered upon a legal career at Erie which continued nearly forty-one years. He was an upright lawyer and tried his cases on their merits rather than upon legal technicalties. He despised quibbles, but was strong on the facts. We were sometimes colleagues and I found him an agreeable and helpful associate. I well recall the case of Frantz v. Lake Shore, etc., Ry. Co., which we won after a stubborn contest (127 Pa. 297). Col. Lynch made a very satisfactory district attorney to which office he was elected in 1866. He had a host of friends but I do not recall that he ever aspired to any other elective office. He was, however, appointed collector of internal revenue for this district in 1876 by President Grant, and held that position for eight years, which interfered somewhat with his professional work.

Col. Lynch was nearly six feet tall, stood erect, with a military bearing, was of athletic build, but not heavy. He had dark hair, somewhat inclined to curl, wore a moustache and was one of the handsomest men at our bar. He was modest, but a most agreeable companion and an outdoor man who enjoyed hunting and fishing, during his later years spent considerable time in the latter recreation.

On September 8, 1869 he was united in marriage with Miss Clara J. Grant, a daughter of Col. and Mrs. Benjamin Grant. They had four children, Faulkner G. Lynch, now and for many years engaged as City Engineer and Assistant City Engineer of Erie, Grant R. Lynch, holding a responsible position in the Erie Post Office, Charles M. Lynch, Jr., and a daughter, Mrs. George T. Bliss. Col. Lynch died of pneumonia in January 2, 1907, in the sixty-fifth year of his age and was buried in the Erie Cemetery. His wife predeceased him by some years.

Hiram Abiff Baker, Esq.

Hiram A. Baker, son of Simeon and Lodema (Benham) Baker, was born at Howard, Steuben County, New York, March 22, 1824. His father's ancestors came to America from England about the middle of the seventeenth century and his mother was of Holland-Dutch lineage. At the age of fourteen years Hiram came with the family to Concord township, Erie County, Pa., where he attended school for four years, then taught school two years (1842-1844) in Michigan. Returning to Pennsylvania he studied law with Hon. H. L. Richmond at Meadville and was admitted to the Crawford County Bar in 1848. After admission to the bar he conjointly taught school and practiced law at Titusville for two years, then removed to Spartansburg, Crawford county, where he practiced law during the first oil excitement. Later he settled in Corry and was admitted to the Erie County Bar, October 1, 1867. Thenceforth he practiced law with office and residence there until his last sickness, being for some years in partnership with Hon. C. O. Bowman, under the name of Baker & Bowman. The firm did a good business. Baker was a fine office and business lawyer and Bowman an expert in the trial of causes. Later Baker had offices for some years with Hon. Manly Crosby. Mr. Baker's practice extended into adjoining counties as well as in Erie county. In his later years he frequently came into court relating to business matters and orphans' court practice, but not often participated in contested trials. He was a sound lawyer of the highest professional character, universally respected and trusted by the public and by his brethren of the bar.

He was a thorough gentleman of the old school, tall, well proportioned and with looks and a manner to inspire confidence. In fraternity, he was a Mason, in religion a Universalist and in politics a Democrat. He never sought public office but served as city councilman, also as school director at Corry. He also acted for some years as notary public. In addition to his law practice Mr. Baker was for some years engaged in the oil business.

On May 14, 1849, he was united in marriage with Miss Arvilla A. Mather, daughter of Luther Peck and Gabrielle (Belmont) Mather. The Bakers had seven children, Cassius L., who became prominent at our bar, a sketch of whom is presented herewith, the late Dr. Willis M. Baker, at one time probably the leading physician and surgeon at Warren and Dr. L. B. Baker, who became prominent in the medical profession at Erie, and later took a law course at Columbia University and was actively engaged in the practice of that profession in New York City, where he died suddenly at the age of forty-eight years. The three daughters, Mrs. Flora L. Sears, and Mrs. Harriet A. Elston, of Corry, and Mrs. Camilla B. Leslie*, of Erie, are living. I am safe in saying that no member of our bar has reared a more worth while family than Hiram A. Baker. He died January 23, 1892, in the sixty-eighth year of his age, and was buried in Pine Grove Cemetery at Corry. His widow survived him for many years and died at the home of her daughter in this city at the advanced age of ninety-three years.

Note: *Mrs. Leslie has since died.

Cassius Leland Baker, Esq.

C. L. Baker, son of Hiram A. and Arvilla A. (Mather) Baker, was born at Titusville, Pa., May 17, 1850, but soon removed with his family to Corry, where he attended public schools. He also attended the Clinton Liberal Institute near Syracuse, N. Y. He read law in the office of Baker (his father) and Bowman, at Corry, was admitted to the bar in 1872 and entered upon the practice of law in that city, where he was notably successful and soon had a fine business and was regarded as a very promising lawyer. He was ever a prime favorite with Corry people and did much of their legal business. He was the Democratic candidate for district attorney when I was elected in 1881 and was the successful candidate for that office against F. M. McClintock, Esq., in 1884. At that time he removed to Erie where he continued in active practice until ill health compelled his retirement about 1920. He was the only Democrat to hold the office of district attorney since 1856, and he filled it with eminent satisfaction; always efficient but never vindicative in the prosecution of criminal cases. During his term of office he took high rank as a lawyer which he maintained until retirement. We were close friends and mutually assisted each other in the trial of important cases, notably those for larceny against L. O. Lindsey and his sons, tried both in Erie and Crawford county, and the Jacob Mets murder case, tried in Erie county. I never had nor could wish a better associate, ever careful and thorough in preparation and wisely efficient at the trial. He was engaged in many important trials, one of the most important, the defense of a personal injury case against a lumber company, tried in Erie county about 1890. Following this trial, Mr. Baker suffered a terrible sickness so that his life was given up by his three physicians, but he made a marvelous recovery and lived for more than thirty years. He was an all round lawyer, equally efficient in his office as in court. He had excellent business judgment, was very methodical and often made investments for clients.

Mr. Baker was his party's candidate for judge in 1896 and one of the first to tender me congratulations. No man exceeded him in public spirit; for some years he was a member of the Erie City School Board and served as its president. He was elected and reelected a city councilman under our present system and because of his business ability was made Finance Director. Both as school director and city councilman, he rendered highly important public services. Recognizing his eminent fitness for public office, Judge Benson and I had determined to appoint him a water commissioner at the earliest practicable opportunity, but Judge Benson's death and my leaving the local bench prevented the consummation of our plans. Mr. Baker was an active Mason of high degree and was chairman of the building committee in the construction of the Masonic Temple in Erie.

In addition to his professional and public duties, Mr. Baker for many years engaged extensively in the lumber business in Pennsylvania and West Virginia with Hon. C. M. Wheeler and his sons under the name of the Baker-Wheeler Lumber Co. He also became largely interested in timber lands in the far west.

In 1874 he married Miss Isabel Gordon of Clyde, New York. They had no children. About 1895 Mr. Baker erected his beautiful home on West Tenth street which they occupied for some twenty-five years; then sold and erected a bungalow in Corry, where he spent his declining years and where his widow now (1927) resides. He was a large handsome man, clean shaven and with an inspiring personality. One of the most dignified men at the bar, yet he was a most delightful friend and companion. He indulged in hunting and fishing, largely to gratify his longing for the great out of doors. I knew him well both at his work and in his recreations and must say that he was as clean living and high minded a gentleman as it has been my good fortune to know. He enjoyed good literature and especially the poems of James Whitcomb Riley. The nervous breakdown which darkened the closing years of his life was one of the saddest tragedies in the history of our bar. He departed this life February 17, 1926, in the seventy-sixth year of his age and was buried at Corry, where he sleeps with the friends of his youth in the land he loved best.

John Calvin Sturgeon, Esq.

J. C. Sturgeon, called "Cal" by his friends, son of Andrew and Eliza Jane (Caughey) Sturgeon, was born in Girard township, Erie County, Pa., October 5, 1841. His branch of the Sturgeon family was founded in Pennsylvania by Jeremiah Sturgeon, who came to Lancaster County in 1720, and whose son Samuel was a patriot soldier of the Revolution. Two of Samuel's sons, William and Jeremiah founded the town of Fairview, Erie County in 1796. Andrew Sturgeon, another son of Samuel located at Towanda, New York, where he served as a soldier in the war of 1812, and in 1820 settled at Girard in this county. His fifth son, Andrew by name, was the father of the subject of this sketch. The Caugheys were also of Revolutionary stock and have been prominent in this county from its earliest settlement. The Sturgeons were English and the Caugheys Scotch, but both came to this country from the north of Ireland. Despite the handicap, if such it be, of working his way through, Cal secured a good education. He worked on his father's farm until about seventeen years of age, during which time he attended district school, then attended the Girard Academy, also a college at Adrian, Michigan, and later Allegheny College, meantime teaching school winters and working on the farm summers. In that manner he attended college each year during the fall and spring terms. He was registered as a law student on July 20, 1861, with Johnson & Payne, attorneys at Erie, but continued his college studies thereafter and finally entered the law office of Hon. S. A. Davenport in 1865, and was admitted to the Erie Bar, Feburary 28, 1867. He immediately entered Harvard Law School where, in less than a year he graduated with the degree of L. L. B. and began practice at Erie. In 1869 he was elected district attorney, in which office he exhibited excellent ability and good judgment. He continued practice at Erie until 1877, when, lured by the McKean county oil development, he located at Bradford and was in active practice in that county for four years, then returned to Erie where he had his residence and office ever after. In 1885, when in the forty-fourth year of his age, he took up patent law, which became the great work of his life. I believe a genius for machinery led him into that field. In a few years he became widely known as a patent attorney and was engaged in the trial of important patent cases before federal courts in this and other states and before the United States Supreme Court. He continued in that branch of the profession and was widely recognized as a successful patent lawyer practically until the end of his life. His time was so occupied with patent matters that he rarely appeared in the local state courts. Occasionally he did however, and I well recall a masterly legal argument he made before me perhaps fifteen years ago. He was enthusiastic and put his whole soul into whatever he undertook.

He was an intense Republican, active in every important campaign and frequently heard on the hustings. Some twenty-five years ago his name was strongly urged and seriously considered for Commissioner of Patents. In 1904 he was a presidential elector and, as such, cast his ballot for Theodore Roosevelt. He was alive to the welfare of the city and took a keen interest in its civic organizations. Was a charter member of the Board of

Trade and later served with great credit as its president. In religion he never departed from the Presbyterian faith of his ancestors. He was rather slim, slightly above medium height of light complexion, wore a moustache and sometimes side whiskers, dressed neatly and was of fine appearance. He was twice married and by his second wife, Eda (Blakesley) Sturgeon, who predeceased him, had two sons, Ralph Andrew, a consulting engineer, and a veteran of the Spanish-American and World Wars, and Barry Albert Sturgeon, Esq., an attorney in California, who also served in the World War. J. C. Sturgeon served in the Navy during the Civil War and was an active member of the Grand Army of the Republic from its inception. For some years he was the nestor of the Erie Bar and the local attorneys, in a body, made him an annual call on each New Year's day. The long, honorable and distinguished career of John Calvin Sturgeon was closed by his death on February 19, 1923, and he was buried in the Lake Side Cemetery. Out of veneration for his memory, his name is still kept as head of the firm by his cousin and former law partner, H. M. Sturgeon, Esq.

Henry Michael Riblet, Esq.

H. M. Riblet was born at Erie, November 6, 1845. He was of French and probably on his mother's side of Pennsylvania German extraction. He was well born, the Riblets being people of distinction in this city, from its early days, including among their number John Harrison Riblet, founder of the Riblet furniture business, George Riblet, formerly a county official and many others. Henry, having received his education in the public schools and the Erie Academy, studied law with Gunnison and McCreary and was admitted to the Erie Bar October 3, 1867. Thereupon he entered upon a diligent legal career which continued without interruption for fifty-two years. He was methodical, painstaking and accurate. He was a good business man and par excellence a good business and office lawyer. He often appeared in court with petitions and other matters pertaining to the settlement of estates, etc., but very rarely in the trial of causes. He did an extensive real estate business, in the course of which he drew many hundreds of deeds, mortgages, bonds, leases, etc. He also acted as agent in charge of real estate and did a considerable collection business. He had many excellent clients and a lucrative practice, but never sought the career of a trial lawyer. I am sure that branch of the profession did not appeal to him. He was a pioneer in the habit, now common, of living in the country and doing business in the city, in that for many years he resided on his beautiful estate in West Millcreek and came daily to the city, many times on foot, a distance of over four miles.

He was of medium size, usually wore a moustache,

had the Pennsylvania German type of face, was of agreeable manners, but, like that race, steadfast in his convictions. He was an uncompromising Republican and a member of the Lutheran Church. On November 18, 1869, he was united in marriage with Miss Pauline Hayes Carpenter. They had three children, all now dead, the last survivor being Pauline Carpenter Riblet, who died in 1922. His wife having died he was, on March 30, 1881, united in marriage with Miss Gertrude Agnes Gaillard by whom he had two children, a daughter, who died in infancy, and a son, Harry Gaillard Riblet, a well known resident of this city. Henry M. Riblet showed his faith in Erie by becoming an extensive owner of city real estate. His residence in recent years was on East Eighth street, near the home of the Shrine Club. There he died March 2, 1920, in the seventy-fifth year of his age, and was buried in the Erie Cemetery. He never sought public office, but for twenty-five years was secretary and treasurer of the Board of Trustees of the Weis Library. He found recreation in his garden and was a great reader.

Hon. Henry Butterfield

Henry Butterfield, son of Jonas and Mary (Gallagher) Butterfield (the father a native of England), was born in Buffalo township, Butler County, Penna., and when a boy came to Erie County with members of his family. He was one of several brothers who became well known residents of this city or county. In 1860 he registered with J. W. Wetmore, as a student at law, of the age of twenty-one years. His fondness for politics and official life, however, was a drag on his legal career and because of his service as Transcribing Clerk in the House of Representatives at Harrisburg and as Clerk of the Erie County Courts, he did not come to the bar until April 2, 1867. He was a brilliant young man, a fine speaker, and promptly won distinction as a lawyer, but he was soon drawn into the vortex of politics and served as a member of the House of Representatives at Harrisburg during the sessions of 1873 and 1874. In 1875 he was elected to the State Senate for the short term and in 1876 for a full term . He not only made an excellent record at Harrisburg, but also many friends throughout the state. However, as has been the experience of many others, it proved a hindrance to his legal career. He continued to practice law, but never attained the eminence in the profession to which his ability entitled him. In 1892 he was again elected to the legislature, where he served with ability, but as his old friends were gone the office did not appeal to him as it had in his youth, and he did not seek re-election, but continued at the bar.

He married the daughter of a naval officer, but while she visited Erie, she never came here as a permanent resident and as he was much alone during his later years, life did not seem to afford him the same thrill as in days gone by. Senator Butterfield was slightly above medium height, wore a moustache and was a handsome man. As a conversationalist he had no superior at the bar. I well recall an evening he spent at our home over forty years ago when we were charmed with his conversation. He was a Republican, but at times, somewhat independent. As the years passed, his health declined, and he died in March 1902, probably in the sixty-third year of his age. He was buried in Pittsburgh, which was the home of a brother and had been that of his parents for many years. His brother, S. J. Butterfield, was admitted to the Erie Bar on the same day as the Senator, but if he practiced law here it was only for a brief period and I have no data concerning him.

Hon. George Ambrose Allen

George A. Allen was born on a farm in Mercer County, Pa., December 31, 1839, the son of Major William and Mary (Steel) Allen. The Allens were Scotch-Irish and settled near Carlisle, Pa., in 1787. Major Allen removed to Waterloo, Venango county in 1843 and remained there practically until his death in 1881. After leaving the common schools George attended Clintonville Academy for two years and the State Normal school at Edinboro for one year, also studied mathematics and the classics under private tutorship. He studied law with W. R. Bole, Esq., a leading attorney at Meadville, and was admitted to the Bar in 1868. The same year he located in Erie, where he practiced law continuously until his death. He was appointed city solicitor in 1872. During his early years he practiced for a time in partnership with T. A. Lamb, Esq., and about 1875 formed a partnership with Louis Rosenzweig, which continued until Mr. Allen's death and was one of the best known law firms in this part of the state. The firm did an exceptionally large business during its entire existence of nearly thirty years.

Mr. Allen gave his entire attention to his profession, and was phenomenally successful. He liked the law and enjoyed the work of a trial lawyer at which he became an expert. I saw him try hundreds of cases, but have no recollection of his losing any he should have won. He was a past master in the art of cross examination, although he never attempted to brow-beat the witness. He was able in the discussion of both law and facts and especially dangerous when he had the last speech to the jury. He never fell down, so to speak, but was uniformly efficient and intuitively grasped the strong points of the case. He usually began his final address to the jury in a conversational manner growing more earnest and more forceful as he proceeded. He was a fine speaker and analyzed the facts of the case but never resorted to spread eagle oratory. In my opinion, George Allen, when in his prime, had no superior at the Erie bar as a trial lawyer. He practiced in both civil and criminal courts, although in the latter he seldom appeared for the Commonwealth, never so far as I recall in a capital case. His kindly nature led him rather to defend than prosecute. President Cleveland, however, appointed him United States Attorney for the Western District of Pennsylvania about 1885 and he served four years with great credit.

He was an ardent Democrat and a delegate to state and national conventions but never held any other political office, although he was his party's candidate for district attorney in 1869 and for congress in 1878, and was a valuable asset to it as a campaign speaker on many occasions. He possessed a remarkably keen wit and if necessary could be very sarcastic. No member of the local bar excelled him at repartee. A juror on one occasion asked to be excused because he was deaf in one ear, when Mr. Allen remarked, "Put him on the grand jury, they only hear one side." His quick wit on one occasion got ahead of his judgment. He was of counsel in the important Hunter will case and during the introduction of evidence, the court, Judge William A. Galbraith, seemed to be ruling against Mr. Allen, who at last continued to argue the question after the court had ruled against him and the judge remarked, "Mr. Allen, if you wish to decide this case you had better take the bench." Quick as a flash, Allen replied, "If your honor wishes to be lawyer in this case you had better take your seat at the counsel table." The judge made no remark at the time but Allen lost the verdict and in overruling his motion for a new trial the court referred to the incident and said in effect that if such a remark were ever made again by any member of the bar, whoever he might be, the offender would be promptly committed for contempt.

Mr. Allen's forensic genius never appeared to better advantage than in Commonwealth v. Gray, tried in the Quarter Sessions Court of Erie county about 1890. Gray was indicted for burning his soap factory near Corry to get the insurance. Hon. A. B. Richmond, the noted criminal lawyer of Meadville, was retained by the insurance companies for the Commonwealth, while Mr. Allen appeared for the defense. When the Commonwealth closed its case, Allen satisfied the court that the indictment was under the wrong section of the statute. This necessitated an amended or new indictment and a continuance; on the second trial Gray was acquitted. Allen's closing address in that case was one of the best ever delivered to an Erie county jury. Gray, however, lost his suit for the insurance, which was tried in Chautauqua county, N. Y. Allen did not always exhibit a thorough mastery of the case in the early stages of the trial but invariably did at the conclusion.

Mr. Allen was a strikingly handsome man, slightly above medium height and well proportioned. He had black, curly hair and wore a moustache and chin whiskers. He came into the court room on one occasion clean shaven and some of his best friends failed to recognize him. He was a well preserved man until a year or so before his death, when his health began to fail; however, he continued his practice to the end.

Mr. Allen was an excellent story teller, a charming companion and close to the hearts of his professional brethren and enjoyed their full confidence and also that of the public. He was of a philosophical turn of mind and in the habit of meeting at his office on Sundays for a social hour with a coterie of congenial spirits, including Professors Missimer, Burns and one or two others, of whom Prof. Missimer, long superintendent of our public schools and now (1927) eighty years of age, is the sole survivor. Mr. Allen was a great admirer of some of the leading Democratic characters in our history and among others of Hon. Jeremiah S. Black, and treasured as a red letter event in his life an evening spent at the home of that great lawyer and jurist at York, Pa., where Judge Black detained him until midnight with the most interesting conversation to which Allen had ever listened. In 1900 there were two vacancies to be filled in the State Supreme Court and Governor Stone tendered Mr. Allen the appointment of one. This the latter declined as he feared it would hurt his chances for the Democratic nomination for which he was a candidate. I think he made a mistake. His appointment would have brought him before the state and his fine appearance on the bench would very likely have led to his nomination. As it was Judge Mestrezat secured the nomination and election and served for eighteen years.

On July 18, 1865, Mr. Allen was united in marriage with Miss Phebe A. Burlingham, of Edinboro, Pa. They had four children, three of whom are living, viz: Mrs. William H. Warner, George A. Allen, Jr., of Erie, and the younger daughter, who is married and resides in Paris. Mrs. Allen died April 1, 1881. Before coming to the bar, Mr. Allen engaged in teaching and also temporarily went upon the road as salesman. He made his own way and secured his education by his own efforts. He was an exemplary husband and father, a good liver and left a very modest estate, but, what was of greater value, a spotless reputation. He died in March, 1905, and was buried by the side of his wife and child in the Erie Cemetery. George A. Allen was probably the best combination of gentleness and force which has appeared at our bar.

"His life was gentle and the elements so mixed in him that all the world might say here was a man."

Louis Rosenzweig, Esq.

Louis Rosenzweig, son of Isaac and Bena (Baker) Rosenzweig, was born April 25, 1844, at Macon, Georgia, where his father was a merchant. His parents were of German birth. When about two years of age, Louis was brought to Erie by his parents, where they located and where the father was a well known merchant for nearly forty years, while the mother lived to a very great age and was a delightful old lady. Louis was educated in the public schools and for some years clerked in his father's store. Deciding to study law, he entered the office of Hon. Edward Camphausen and was admitted to the Erie Bar April 6, 1872. For the next forty-three years he was in active practice at our bar, being admitted in due course to the state appellate courts and to the federal courts. In 1876 he formed a partnership with Hon. George A. Allen, as Allen & Rosenzweig, which continued twenty-nine years, was one of the strongest in this part of the state and did an immense business. In all departments of the profession Rosenzweig was an outstanding success, and in the management of a business proposition, such as a stock of merchandise or a sheriff's sale thereof, he was unrivalled at our bar. He was also a fluent speaker and fine trial lawyer, especially expert in the examination of witnesses and was a rapid fire cross examiner. He was sometimes spoken of as the ablest lawyer at our bar, but, while entitled to a place in the front rank, in my opinion Allen's methods were slightly more effective before a jury. Both were great lawyers and they made a wonderful combination. Rosenzweig was a tireless worker, always prepared his cases with great care, and presented exhaustive briefs. He had an enormous clientage representing many of the most important interests in the city. No member of the bar was more trusted or more worthy of trust than he. To use a common expression, he was "true as steel." He never forgot a promise. He was probably the most careful man at our bar to see that the fees of opposing counsel were taken care of in any adjustment or compromise. No man at the bar stood higher among his professional brethren. The memorial services following his death presented a scene never to be forgotten. The remarks and there were many, every one wanted to say something, exhibited true sorrow as at the loss of a brother. Rosenzweig was probably the best spender at our bar. He earned large fees but never hoarded his money. He lived like a prince and died comparatively poor. He typified the old saying of the true lawyer in that "He lived well, worked hard and died poor," although, of course, he left some estate.

On October 19, 1864, Mr. Rosenzweig was united in marriage with Minnie Newberger, daughter of Jacob Newberger, a merchant of Cumberland, Indiana. They have four children, Grant I., now and for many years a prominent lawyer of Kansas City, Mo., Bert R., of Cleveland; Eta, wife of Isadore Levi, and Harriet, wife of Fred Davidson, of Schenectady, N. Y.

On November 25, 1883, he visited Cleveland, Ohio, where he boarded an evening train for home, but when in the railroad yards, about a mile east of the station, the conductor forcibly ejected him from the train, because his return trip ticket was not good on that limited. Rosenzweig offered to pay cash fare and protested as did other passengers about his being ejected in that dangerous place—a dark railroad yard, but in vain. In attempting to walk back to the station he was so seriously injured as to necessitate the use of crutch and cane for many years. This resulted in the most notable personal injury case ever tried in Erie county, wherein Mr. Rosenzweig recovered a verdict of $48,750, which was affirmed by the state supreme court in 113 Pa. 519. Notwithstanding the handicap of this disability, he continued faithfully at his profession until fatally stricken in court. He died March 6, 1915, in the seventy-first year of his age and was buried in the Hebrew Cemetery at Erie.

He was a medium sized man, well but not strongly built, with a striking face and personality. He wore a full black beard, becoming sprinkled with gray as the years passed, always neatly trimmed. A fine portrait of Mr. Rosenzweig, as he appeared in later years, is found in Miller's History of Erie County, Vol. 2, page 65. He wore spotless apparel, including a frock coat and usually a white necktie and white vest and was beyond question the best dressed member of the bar, possibly excepting Col. Thompson. Being disabled from active exercise he often indulged in such games as cards, both at home and in the clubs. He was a prominent and popular member of the Erie Club and usually found there, surrounded by congenial friends, at the lunch hour.

About 1882, he built his beautiful home on Seventeenth street, west of Peach, where the family resided for some thirty years. Probably as near an ideal home as could be found. He and his wife were chums and so devoted that she never recovered from the shock of his sudden death and only survived a few weeks. He was proud of his race and his religion and an honor to both, and his ability to speak the German language, which he acquired in childhood, was ever a help to him. He was an active Democrat, but never sought public office, although when young he served a term as alderman and two as school director. He was a member of the Masonic Fraternity and one of the organizers and original trustees of the Erie Public Library. In honor of his admission to the bar, his father gave a notable banquet to lawyers and friends, at his residence on Peach street, at which venerable lawyers and judges forgot their dignity and all had a royal night. Again, about the end of the year 1886, Mr. Rosenzweig gave a dinner party at his home on Seventeenth street, which was largely attended, wonderfully enjoyable, lasted until nearly morning and became historic. The last large banquet he gave was at the Country Club, in the summer of 1910, which was also largely attended and at which Hon. Robert von Moschzisker, then recently elevated to the state supreme court and now its Chief Justice, was guest of honor. It proved as notable and became as historic as those above mentioned. It may safely be affirmed that no member of our bar treated his legal brethren better socially or professionally than did Louis Rosenzweig.

Hon. Manly Crosby

Manly Crosby, son of Mr. and Mrs. Alanson Crosby, was born at Franklinville, New York, March 3, 1834, educated at the Cattaragus county schools and studied law with A. V. Boolius, Esq., at Ellicottville, N. Y. He also attended the Albany Law School, which conferred upon him the L. L. D. degree. He was admitted to the New York State Bar in 1861 and to the Erie County, Pa., Bar in 1868 and thereafter, until his death, practiced in this state, having his residence and office in Corry. He enjoyed a fine practice to which he gave painstaking care. He was a good business lawyer and could try cases well, although in his trial work he usually had an associate. His court papers were uniformly prepared with scrupulous care and his conduct, both in and out of court was such as to challenge admiration. He was a perfect gentleman on all occasions and, having most agreeable manners and a charming personality, was a favorite wherever known. Had he belonged to the majority party he might have had a congressional or judicial career.

He wore a moustache and was very handsome, slightly under medium height and trim built. His dress and bearing were ever appropriate. In addition to his professional work he was engaged in the oil and lumber business and greatly interested in horses and cattle. He was a Democrat and not a seeker of public office; although he was chosen and served as Mayor of Corry. He was very companionable and a member of the Masonic fraternity, also an Elk. His religion was that of a Universalist. In 1862 he married Frances Clarke of Ellicottville, N. Y. They had a large family of boys, several of whom, including William G. Crosby, Esq., of our bar, are still living. His wife having predeceased him, Mr. Crosby died December 3, 1909 at the age of seventy-five years and was buried at Buffalo, N. Y. In every relation of life he stood the test of real manhood.

Rev. Samuel Price Longstreet

S. P. Longstreet, son of Lewis and Elizabeth Roy (Goble) Longstreet, was born at Milford, Pike County, Pa., February 1, 1829. The parents on both sides were of old and unusually prominent New Jersey families. His paternal great grandfather was Colonel Christopher Longstreet of Sussex County, N. J., which for many years he represented in the state legislature, and later removed to northeastern Pennsylvania. After receiving the usual education, S. P. Longstreet studied law at Wilkes-Barre with Hon. W. W. Ketcham and was admitted to the Luzerne County Bar August 6, 1855. For about ten years thereafter he was actively engaged in legal practice in that county with such success as to become one of the leaders of the bar. He was a hard working lawyer, prepared and tried his cases with great care and ability. About 1864, however, he embarked in the coal business both in Schuylkill county and in Erie, to which city he removed. At first this business was successful and he accumulated a fortune estimated at $200,000; but later reverses came upon him and all his property was swept away. Then, January 25, 1869, he was admitted to the Erie Bar and took up the practice here, which he continued for about seven years. In this he was quite successful and exhibited the same characteristics which had given him prominence at the Luzerne County Bar. Before coming to Erie, Mr. Longstreet had become an active member of the Methodist Episcopal church, and, being a forceful speaker, developed into a local preacher. While practicing in Erie the call to the pulpit became so strong that, in February 1876, he abandoned the law, located in

Salt Lake City and was pastor of a Methodist church there, but after eighteen months resigned his pastorate and resumed the practice of law in that city. In 1880, however, he was appointed pastor of the Broadway Methodist church at Helena, Montana, and so continued until his death, April 5, 1881, at the age of fifty-one years. I am sure he was an able clergyman, for my former partner, Judge Vincent once said, "A lawyer because of his practical experience always makes a good preacher, while a preacher because of his theoretical tendencies seldom succeeds at the bar."

March 9, 1851, Mr. Longstreet was united in marriage with Miss Laura Babcock, daughter of Ezekial Babcock of Montrose, Pa. She survived him. They had no children. The first death of a minister of the gospel at Helena was that of Mr. Longstreet. When I came to Erie as a law student he had recently left the city and his name was often and favorably mentioned by members of the bar.

Francis Price Longstreet

Francis P. Longstreet, brother of Samuel P. Longstreet, was born at Hawley, Wayne County, August 2, 1843, and received his education at the Wyoming Seminary. He was the first man in his town to volunteer his services to the Government at the beginning of the Civil War. He was regimental clerk during his term of service and was complimented by General Hancock on the accuracy of his work. After the war he studied law and was admitted to the Erie Bar August 22, 1871, where he practiced with his brother until 1876, meantime being admitted to the United States Court. He was not robust and in the year last mentioned removed to Lehighton, Carbon County, where he continued to practice law until his death, becoming one of the leaders of the bar of that county. Despite his ill health he was a fine lawyer with a good clientage and was universally respected in and out of the profession. Inspired by the teachings and example of his mother and an elder sister, he early joined the Methodist Church and later became a pillar therein. While he declined a preacher's license, his inspiring voice was often heard in the church, and his home was a Mecca for the clergymen of that denomination. He died of tuberculosis on April 4, 1880, and his funeral was the largest that had ever been held in that town. It was attended not only by the bench and bar, but by members of the Masonic fraternity and citizens generally. The funeral services were conducted by seven ministers and the resolutions adopted by the bar association gave full utterance to the high regard in which he was held. He was survived by his widow and three children, also by his aged mother.

Hon. Samuel Myron Brainerd

S. M. Brainerd, son of Samuel and Olive L. Brainerd, was born in Conneaut township, Erie County, Pa., November 12, 1842. His parents lived on a farm and both died before he reached his majority. He had a sister who married and lived for many years near Cranesville. Brainerd attended the academy at Albion, some three miles from home, sometimes walking and sometimes going on horseback. Later, for about two years, he attended the State Normal School at Edinboro. He was there engaged in some business by which he earned his way and later earned money to prosecute his legal studies by selling nursery stock. He began his legal studies with Hon. George H. Cutler at Girard and finished with William Benson, Esq., of Erie. While a law student he was united in marriage with Miss Lovina Chapin, daughter of Mr. and Mrs. Plinney Chapin, who, although a Wattsburg family, then resided on a small farm on the Buffalo road, about two miles west of North East boro. There the Brainerds lived for some time with her parents, while he opened an office in the boro, and tried cases before magistrates, etc., for some two years before admission to the bar. He then looked very young. I heard him try one of his first cases. In September, 1868, he and Cushman Brothers began the publication of the North East Star, soon after changed to The Sun, of which D. R. Cushman, Esq., was editor for nearly sixty years. Brainerd became a full fledged lawyer upon his admission to the Erie Bar, December 22, 1869. About that time, or before, the Brainerds established a home in North East boro. He was a finely built young man of medium height, strikingly handsome, had a magnetic personality and made numerous friends. He was a fine speaker and soon became recognized as a trial lawyer. In 1872 he was elected district attorney and the county never had a more vigorous prosecutor. His fault, if any, was an excess of zeal. When he started to convict a defendant he never conjured up doubts as to his guilt. His campaign for this office and efficiency in the discharge of its duties, made him familiarly known in every part of the county. In 1874 he moved to Erie and formed a partnership with William Benson, Esq., as Benson & Brainerd, which continued many years. It was a very strong law firm; both were excellent trial lawyers. Brainerd had a good knowledge of law, while less profoundly learned therein than Benson, was more spectacular in his methods and very popular. He acquired a great reputation as a cross examiner, but it was quite often of the brow-beating type and not always successful. He was bold, self-confident and very earnest. In style he was dramatic and sometimes reached a climax that swept everything before him and carried the jury by storm; but here again he was not always successful. When I was a student in their office in 1877-8 they were doing a tremendous business, in fact, their office was literally thronged with clients and their cases on the trial lists were legion. Brainerd had dynamic energy, would be at his office by eight o'clock in the morning and remain until after nine in the evening. He tried civil and criminal cases at every term of court. If he had any preference it was for the latter. He was quite generally for the defense, but not infrequently was retained for the prosecution, in which latter capacity he was relentless and had no superior if, indeed, he had an equal at our bar.

Brainerd was an expert on the rules of evidence and could give plausible reasons to sustain his position as to the admission or rejection of testimony. He probably never did a finer piece of professional work than in the defense of a homicide case many years ago. The commonwealth relied for conviction upon alleged incriminating statements made by the defendant at the coroner's inquest and while on his way from there to the jail. The commonwealth relied upon these statements as plenary proof of the fact, but when proof was offered as to the testimony before the coroner it appeared the defendant had been directed to be sworn and testify there; whereupon Brainerd objected and produced an authority that under such circumstances what a defendant said could not be used against him. After argument the objection was sustained. Then the commonwealth called an officer and offered to prove what the defendant said to him on his way from the coroner's inquest to the jail. Brainerd again objected on the ground that the testimony before the coroner being incompetent, what defendant said to the officer, based thereon, was also incompetent, and cited an authority. This was also sustained and a verdict of "not guilty" directed. This illustrates the value of preparedness in trial practice.

In 1882 after a memorable contest Mr. Brainerd was nominated and elected to congress and during his term made an excellent record, secured large appropriations for our harbor and post office building, got the land light house restored and in many ways indicated great efficiency. He came up for reelection, backed by a united Erie county delegation, but Captain Mackay, of Franklin, who had thrown his delegates to Brainerd two years before, insisted that the compliment should be returned. This Brainerd declined to do and after a protracted contest, Mackay was nominated, which caused much ill feeling and resulted in the election of our foremost citizen, Hon. William L. Scott, on an independent ticket, although a Democrat. Two years later, Mackay again received the Republican nomination and was again defeated by Mr. Scott. In a way it was not a misfortune, as Grover Cleveland, a Democrat and personal friend of Mr. Scott, was President during the latter's service in Congress. In addition Mr. Scott was a national figure and a leader in Congress. Mackay made a great mistake in opposing Brainerd's second nomination. No man fit to go to Congress should be cut off with one term. At the end of a second term, under the circumstances, Brainerd should have retired in Mackay's favor. Brainerd did nothing to assist Mackay against Scott, and in fact was accused, I know not how justly, of favoring the latter and lost standing with his own party.

He never again sought public office, but devoted himself to his practice; the partnership with Benson having been dissolved, and after being in company with Isador Sobel, Esq., for a time he joined in practice with George H. Higgins, Esq., about 1893, and the firm of Brainerd & Higgins did a good business for some years. I was associated with them in several important cases, including Woeckner v. The Erie Electric Motor Co., and Murphy against the same defendant. I knew Mr. Brainerd intimately; we hit it up all right. We were colleagues in important criminal cases, including the murder case of Patrick Ward and also that of Philip Stein, and we were opposed in the Hugh Brown murder case and also that of Jacob Metz. He was an agreeable associate and a hard fighting opponent. He was a stronger lawyer before he was forty-five years old than he was thereafter. About that time the great strength and dynamic force of his earlier years began to disappear. Those who knew Brainerd only after he was fifty had little conception of his former ability and fine presence. In his prime his fresh, handsome face, with dark moustache and gray hair, presented a striking appearance. Mrs. Brainerd, a woman of remarkable beauty and charm, died before he was fifty. He later married Mrs. Videto, a lady of excellent family and high standing. This marriage, proving unhappy, ended in a divorce. Then, shortly before his death, Mr. Brainerd married Miss Ida Hall, a friend of the family and a most excellent woman, who survived him and since, I believe, has been engaged in teaching.

When the Brainerds came to Erie they lived in the Amos Williams house, 238 West Eighth street, but in the spring of 1878 they rented a fine new brick residence on the northeast corner of Tenth and Chestnut streets, owned by James Casey. That was their home for some fourteen years. The rent, forty dollars a month, Brainerd thought too high, but he took the place because it appealed to him. When they got settled there he sent me over to his home, ostensibly to get some papers he had left in his blue coat pocket, but I think in reality to see what a charming home he had. At least, she showed me their home and it was beautiful, a large new house, newly furnished and everything of the best. The sun was then shining on the Brainerds, who had a very interesting family of growing children, while he had won a commanding position at the bar and had ample income to gratify every wish. Those were their happiest years. We lived across the street from them for some time and knew something of the family. He did all the marketing. She never knew what they would have for dinner until he sent it over, as he did in lavish abundance.

On the twenty-fifth anniversary of their wedding, the lawyers and other friends gave them a surprise party and a beautiful silver tea set. It was a delightful occasion and the only time he was ever so taken by surprise he could practically say nothing; for in court he could adopt a new theory of the case whenever necessary to meet the emergency. No advocate in our court, when driven from his position, could reform his line of battle with more alacrity. He was uniformly kind to his juniors at the bar, except when opposing them in court.

When in his prime he had a fine professional income, but never saved much, and in his latter years, when failing health limited his activities, was not always prompt in paying his bills, and during the last years in the Casey house he got behind in his rent and Casey said to him on one occasion: "I have bad news for you. I am going to raise your rent." To which Brainerd promptly replied, "Well, if you can raise the rent you will do a d—n sight better than I can." However, when he died he left sufficient life insurance, payable to his executor, to liquidate every claim.

He was an ardent Republican and effective on the stump, where he was often seen in his younger days. He also served as chairman of the Republican county committee in 1882. He was fond of fine horses and cattle and found much recreation in driving his beautiful mare. He bought a farm on the Saltsman road, south of the Buffalo road, in Harborcreek township, where for a time he found pleasure in raising fine stock; but it became a financial drag and he sold it to the late T. M. Nagle, who also bought much adjoining property, most of which he sold afterward. Brainerd enjoyed the trial of cases even before magistrates and would frequently leave his office for an entire day to try some not very important case in a remote part of the county, to his financial disadvantage. He had an abundance of important business, including for some years the local solicitorship of the Lake Shore Railway. He had this characteristic, that he would try a small case just as ably as he would a large one. I heard him sum up hundreds of cases but never more effectively than the important malpractice case of McWilliams vs. Dr. Hotchkiss, tried in the Erie county court, in which I assisted Hon. A. B. Richmond, of Meadville for the defense.

The Brainerds had four children, the eldest daughter died when a small child, while the eldest son, Samuel B., lived until recently and left a family. He was for many years deputy postmaster at Erie. Carlton, the younger son, lives in this city and has been a faithful employee of the local street railway company for a good many years. Anna, the younger daughter, is married and resides in this state, but not in Erie. Mr. Brainerd died November 21, 1898, aged fifty-six years, and was buried by the side of the wife of his young manhood in the Erie Cemetery.

Colonel William Wallace Brown

Wallace Brown, commonly so called, the son of Rasselas Wilcox and Mary Potter (Brownell) Brown, was born at Sumner Hill, Cayuga County, New York, April 22, 1836; but when two years of age was brought by his parents to Elk County, Pa., where the father bought a tract of land, of which he made a farm, was a pioneer settler and a prominent citizen. After his common school education, Wallace, attended the Smethport Academy and later was a student and also a graduate of Alfred University in the class of 1861. He had responded to President Lincoln's first call for troops and was graduated in the uniform of a volunteer soldier. He enlisted in the Twenty-third Regiment, New York Volunteers, known as the "Southern Tier Riflemen," but after one year, through the influence of General Thomas L. Kane, was transferred to the famous Penna. Regiment, known as the "Bucktails." After his military services, he took up the study of law and was admitted to the McKean County Bar in 1867, having served as recorder of deeds of that county 1864-1866. He also served as superintendent of schools of the same county 1866-1867 and as district attorney 1867-1869. Then he removed to Corry in this county and was admitted to the Erie Bar August 31, 1869, and began practice here with offices at Corry and so continued until some eight years later, when lured by the McKean County oil excitement, he removed to Bradford, where he had his home and office for about fifty years. While the duties of numerous public trusts with which he was honored took Wallace Brown much away from his office, he never gave up the profession and his name was at the head of a law firm in Bradford up to, or nearly to, the date of his death. He was a good lawyer and I recall being impressed by the ability he displayed in the trial of a cause in the Erie County Court, after he had located in McKean County. He was reliable, industrious, capable, a good speaker and had every element of a successful lawyer. Had he given his undivided attention to the profession he would undoubtedly have been of the highest rank. In any event, he was sufficiently eminent to be appointed Assistant Attorney General of the United States by President Roosevelt, without solicitation, and made a fine record in the adjustment of the Cuban and other claims growing out of the Spanish-American War. This was probably the most important professional service of his career.

While a resident of Erie County he was elected and reelected to the state legislature and served with distinction during the sessions of 1873, 1875, 1876. After locating in McKean County he was elected and reelected to Congress, where he also served with distinction. He served with the rank of Colonel on the staff of Governor Hartranft. He also served as Auditor of the War Department, having been appointed thereto by President McKinley and later held the same position in the Navy Department. Wallace Brown was ever an active member of the Baptist Church, faithful and efficient in all its work, including that of the Sunday School. In politics he was a steadfast Republican. He was most loyal to his alma mater and for over fifty years a trustee of Alfred University, which in 1886 conferred upon him the L. L. D. degree. Personally he was tall, well proportioned and an exceptionally handsome man with a most attractive personality.

On March 18, 1862, while at home on recruiting duty, Wallace Brown was united in marriage with Miss Ellen Crandall, of Independence, Allegheny County, New York, who was also a graduate of Alfred University. After more than forty-eight years this union was broken by her death, September 5, 1920. Colonel Brown died on November 4, 1926, as the result of an accident, in the ninety-first year of his age, and both he and his wife were buried in the Alfred Cemetery near the University, so dear to both. They had one daughter, Jessie Lincoln Brown, who became the wife of Hon. Frederick P. Schoonmaker, for many years City Solicitor for the city of Bradford and now a Judge of United States Court for the Western District of Pennsylvania. Mrs. Schoonmaker died in 1921, survived by her husband and three children.

Major Isaac Brownell Brown

Isaac B. Brown, usually called Major Brown, son of Rasselas Wilcox Brown and Mary Potter (Brownell) Brown, was born at Rasselas, Elk County, Penna., February 20, 1848. He was of distinguished New England ancestry; his great grandfather, Isaac William Brown, having rendered many perilous and heroic services as a soldier in the Revolutionary War. Isaac Brown, grandfather of the subject of this sketch, was born and spent his life in New York state to which his father came from Connecticut about 1780. There the above named Rasselas Wilcox Brown was born, grew to manhood and married, but in 1838 removed to Elk County where for half a century he was a prominent citizen and the town was named Rasselas in his honor. The American founder of the mother's family was Thomas Brownell who came early to this country from England. Major Brown was reared on the farm, attended district school, the Smethport Academy and later, Alfred University, graduating therefrom in the class of 1869. Prior thereto when sixteen years of age he enlisted in the 211 Regiment Penna. Volunteers and with it engaged in several important engagements during the closing year of the Civil War, including the siege of Petersburg. After the war he taught school for some years, locating at Corry, and studying law in the offices of Crosby and Brown, was admitted to the Erie Bar, May 6, 1875, and entered upon the practice at Corry. He had, however, a natural gift for politics and his election to the state legislature in 1880 was the beginning of one of the most notable public careers in the history of the State, extending over a period of approximately thirty years. He soon rose to a commanding position in the legislature. During his third term there (the session of 1885) I was a member of the state senate. At that time few if any members of the House wielded greater influence. When he spoke, as he did only on important matters, he was listened to with marked attention and carried great weight. He was a clear, logical forceful speaker and his high character and excellent judgment added strength to his conclusions. He gained such a wide reputation by his six years' services in the legislature as led to his appointment as Deputy Secretary of Internal Affairs. He rendered such distinguished services therein as made him the logical candidate for Secretary of Internal Affairs to which office he was elected by the people. For years he held many other important offices, including that of Superintendent of Bureau of Railways, member of the Board of Pardons, President of the Pennsylvania Medical Council, President of the Board of Property, Commissioner from Pennsylvania to the World's Exposition at St. Louis, a Commissioner of Forestry of Pennsylvania, President of the National Convention of Interstate and State Railroad Commissioners, and other positions. In 1885 he introduced in the House the bill for the establishment of the Soldiers and Sailors Home at Erie and was for many years a Trustee of that institution. He filled with credit all the numerous positions to which he was called as he would that of Governor for which his name was often mentioned. Major Brown's manifold public services absorbed his energies during the active years of his life and deprived him of the professional career which might have been his. He performed so many valuable official services as probably compensated him for the loss. In any event the public was the gainer.

It is worthy of note that he and his brother Jefferson L. Brown were serving at the same time in the legislature, while his other brother Col. Wallace Brown was serving in Congress; also that the three brothers, while serving under different commands near the close of the Civil War, all accidentally met on the same spot.

Major Isaac B. Brown was a large, fine looking gentleman of commanding, but ever genial personality. On June 25, 1870, he was united in marriage with Miss Hannah Partington. They had three children, two of whom, Sara Mary Brown, now Mrs. Harold A. Gilbert, of Williamsport, and Rasselas W. Brown, of Corry, are living. Major Brown ever took a deep interest in matters pertaining to the veterans of the Civil War and was greatly beloved and honored by them. For many years he was President of the Survivors' Association of the Third Division, Ninth Corps, Army of the Potomac, and delivered the oration at the unveiling of the Division Statue on the Battlefield of Petersburg, Virginia. He was an officer in the National Guard of Pennsylvania, and retired with the rank of Lieutenant Colonel.

Major Brown was justly proud of his lineage and spent his leisure hours for nearly forty years in collecting and compiling data for his book entitled "Genealogy of Rasselas Wilcox Brown and Mary Potter Brownell Brown, their Descendants and Ancestral Lines," a wonderful book of genealogy which he published in 1920. It states they had common ancestry with Commodore Perry, President Grant, Admiral Dewey and other notables. The Major asserts, this New England stock contains America's best blood, and being of that general ancestry, I cannot too strongly dispute it; but our country contains much other good blood, for example, that of the Scotch-Irish. Major Brown never abandoned his Corry residence or his interest in the home town. He established the Corry Water Supply Company in 1886 and was its president until his death. He was a Republican and a member of the Episcopal Church. His principal recreations were hunting, fishing and golf. In 1900 the Alfred University conferred upon him the L. L. D. degree. During his later years, like many other old veterans, he was troubled with rheumatism and spent his winters at a beautiful spot on the west coast of Florida, near Clear Water. He died January 16, 1925, in the seventy-seventh year of his age, and was buried in the family mausoleum in Pine Grove Cemetery at Corry.

As indicative of Major Brown's resolute spirit, we may note that while attending the World's Fair at Chicago in 1893, he deliberately took down a Confederate flag, which was floating over a southern engine. His reasons for so doing appear in Sanford's History of Erie County, page 447.

John Keese Hallock, Esq.

John Keese Hallock, son of Rev. John Keese and Malissa Griffith Hallock, was born at Chagrin Falls, Ohio, April 24, 1844. His father was an itinerant Methodist minister and the son attended school wherever the family happened to reside. He, however, graduated at the Waterford Academy and studied law with Hon. Benjamin Wade and Hon. Joshua R. Giddings, at Ashtabula, Ohio, at about the time of the impeachment trial of President Johnson, which had it succeeded, would have made Senator Wade, who was President pro tem of the Senate, President of the United States. In such an atmosphere young Hallock could not be other than a Republican and so remained during life. He furthermore inherited the Methodist religion, to which he remained steadfast. He also studied law with Hon. A. B. Richmond, of Meadville, and may there have imbibed his fondness for patent law, as Mr. Richmond, among his varied accomplishments was a patent lawyer. Mr. Hallock was admitted to the Erie Bar in 1868. He was also later admitted to many other courts, state and federal, including the United States Supreme Court. He became an exceptionally well known and capable patent lawyer, whose practice extended into many jurisdictions. In later years, Hugh C. Lord, Esq., of this city, became Mr. Hallock's partner.

On October 2, 1871, Mr. Hallock was united in marriage with Louisa C. Arbuckle, of this city, a sister of Richard H. Arbuckle, who for fifty years has been one of Erie County's foremost men.* They had three children,

---

Note: *Mr. Arbuckle died recently at the age of ninety-two years.

one of whom, J. Keese Hallock, is now a well known business man in Pittsburgh. Mr. Hallock was of medium height, strongly built and a gentleman of exceedingly fine looks and manners. In his later years he had an infirmity of hearing, but was a great reader, a fine story teller, very companionable, and always enjoyed a good joke. He was an Elk and member of the Erie Club. He died, all too soon, on April 2, 1897, at the age of fifty-three years, and was buried in the Erie Cemetery. He enjoyed the entire confidence of his professional brethren and of the courts before whom he appeared.

John L. Hyner

J. L. Hyner was born at Heiner, Penna., in 1839. He served in the Civil War as a member of a New York State volunteer regiment. After the war he became a student of law with Col. Grant, at Erie, and was admitted to the Erie Bar April 4, 1870. After probably the most exciting contest ever waged in this county for that office, he was elected sheriff in 1872. Hyner had the Republican nomination and Wilson Moore, father of Harry L. Moore, Esq., that of the Democratic party. Moore was exceedingly popular among the farmers, from whom he had bought cattle for years. The victor was not known until the official count determined that Hyner had won by a majority of seven votes. He made an exceptionally capable sheriff, but his health became impaired, and after the expiration of his official term he sought restoration by a temporary residence in or near Arizona. This failing to produce the desired result, he returned to Erie and on April 2, 1878, died in his beautiful home on Twenty-first street, at the age of thirty-nine years, and was buried in the Erie Cemetery. He was survived by a widow and four children, one of the latter being P. Dale Hyner, Esq., a well known member of the Erie Bar. Mr. Hyner's untimely death, without an opportunity of making a record in his profession is another sad incident which we are called upon to record.

Samuel B. Brooks, Esq.

Samuel B. Brooks, the son of parents of Irish and English extraction, was born in Tompkins County, New York, May 18, 1823, and reared on a farm. He was educated in the common schools and at the Groton (N. Y.) Academy and having studied law with Hon. John W. Ryan of Lawrenceville, Penna., was admitted to the Tioga County Bar in 1854. For fourteen years he practiced his profession in that county, meantime serving five years as justice of the peace at Lawrenceville. He removed from there to Corry and was admitted to the Erie County Bar September 29, 1868, where he thenceforward pursued his profession. The following year (1869), however, he was made a justice of the peace at Corry and served as such for ten years and thereafter until his death as alderman, being practically a continuation of the same office under a new name. He was one of the best magistrates in the county, being uniformly courteous, dignified and just. His practice after coming to this county was interrupted to some extent by official duties and I believe consisted largely in the settlement of estates and other office business. He rarely appeared in court, although he had law students and kept in touch with the profession.

He was of medium height, of stout build, had a remarkably fine face and a personality that inspired confidence; he looked every inch a judge. Esq. Brooks held an appointive office in the state legislature for four years and for one year was clerk in the state treasury department.

On April 1, 1843, he was united in marriage with Miss Sarah E. Miller, a native of the state of New York. They had a family of nine children, one son, H. Isaac Horton Brooks, is living in Corry and a son and two daughters in Erie. He has fourteen granchildren, three living in Corry and eleven in Erie. For many years he was a Republican, but supported Horace Greeley for president in 1872 and thereafter was an independent in politics. He was a member of the Presbyterian church. Samuel B. Brooks died January 30, 1887, and was buried in Pine Grove Cemetery at Corry.

Alphonzo William Covell

A. W. Covell, son of William W. and Ellen E. (Barber) Covell, was born at Westfield, New York, November 23, 1847, of English and Scotch-Irish extraction. When five years of age, he came with his family to Concord township, near Corry, where his father followed the occupation of farmer and carpenter. The son received his education at the public schools and the Westfield (New York) Academy, from which he graduated in 1864. For a time he followed the pursuits of his father, then studied law with Hon. C. O. Bowman at Corry and was admitted to the Erie Bar, May 25, 1870. At first he located at Rouseville and practiced law in Venango County, but in 1873 returned to Corry and became associated in practice with his brother, C. L. Covell, Esq. This continued until A. W. Covell moved to Erie about 1878. Thereafter he practiced at Erie and was apparently doing well, as he often appeared in the trial of causes, especially in the criminal courts. He was above medium size, had a good personality, spoke with confidence and I thought was the making of a good lawyer. About 1885, however, he removed from Erie. Just where he located or what he did thereafter is not known to the writer. I have an impression he engaged in some other line of business, perhaps with his wife's father, Mr. J. H. Rathbun, at one time warden of the Erie County jail. In any event he withdrew from practice here and so far as I know never resumed it, although he returned to Erie about 1900, where he remained until his death. In 1871 he was united in marriage with Mabel H. Rathbun. They had no children and Mr. Covell died in Erie, October 7, 1903, at the age of fifty-six years and was buried at Corry.

Clarence Lewis Covell, Esq.

C. L. Covell, of Scotch-Irish and English extraction and the son of William W. and Ellen E. (Barber) Covell, was born on a farm near Westfield, New York, May 3, 1849, and when a small boy, came with his parents to Corry where his father, a pioneer there, followed the calling of a farmer and carpenter, in the latter capacity erecting the first frame building, worthy of the name, in what is now that city. Clarence grew up on the farm and after attending the schools at Corry and at the Westfield Academy took up the study of law in the office of Hon. C. O. Bowman and was admitted to the Erie Bar March 27, 1873. He then entered upon the practice of law with residence and offices at Corry and so continued for over thirty years. In due time he was admitted to the state appellate and federal courts and was soon recognized in this and adjoining counties as an able and successful practitioner. In addition to his general practice he was for some years city solicitor for Corry and made one of the best that city ever had. He was an exceedingly careful and painstaking lawyer. I was associated with him in some important cases and never had a more agreeable colleague or one who prepared his cases better. He was a man of strict integrity and enjoyed the confidence of the profession and the public. He enjoyed the trial of civil cases but seldom appeared in the criminal courts. We did, however, have a memorable contest in the successful prosecution of the Berliner tannery as a nuisance, a case stubbornly defended by Brainerd and Olmsted, in a trial which lasted eight days. It was there "Charley" White, as a witness for the commonwealth said, "The tannery was the prince of stinks."

Clarence Covell was slightly under medium height, wore a dark moustache, had a strikingly handsome face and rotund figure. He was uniformly genial and of most agreeable manners. In other words, had a very likeable personality. He was a most loyal citizen of his home town and took an active interest in whatever might promote the welfare of Corry. He was one of the founders of the Corry Iron Works and a charter member of the Northwestern Oil Company; he also became a large real estate owner.

On March 19, 1873, he was united in marriage with Miss Sarah Louisa Rathbun, of Erie County, New York. This union was blessed with two children, a son and daughter. The son, Alvah W. Covell, is one of Corry's substantial citizens and for many years has been in the service of the United States as a railway mail agent. The daughter resides in Pittsburgh, where her husband, Walter E. Guignon, is a railway superintendent.

While yet apparently in the midst of a useful and honorable career, Clarence L. Covell died December 20, 1904, at the age of fifty-five years and was buried at Corry. He was survived by his widow and the two children. An excellent sketch of the Covell family appears in Miller's History of Erie County, Vol. 2, Pages 419, 420. Mr. Covell was a Democrat and attended the Methodist Church. He was a member of the Knights of Pythias and of the K. O. T. M., and his principal recreation was the study of history. As a mark of the confidence reposed in Mr. Covell it may be proper to state he was treasurer of the Corry City school district for fourteen years.

George William Lathy, Esq.

George W. Lathy, son of Doctor William Kent and Mary (Wallis) Lathy, was born in Northumberland County, Penna., February 20, 1809, being eight days younger than Abraham Lincoln. His father came from England and settled in that county and his mother, of Philadelphia, was a member of the Society of Friends. He had one brother, Dr. Henry Kent Lathy, who adopted the father's profession, located at Alton, Ill., and died from smallpox, contracted while ministering to those stricken during an epidemic of that malady. George W. chose the legal profession and, after practicing a few years at Muncy in his native county, about 1840, moved to Clarion, Penna., where he practiced successfully and was a leader of the bar of that county for over thirty years. He was an active Republican and during this time became the leader of the party in Clarion County, which on two occasions put him forward as a candidate for Congress, but he failed to secure the district nomination.

When a young man, George W. Lathy was united in marriage with Miss Letitia Derby, daughter of Edward Derby, an architect and native of Massachusetts, then residing at Franklin, Penna. To them were born ten children, nine sons and one daughter. The eldest son, William E. Lathy, adopted his father's profession and, locating in Erie, was admitted to our bar March 7, 1871. At the son's request, the father removed to Erie and was admitted to our bar December 18, 1871. At that time a law partnership was formed under the name of George W. Lathy & Son, which continued for nearly ten years. The firm did a fair business and was for a time solicitors of Erie City. While Mr. Lathy had a good standing here, he never attained the leadership he had enjoyed in Clarion County. The legal business in Erie County was then largely in the hands of well established lawyers of rare ability and it was difficult for an attorney, however able, coming here in his sixty-third year, to acquire a large practice. I well recall Mr. Lathy during my law student days as a thorough gentleman of the old school, with a most kindly and genial personality. In 1881 the firm was dissolved, the son removing to Kansas and his parents going to Philadelphia, where their declining years were passed in the home of their son, Henry Kent Lathy, who now has been deputy collector of customs at the port of that city for nearly sixty years. George W. Lathy died in 1890 at the age of eighty-one years.

William Edward Lathy, Esq.

William E. Lathy, son of George and Letitia (Derby) Lathy, was born at Clarion, Pa., April 2, 1846. He was educated for the bar and for a short time practiced with his father at that town. Thereafter for three or four years he practiced in Forest County, residing at Tionesta, the county seat. Then coming to Erie, he was admitted to our bar March 7, 1871, and the same year formed the partnership with his father, to which we have referred. After ten years active practice at Erie William E. Lathy removed to Newton, Kansas, where he took a good position at the bar and served as district attorney of Harvey County. Later he removed to Kansas City, Mo., where for some years and to the time of his death he was assistant district attorney. He was undoubtedly a fine gentleman and good lawyer, but possibly too greatly inclined to move from place to place, forgetting, perhaps, the old maxim that "A rolling stone gathers no moss." He married the daughter of a prominent citizen of Tionesta, but they had no children. William E. Lathy died in Kansas City, in 1896 at the age of fifty years.

Henry W. Blakeslee, Esq.

Henry W. Blakeslee, son of Dr. William V. and Lorene (Cook) Blakeslee, was born in Concord township, Erie County, Penna., February 11, 1848. He was educated at the public schools and Corry High School. In 1870 he became a law student in the office of S. B. Brooks, Esq., at Corry, but probably completed his law course with Col. Thompson at Erie. In any event, after his admission to the Erie Bar, November 22, 1872, he had his office with or adjoining that of the Colonel in Erie. He soon acquired a good practice and when I was a law student here—1877-8—he was generally regarded as one of the most promising young men at the bar. He was above medium size, wore a black moustache, was strikingly handsome, and of engaging manners.

After practicing law eight or ten years he left Erie and soon thereafter embarked in the oil business. This he successfully continued for over forty years and thereby accumulated a very handsome fortune. The last time I saw him was when he called at my office while on a visit to Erie some fifteen or more years ago. Soon thereafter he traveled around the world and during the journey sent the writer and other Erie friends mementoes from abroad. He never forgot his old Erie associates and remembered some of them in his will. At the time of his death, Mr. Blakeslee had large property interests in Oklahoma. He died April 13, 1927, at the age of seventy-nine years, and was buried in the McCray Cemetery in Concord township. He was never married. Speaking of Mr. Blakeslee, I have two regrets. First, that, although successful in other lines, he abandoned the legal profession and, second, that so fine a type of man should have left no descendants.

Colonel James Oliver Parmlee

Colonel James O. Parmlee, son of Aaron Stafford and Martha Louisa (Brown) Parmlee, was born at Warren, Penna., July 10, 1845. He was of a very prominent family, his mother being a sister of Judge Rasselas Brown, for more than fifty years a leader of the Warren Bar, and his father's brother, George Parmlee, being one of Warren's most prominent citizens and for many years a trustee of the State Hospital for the Insane at North Warren. James attended school at Warren, also at Brownsville, New York, and later took a full course at Allegheny College from which he graduated with the A. B. degree. Thereafter he took up the study of law in the office of Johnson & Lindsay at Warren and was admitted to the bar of that county, and in 1871 came to Erie, was admitted to our bar (Oct. 7, 1871) and formed a partnership with Albert B. Force, a classmate in college, under the name of Force & Parmlee. The partnership continued for some years and did a good business, meantime Force serving a term as district attorney. Mr. Parmlee was a quiet, gentlemanly young man of sterling qualities and highly regarded by bench and bar. He was selected as master, auditor, etc., frequently, and in those capacities showed a high order of ability. He was industrious and regarded as an exceptionally sound lawyer; but about 1878 Force, who had married a Pittsburgh lady removed to that city and is now (1927) living in Seattle, Washington, at the age of eighty-two years[*]; Parmlee returned to Warren to become a member of the law firm of Johnson, Lindsay & Parmlee. Judge Johnson, the senior

---
[*]Mr. Force died Sept. 24, 1928.

member of the firm, who had served a term as President Judge of the district and was for many years thereafter one of the leaders of the bar of northwestern Pennsylvania, was Parmlee's stepfather, while Lindsay, a very able lawyer, later served a term as judge of his district. As the years passed, Judge Johnson died and Hon. Edward Lindsay came to the bar and the firm became that of Lindsay, Parmlee and Lindsay and when W. M. Lindsay went upon the bench, the firm changed to Parmlee & Lindsay and so continued until the former's death. At a later period, Hon. Edward Lindsay served as judge of his district by appointment. These continuous partnerships, extending over a quarter of a century, with members of the bar, all of whom were sometime honored by judicial service, speaks well for Colonel Parmlee both as a lawyer and a man. The standing of those law firms was ever of the highest. I well remember Colonel Parmlee's conduct of an important case in Erie county about fifty years ago, and of many years later hearing him argue a case before the superior court and also of listening to his trial of an equity case in Warren county and in each instance I was impressed with his ability.

Colonel Parmlee was a soldier in the Civil War and acquired his title by serving as a captain and lieutenant-colonel of the Sixteenth Regiment National Guards of Pennsylvania; while living in Erie he was a member of the McLean Guards. He had a striking personality, being of medium size, clean shaven, except for closely cropped side burns, with exceptionally good features, stood erect and had a military poise and carriage, befitting a major general. After returning to Warren, Colonel Parmlee was united in marriage with Miss Honore Temperance

Stevens and for the balance of his life resided there. He was a Republican, but so far as I know never sought public office. He was a faithful member of the Presbyterian Church. As a lover of the woods he indulged in hunting and fishing. In addition to his professional work he was for some time engaged in the lumber business. It may be well said of Colonel Parmlee that he had very high professional and personal ideals to which he was ever true. He died September 9, 1903, at the age of fifty-eight years and was buried at Warren. In addition to his widow, who is still a well known and highly honored resident of Warren, he was survived by a sister and other collateral relatives.

Theodore Albert Lamb, Esq.

T. A. Lamb, son of Lyman Lorenzo and Miranda (Town) Lamb, was born at Townville, Crawford county, November 2, 1846. His forbears on both sides were early settlers in New England as they were, perhaps one hundred and fifty years later, early settlers in Crawford County. Lyman L. Lamb, the father, was a prominent citizen of Townville and early became interested in the oil business at or near there, removing to Erie in 1865, he for some years occupied the home at Eighth and Peach streets, now the site of the Masonic Temple.

For many years after coming to Erie, Lyman L. Lamb was engaged in the coal business. He also helped to organize and was a director of the Keystone National Bank and was one of the organizers of the Erie Dime Savings and Loan Company, now the Erie Trust Company. He died in 1890. The Town family, of which Theodore Lamb's mother was a member, is one of the pioneer and most prominent families in Crawford and Erie counties. She survived her husband twenty-seven years and died at the age of ninety-three. Theodore secured his education in the public schools and at Allegheny College, of which he was a graduate. It was his intention to become a banker, but while waiting for a favorable opportunity, took up the study of law in the office of Spencer and Marvin at Erie, and was admitted to our bar August 22, 1871, and pursued that profession for the balance of his life. In the early years of his practice he was for a short time in partnership with Hon. George A. Allen. Mr. Lamb was solicitor for Erie City for twelve years, beginning in 1877, during which time he became an expert on all matters relating to city government and was recognized throughout the state as one of its ablest city solicitors. He won several important cases for the city, one of the most notable being that of Magill v. Erie City, 101 Pa. 616, where he secured a reversal of the lower court. Judge Trunkey, then a member of the supreme court, told me Lamb's argument in that case was a classic. After leaving the solicitor's office he continued to practice law with an ever increasing reputation and business. In the spring of 1894 we formed a partnership as Lamb & Walling, which continued until I became judge of Erie county, January 1897. He was in my opinion the best book lawyer in the history of the county. He loved law books, bought them freely and studied them diligently. He not only kept abreast of the Pennsylvania decisions and those of the United States Supreme Court, but he read the decisions of other states, including those of New York and Massachusetts. He also read the American Decisions and American Reports, as they were published. Lamb could grasp a decision readily and retain the principle it enunciated indefinitely. He possessed in a high degree a discriminating mind and in making briefs referred only to such cases as were applicable. Thus he gradually became recognized by bench and bar as an exceedingly sound lawyer. His method in presenting the facts was somewhat similar in that he never called an unnecessary witness or attempted to prove something foreign to the case in hand. He was, however, stronger on the law than on the facts. Other members of the bar could try jury cases as well, and a few, perhaps, better, but none had a better knowledge of the law or could state it more clearly. As a trial proceeded Lamb had the remarkable faculty of making up the record so as to show clearly what the issue was in case of review; yet he never troubled the trial judge with frivolous objections, or unnecessary requests for charge. He was a master of Pennsylvania practice and his advice thereon, as well as on general questions of law, was often sought by and freely given to his professional brethren. Frequently he was selected as master, auditor or referee and uniformly gave the highest satisfaction. On one occasion he was complimented by being selected as master in an important equity suit in Crawford county and acquitted himself with great credit. He rarely appeared in the criminal courts, although he and I successfully defended one of Erie's most prominent citizens, when indicted for libel. Lamb was a lawyer who scrupulously lived up to the very highest code of professional ethics. He never wronged any one.

He was so modest and retiring that it was some time before his real ability became known to the profession and still later to the public. His worth was not fully recognized until he was forty-five years old. Thenceforward, he enjoyed a large and lucrative practice, representing many important clients and interests and acting for many years as trustee of the Reed Estate. He illustrated the fact that in the law unassumed individual merit will in the end reap its reward. He was conservative and exercised good judgment in looking after his clients' affairs. Once he said to me, "Whatever I do with my own money, I will never fool away that of my clients." Lamb was of medium height, not stoutly built and, while enjoying fair health, never what would be called robust. So far as the writer knows he took no athletic exercises, had practically no recreations, could always be found in his office or at the court house, and was ever at work or ready for it. No member of the bar kept closer to his profession than T. A. Lamb, for he never divided his attention with any other work or, rarely, play. He was a member of the Presbyterian Church, and a Democrat, but never sought political office, although he was his party's candidate for judge in 1886 and came near being elected. That he would have made a great judge no one who knew him doubted. He was a delightful man personally to those who knew him, but not what would be called a good mixer.

On June 20, 1872, Mr. Lamb was united in marriage with Miss Fanny T. Bond. They had two children, daughters, Grace, the elder, married Frederick T. Borst, and they have two children, one a son named Theodore Lamb Borst. Florence, Mr. Lamb's younger daughter, never married and was a teacher, but lives now in Boston, Mass. Long years of continuous toil finally began to tell on Mr. Lamb and his health gradually failed, but he kept at his life work until he died on January 9, 1920. He was buried in the Erie Cemetery. The wife, who survived him, has since died. He was immensely fond of his little grandchildren, who were a great comfort to the closing years of his life. He had one of the most kindly dispositions imaginable. I never heard him speak unkindly but once, then we were coming from the court house where he had an unpleasant controversy with one of the leaders of the bar, and he said, "That man takes excellent care of his health, but he need not do so on my account."

Judge Henry Souther

Henry Souther, son of Joseph and Hepsie (Armisted) Souther, both of English ancestry, was born at Charleston, Massachusetts, March 5, 1826. The father, a manufacturer of morrocco and kid leather, died in 1866. Henry had good educational advantages, being a student at an academy in Fryeburg, Maine, also attended school at Charleston and in Boston. In 1842 he came to Elk County, Pa., to assist his father in a lumbering operation, and in 1845 Henry was entered as a law student by Col. C. B. Curtis of Warren and was admitted to the bar in 1848. He located at Ridgeway where he successfully practiced his profession for over twenty years. In 1847 he was elected Treasurer of Elk County. He also served as deputy attorney general and district attorney of Elk county for seven years, beginning in 1848. In 1855 he was elected state senator for his district, embracing seven counties. He was an active Republican and in 1860 was a delegate to the national convention which nominated Abraham Lincoln for President. In 1861 Governor Curtin appointed him surveyor general of the state, an office he held for two years. In 1868 he was a delegate to the national convention which nominated General Grant for President. In 1871 Gov. Geary appointed Mr. Souther a law judge of Schuylkill county, which office he held until the end of the year. He located in Schuylkill county to take up the duties of judge and in 1872 removed to Erie and was admitted to our bar where he practiced for some fifteen years. His home during that time being on the east side of French street, north of Eighth street. His office during most of that time being in the

Dime Bank Building, opposite the post office. He was a good lawyer but never had a large practice in this county. Being a man of ample means it is doubtful if he desired a large practice. The late Judge A. G. Olmsted of Potter county informed me that Judge Souther had a large practice in his younger days and he often met him in the trial of causes in Elk and other counties.

Judge Souther was all his life a practical joker and, as the creator of innocent fun, highly entertaining. Judge Olmsted said Souther's ability to discover and describe the humorous side of a situation, while intensely amusing, sometimes detracted from the effect of his advocacy. Judge Souther had such an exuberance of good spirits that it was sometimes difficult for him to be serious. He was ever a most charming companion and frequently the life of the company. He had, however, a serious side, was a man of the highest ideals and stood firmly for the right as he saw it. He was a stout built man of medium height with a handsome face, smoothly shaven, except for well cropped side burns, gray when I knew him. He was always neatly dressed and presented the appearance of a gentleman of the old school.

In 1850 he was united in marriage with Miss Letitian Patterson, daughter of John Patterson, of Warren. They had no children, except an adopted son. While residing in Erie he owned a valuable farm in Millcreek township, which he finally sold and later exhibiting to a brother lawyer a roll of some four hundred and fifty dollars, said, "This is the interest on my farm mortgage and is the best way to farm it." About 1888 Judge Souther removed to Fredericksburg, Va., where some years later he suddenly dropped dead upon the street.

Judge and Mrs. Souther were devout members of the Episcopal Church. She and the adopted son outlived the judge, but are now dead. The sunshine and mirth-giving spirit of Judge Souther added to the sum of human joy. On locating at Fredericksburg he renewed his interest in agriculture and acquired a large farm near that city.

Major Bernard J. Reid

Perhaps our bar presents no more remarkable career than that of Maj. B. J. Reid, born in Westmoreland County, Pa., April 25, 1823; the son of Meredith and Eleanor (Hanlon) Reid, who came from Ireland in 1817. The father was a land surveyor, merchant and school teacher, and the son was educated in public and private schools and in an academy near Fayetteville, Ohio. Bernard was an apt pupil and before sixteen years of age became a teacher, which occupation he followed intermittently for some years, as he also did that of land surveyor, holding at one time the office of Clarion County surveyor by appointment of Governor Shunk. For two years, beginning in 1847, he was employed at St. Louis in the office of the Surveyor General of Public Lands for Illinois and Missouri. In the historic year of 1849 he made the overland trip to California, which took five months. For a time he engaged there in gold mining, then for a year taught school, being for a time professor of English, Spanish and mathematics at Santa Clara, also engaged in newspaper work, as he had previously and did subsequently in Clarion County, Pa. In December, 1852, he returned to Clarion County and resumed his law studies under Thomas Sutton, Esq., being admitted to the bar of that county in 1853, where he practiced law, except when engaged in military service, until he removed to Titusville in 1871. Maj. Reid was admitted to the Erie Bar in 1872 and became a resident member here in 1874, with offices in the Noble Block, now the Penn Building. During his residence here he represented Hon. Orange Noble in several matters, also the Casey estates and other important interests. He was regarded by our bench and bar as an able lawyer of high standing. In 1877 he returned to Clarion where he continued in practice until he located in Pittsburgh in 1900, and closed his professional career at the Allegheny County Bar. He died November 15, 1904, at the age of eighty-one years and was interred in the Calvary Cemetery at Pittsburgh. Wherever he engaged in practice, as he did in many counties, he was known as an excellent lawyer and a man of the highest character. His experience as a surveyor came to his aid as a land lawyer and in that branch of the profession he had few equals. He belonged to that coterie of Pennsylvania land lawyers of fifty years ago, of whom Thomas Murray of Clearfield, John H. Orvis of Center and Simon P. Wolverton of Northumberland counties were notable examples. On the completion of his fiftieth year as a member of the Clarion County Bar, his fellow members thereof, in token of affection, and with appropriate ceremonies, presented him with a beautiful gold headed cane.

On the breaking out of the Civil War Maj. Reid recruited a company of men known as "Company F. 63rd P. V. I," of which he became captain and participated in many battles during the early years of the war. Again in 1863, when Governor Curtin called out the state militia to repel Lee's invasion, Maj. Reid joined as Captain of Company D, 57th Penna. Militia, and became major of the regiment. Maj. Reid was a war Democrat, became an active Republican, served as chairman of its county committee, but later became independent in politics. He was a devout member of the Roman Catholic Church. As I recall him, after the lapse of half a century, he was an exceedingly fine looking gentleman, not large, although perhaps above medium height, well groomed, with gray short cropped side burns.

On February 21, 1854, he was united in marriage with Miss Letitia M. Farran, who predeceased him, leaving surviving six of their nine children, including Hon. A. B. Reid, for many years and still a judge of the Common Pleas Court of Allegheny County. During his long practice Maj. Reid had a number of law partners, the last being the son just mentioned. The major was fond of English literature, the study of which formed his principal recreation.

Captain William Brooks Chapman

Captain William Brooks Chapman, usually called W. B. Chapman, was of New England extraction, his ancestors coming from England in 1643. In 1774 Uriah Chapman, Sr., with his family, and some thirty other Connecticut families, settled in Pike County, Penna., where he served as justice of the peace and where he died in 1816. His son, Uriah, Jr., born in 1758, who served under three enlistments and was seriously wounded in the war of the Revolution, was the grandfather of W. B. Chapman. Among the thirteen children of Uriah, Jr., was Daniel St. John, born in Pike County in 1796, who moved to Ohio where, in 1823, he married Margaret Burtt, a native of Connecticut. Among their eight children was William Brooks Chapman, born in Cleveland, October 8, 1826. Daniel St. John Chapman served with distinction under General Scott in the War of 1812 and was seriously wounded in the battle of Lundy's Lane. In 1835, William moved with the family to Conneaut, Ohio, where he grew to manhood and where, being the eldest child, he at an early age, by manual labor, assisted in the support of the family. He worked on the construction of the Conneaut Academy where he afterwards attended school. Although a diligent student, his educational advantages were meagre. By hard work and rigid economy he had saved enough on attaining his majority to buy eleven acres of land on the Ridge Road east of Conneaut, upon which he built a log house where, having married Cynthia (Pitney) Olds in 1847, they began housekeeping. Soon thereafter he became enrolled as a student at law and while supporting his family by manual labor, so diligently studied law at night that he was admitted to the Ohio bar in 1853. Later he became a member of the bar of the United States Supreme Court, also that of the Supreme Court of Pennsylvania and elsewhere. He opened an office at Conneaut and practiced his profession with marked success until he joined the 2nd Ohio Battery Light Artillery in July 1861, in response to President Lincoln's first call for volunteers. Mr. Chapman was commissioned First Lieutenant and, while serving as Captain in command of the Battery at the battle of Pea Ridge in March, 1862, was seriously wounded, a one ounce bullet having passed through his body. The general in granting his leave of absence, wrote: "Application for leave of absence is hereby granted to Lieut. Chapman, who contributed no small part in checking the advance of an elated enemy on the evening of March 7th, 1862."

He soon after rejoined the Battery and was commissioned as "Captain," but was later compelled to retire because of the continued disability resulting from his wound. He renewed the practice of law in Ohio until he removed to Erie and became a resident member of our bar in March 1873. He was so well and favorably known here that he was admitted at once without waiting the year required by the then existing rule as to non-resident attorneys. I was a student at law and admitted to the bar while he practiced at Erie and knew Capt. Chapman intimately. He was of medium size with a large head, smooth shaven face and a personality which inspired confidence, ever approachable, ever kindly and ever genial. To know Captain Chapman was to like him. He had a good voice, was an excellent speaker and a fine trial lawyer. He tried many cases during his residence here and was uniformly clear, fair and strong in their presentation, and was always well prepared. His removal to Bradford, Pa., in 1879 was a distinct loss to our bar, but he was lured by the oil excitement which was there then at its height and he joined many others. However, he acquired a good practice in that part of the state and so far as known never regretted locating there. He took a prominent position in that district and was at one time brought forward as a candidate for judge against Hon. Thomas A. Morrison. He continued in active practice until his death on October 27, 1895, resulting from an accident. Thus closed a highly patriotic, honorable and useful career in the seventieth year of his age. He was buried at his old home in Conneaut, Ohio, where his father, who lived to the age of eighty-six years, also sleeps.

Captain Chapman was an ardent Republican and his services were in great demand as a campaign speaker. He never resorted to personal abuse, rarely related anecdotes, but held his hearers by clear logic and sound reason. He had a strong leaning toward the Methodist Church of which his wife was an active member. He was a Mason and master of his lodge when he joined the army. When in Erie his home was 420 West Seventh street. He had a family of five children, of whom John B. Chapman, Esq., is a practicing attorney at Cincinnati, and William B. Jr., of Pittsburgh, is in the oil business.

It is noteworthy that Henry S. Chapman, son of John B., made a brilliant record in the World War. So Captain Chapman, his father, grandfather, and grandson have respectively been conspicuous in the four great wars which have involved the destinies of our country.

Judge Johnathan Bone Cessna

Hon. J. B. Cessna, a member of the prominent Cessna family of southern Pennsylvania, and a brother of Hon. John Cessna, a former congressman from the Bedford district, was born at Rainsburg, Bedford County, Pa., March 24, 1840. He was educated at Franklin and Marshall College, Lancaster, Pa., and was admitted to the Bedford County Bar in 1865, where he was actively engaged in legal practice for about eight years. Then locating at Hastings, Nebraska, he continued practice and for a time was judge of the orphans' court. His fine ability, tireless energy and exceptional power of clear statement gained him such prominence at the bar that he was retained in many jurisdictions, including California, where he was counsel in the Spanish Land Grant Cases. He appeared before many courts, including the United States Supreme Court. In 1905 he located at Erie, Penna., where he continued in active practice for twenty-one years. In fact he had been admitted to the Erie Bar in 1873. His most notable local victories during the twenty-one years above mentioned were in Schofield vs. The Railroad Company, for personal injuries, where he recovered and sustained a large verdict, and in the equity suit of Brown vs. Culbertson, involving the title of a large tract of land in South Erie. In the latter case he submitted probably the most elaborate printed brief ever presented to an Erie County court, which he supplemented by the most extended oral argument in the history of the county. In the investigation and presentation of intricate legal questions the judge must be given high rank.

Judge Cessna was of medium height and in his younger days, with dark moustache and burnsides, presented a striking appearance. Even when the years had frosted his hair and beard he was still a man of marked personality and his portrait in the assembled pictures of the Erie Bar prepared in 1920, is one of the best in the collection. He was of genial personality and during his twenty-one years of residence in Erie made many friends. He was often seen at the rooms of the Erie Chamber of Commerce where he was ever a popular member. An ardent Republican, he never sought public office. A devout Presbyterian, he was ever faithful to his church.

On June 12, 1872, he was united in marriage with Miss Catherine Brown, daughter of a very prominent Erie family, and sister of Conrad J. Brown, for many years officially identified with Erie City and County. In 1926 Judge and Mrs. Cessna removed to Kansas City, Mo., where he died January 13, 1928, in the eighty-eighth year of his age and was buried at Kansas City, Mo. He was survived by his widow and two sons, W. B. Cessna, of Council Bluffs, Iowa, and Reon B. Cessna, of Kansas City— both successful business men. By continuing at his life work at a great age, Judge Cessna set a good example to his brethren of the bar, as had Hon. Elijah Babbitt and Judge Vincent before him. Judge Cessna was a great student of history, and traced his ancestry back to the year 1300, when in Normandy Jean Cessna partook of a heritage from William Cessna, chaplain and secretary to the king of France. The family has been prominent in Bedford County since coming there as refugees during the French Revolution. It was one of the judges fondest memories that he heard President Lincoln deliver the Gettysburg address.

Captain Myron Erastus Dunlap

Captain M. E. Dunlap, son of Jacob Dunlap and his first wife, was born at Lockport, New York, July 19, 1842. He was educated in the schools at Niagara Falls and at the United States Military Academy at West Point. In the early days of the civil war he left the latter to join the Union Army and served under two enlistments, from which he derived the title of "Captain." Upon entering the service he was commissioned First Lieutenant by Governor Morgan of New York State. After the war he took up the study of law and became a member of the New York State Bar, removing to Erie, Pa., he entered the office of Hon. James Sill and was admitted to the Erie Bar, December 12, 1873. For some twelve years thereafter he practiced his profession at Erie. Being fond of the study of law he and Ulrich Blickensderfer, Esq., in 1874 prepared and published a book, called an "Abridgement of Elementary Law." This proved very popular with law students, especially those preparing for final examination, and a few years later Captain Dunlap brought out a greatly enlarged and improved edition, known as "Dunlap's Abridgement."

The Captain was a tall, handsome man of polished manners, remarkable personal charm, and ever retained the military bearing acquired in youth. He was a very fine conversationalist, also spoke well in public and had many elements of a successful lawyer.

He had a fondness for politics and was one of Senator Sill's most trusted associates therein, especially so far as related to the city of Erie. Captain Dunlap enjoyed the open and his great fondness for the bay and lake caused him to engage at one time in the fishing business. In fact, he was the pioneer pond net fisherman at our port. This angered the grill net fisherman so they caused his arrest. He lost in the lower court, but, acting as his own lawyer, appealed the case and finally won in the United States Supreme Court.

After coming to Erie Captain Dunlap was united in marriage with Miss Catherine D. Saltsman, a near relative of the late Hon. Robert J. Saltsman, twice mayor of Erie City. The Dunlap home was at 127 West Ninth street, now the residence of Mrs. W. B. Trask. They had one son, Erskine S. Dunlap, now and for many years a prominent resident of North East township and trusted employee of the General Electric Company.

After leaving Erie some forty years ago, Captain Dunlap resided in Washington, D. C., where for years he filled with credit an important government position. He died there on February 28, 1901, in the fifty-ninth year of his age and was buried in Arlington Cemetery. Thus ended the career of a man of brilliant intellect, who failed to gain the height in the legal profession to which his fine abilities entitled him. I accidentally met Captain Dunlap in Chicago in the spring of 1893 and spent a most delightful day with him, on the grounds being prepared for the world's fair. I never saw him again. Politically he was a Republican.

Ulrich Blickensderfer, Esq.

Ulrich Blickensderfer, son of Nathan and Katherine Mary Blickensderfer and grandson of Judge Jacob Blickensderfer, was born at New Philadelphia, Ohio, May 8th, 1845. His father was educated for the bar, but never entered upon the practice and, when Ulrich was young, removed to Crawford County, Penna., and later to Erie County and bought a beautiful lake front farm in Springfield township. Here Ulrich grew to manhood and this was the family home for many years and is yet known as "The Blickensderfer Farm." After graduating at Allegheny College, Ulrich read law in the office of Hon. James Sill and was admitted to the Erie Bar Dec. 12, 1873. Captain Dunlap and he were fellow students with Mr. Sill and sometime after their admission jointly published the "Abridgement of Elementary Law," which we have mentioned in speaking of the Captain. Mr. Blickensderfer was a very active young man and seemed fond of the law, but after practicing here eight or ten years, located at Hammond, Indiana, where, for the balance of his life, he devoted his energies to the real estate business.

Of medium height, light complexion and slight build he ever presented a neat appearance and was of engaging manners. When a young man he was united in marriage with Miss Susan Hurd, daughter of Gilbert Hurd, Sr., Esq., a prominent resident of Springfield township. Ulrich's brother George invented the Blickensderfer typewriter, which was successfully manufactured for many years.

Ulrich died childless on October 17, 1918, at the age

of seventy-three years and was buried at Hammond, Indiana. His wife had died about three years previously. He was survived by two brothers, two sisters and other relatives. His brother, Charles, is a well known resident of Conneaut, Ohio, and his other brother is a prominent citizen of Stamford, Conn.

James W. Sproul, Esq.

John and Jane (Woods) Sproul, parents of James W. Sproul, came from Donegal in the north of Ireland and settled in Summerhill township, Crawford County, Pa., where James was born October 24, 1849. He grew up on the farm, attended district school and later the State Normal School at Edinboro. He also attended a commercial college at Meadville, taught school and attended Allegheny College one year. Having finished his schooling, he entered the law office of Hon. H. L. Richmond & Son, at Meadville, and was admitted to the Crawford County Bar in 1872. At Meadville he became acquainted with Hon. A. F. Bole, then also a law student, and after a practice of about a year there they decided to locate at Union City, in this county, under the firm name of Bole & Sproul. The latter was admitted to the Erie Bar, April 13, 1874. The firm was dissolved in 1875 and Sproul continued to reside and practice law at Union City, until he moved to Erie city in 1898. The last five years he lived at Union City he was in partnership with his nephew, W. O. Morrow, Esq. Even while young Sproul became recognized for ability in the trial of causes in this and other counties, and had a large general practice. He took high rank at our bar long before moving to this city, and thereafter continued in active practice here until his death. He participated in many important trials, was equally able on the law and the facts. In a general way he was not a hard worker and never seemed anxious for a large practice, but every paper he presented to the court was drawn with accuracy and every litigated case he had was fully prepared and tried with signal ability. He spoke with ease and confidence and was wonderfully persuasive with jurors. He was one of the four or five strongest trial lawyers at our bar and was never more conspicuously able than in the trial of what is known as the Swails Will case, where he secured a verdict and judgment setting aside the alleged will of Moses Reynolds, of Waterford township, and was sustained by the State Supreme Court in a vigorous opinion by Judge Paxson, Swails v. White, 149 Pa. 261. T. A. Lamb, Esq., after having a half day's legal battle in court with Sproul, on some important case, expressed to me the opinion that no other member of our bar could have argued the case better than Sproul did. He combined an acute legal mind with great forensic power, and while never a leader of the bar, in the extent of his practice, no local lawyer could try cases better than he.

J. W. Sproul was not above medium height or size, of light complexion, wore a large moustache, was good looking and of most charming personality. He was immensely popular, enjoyed a good joke or story, had an exceedingly keen wit, was a fine after dinner speaker, and unexcelled as a toast master, while as an all round companionable man he was hard to beat. His resemblance to the late George W. Evans, former sheriff of Erie County, led to an amusing incident. A man from the country, standing on State street was looking for some one to endorse his note to the bank for one hundred dollars, saw Sproul across the street and said, "George, come over here." Sproul, realizing the mistake, complied and assuming it was some friend of Mr. Evans, signed the note. The joke was, Sproul had to pay it, but was later reimbursed, at least in part, by the real debtor.

Sproul was a member of the Methodist Church, of the I. O. O. F., of the F. & A. M., including the Chapter, Commandery and Shrine. He was an active Republican and sometimes made campaign speeches, and was at least twice sent as delegate to state conventions, but never sought public office. He might, I think, have been state senator, congressman, or president judge, but would never allow his name to be used. He was fond of fishing and hunting, in pursuit of which he repeatedly visited Canada and the mountains of Pennsylvania. He was an authority on birds. I recall riding with him on one occasion from Union City to Lowville, when he frequently stopped the horse to call my attention to some kind of bird he saw or heard along the way.

Following his location in Union City, he, in 1874, married Ida Cooper, daughter of Ezra Cooper, who was the largest real estate owner in that part of the county. She was a beautiful woman, but died, childless, August 17, 1895. He later married Estelle Walden, by whom he had four children. J. W. Sproul, with Mr. Joseph A. Stern, of this city, were delegates to the National Shrine convention in California in May 1907. Just before starting, Mr. Sproul came up to the bench, told me of his proposed trip and the occasion, and smiling said, "Don't allow any advantage to be taken of my absence." To which I replied, "We will take care of you; don't give it a thought." They returned from California by way of Dakota, where they stopped to visit friends and after leaving there Mr. Sproul became suddenly and violently sick. Stern managed to get him as far as Chicago and into a hotel there, where he received proper medical treatment and seemed to rally somewhat. In compliance with his urgent request they put him aboard a train, gave him every possible comfort and Mr. Stern brought him home, where he was put to bed and died in a few days. His funeral, held in the Methodist Church at Union City, was a memorable occasion. The friends and neighbors where he had lived for a quarter of a century taxed the capacity of the church. Every face was a picture of gloom. Many women and some men wept like children. That funeral spoke louder than words of what "Jim" Sproul really was and what he had been during all the years. He was buried in the Evergreen Cemetery at Union City. His children, save one who died many years ago, are grown and their mother is living. Twenty years have passed and yet no one has appeared who quite fills the place at the bar and elsewhere made vacant by his death. I have never become fully reconciled to the untimely death of James W. Sproul.

Hon. Andrew Fayette Bole

A. F. Bole was born June 13, 1849, in Venango township, Crawford County, and was a younger brother of W. R. Bole, Esq., in his day one of the leaders of the Crawford County Bar. A. F. Bole attended Allegheny College for three years ending in 1870. He began the study of law with Christian M. Bouch at Meadville in 1869 and was admitted to the Crawford County Bar November 11, 1871, on motion of Judge Derrickson. He practiced law for a time at Meadville and early in 1874 came with J. W. Sproul, Esq., to Union City and was admitted to the Erie Bar February 27, 1874. He and Sproul were law partners for about a year. Later Bole continued practice there alone for some years. In 1882 he removed to Corry and formed a law partnership with Hon. C. O. Bowman, and continued to practice there until his death. He was elected and served acceptably as Mayor of Corry, succeeding Hon. W. Ed. Marsh, in that office in 1889. Physically he was very large, probably the heaviest man ever a member of our bar, and he had quite an imposing presence, but never had a very large practice.

During the early years of his residence in this county, he married Maggie L., the daughter of Perry G. Stranahan, one of Union City's most prominent citizens. I have not been able to learn more about Mr. Bole's family. He died October 6, 1891, and was buried at Meadville.

Charles E. Lovett, Esq.

Charles E. Lovett, son of Joseph and Sarah Ann (Dutton) Lovett, was born at Clymer, Chautauqua County, New York, April 14, 1851. His father, a native of Maine, of Scotch lineage, after having been an actor of note in his youth, followed the business of a merchant tailor. The mother was a native of New York State of English extraction. When Charles was young, the family moved to Madison, Ohio, where he attended district school and the Madison Seminary. He then entered the law department of the Michigan University from which he graduated with the L. L. B. degree in the class of 1874. Coming to Erie he registered with Col. Lynch and after spending some time with him and in the office of Charles Burnham, Esq., was admitted to the Erie Bar October, 10, 1874, and here entered upon the practice of law. His brother Dr. A. S. Lovett, was then a popular young physician in South Erie. In 1878, after a spirited contest in which he received more votes than his two opponents, Charles E. Lovett received the Republican nomination for district attorney and was duly elected. It was then considered a one term office and so he was not a candidate of reelection, although his conduct of the office had given general public satisfaction. In 1882, following Horace Greeley's advice, he went west and located at Lamoure, Dakota, where, in addition to the practice of law he did a very successful real estate business.

After about four years residence in Dakota he removed to Duluth, Minn., then in its infancy, but giving promise of the remarkably fine lake port city it has since become. For about twelve years he was actively and extensively engaged there in the real estate business. He was public spirited and took such high rank as a citizen that in 1898 he was elected Comptroller of Duluth and served as such for a full term. He was universally respected and looked up to as a pioneer resident of that city. He continued in the legal profession so much as permitted by his other duties. He was ever noted as a fraternalist and in 1897 was one of the founders and perhaps the leading spirit in establishing the fraternal order known as the "Modern Samaritans," and from 1913 until his death (1925) was its Supreme President. This was the crowning work of his life, and under his capable management, the order grew into a great fraternity, both in the United States and Canada. Lovett became known as one of America's leading fraternalists and took high rank in national fraternal conventions. To the writer, Mr. Lovett's most striking characteristic was his unusual faculty of making and retaining personal friends. While in Erie he had hundreds of warm personal friends, scattered over the county, and in the west came to have thousands spread over a vast territory.

December 18, 1879, he was united in marriage with Miss Sarah H. Roe, of Madison, Ohio. This union was blessed by two children, a daughter, now Mrs. Roella Watts, of West Palm Beach, Florida, and a son, Carl H. Lovett, of Hudson, Wisconsin. On September 10, 1925, while on a visit to his old home and friends at Erie, Mr. Lovett was accidentally struck and killed by an automobile, and was buried at Madison, Ohio. In addition to his widow and the children above mentioned he was survived by two brothers, Dr. Arthur S. Lovett, of West Palm Beach, Florida, and Irving D. Lovett, of Fort Dodge, Iowa. His sudden death called forth many eulogies of an unusual character. The Samaritan, official organ of the fraternity of which he was supreme president, got out a special edition devoted entirely to a description of his life and services, while the press of Duluth gave full utterance to the loss and sorrow of the city at the passing of such a highly distinguished and ever loyal citizen. One editorial closed with the bautiful lines:

> "There is no death! The stars go down
> To rise upon some fairer shore;
> And bright in Heaven's jeweled crown
> They shine forever more."

Hon. Paul Hugus Gaither

Paul H. Gaither was born in southern Pennsylvania, March 26, 1852. His father, Samuel Gaither, was a prominent lawyer and personal friend of Judge Jeremiah S. Black. Paul came to the bar before he was twenty-one years old and had the distinction of arguing a case before the state supreme court when he was but twenty-three. He located in Erie and was admitted to our bar November 19, 1874. He became highly regarded here by our bench and bar, but to find a less rigorous climate, returned to southern Pennsylvania in 1876, and ten years later became associated with John A. Marchand; later with Hon. Cyrus E. Woods, one time United States minister to Japan and, still later with Hon. Charles E. Whitten, now one of the judges of Westmoreland county. Mr. Gaither and Judge Whitten made a remarkable legal firm, each considered the other the best lawyer in Westmoreland county. Mr. Gaither had such a remarkable legal career that I am glad he was a local member at our bar even for a brief time. He became one of the best lawyers in his part of the state. A tireless worker, a clear cut forcible advocate, equally strong before court or jury. There were few members of the Pennsylvania Bar who could state a legal proposition clearer or argue a question of fact more convincingly than he and none who exemplified in the practice higher professional ideals. He never sought or held public office, but gave his entire life to the profession and gradually the bar of the state came to regard him as one of its brightest ornaments. This feeling was so general that in 1920 he was unanimously chosen President of the State Bar Association, a position he filled with marked ability. During his long professional career he was counsel in an unusually large number of important cases and won many notable professional triumphs; but he was ever the same unassuming Christian gentleman.

He was a devout Presbyterian and for many years an elder in that church, also superintendent of the Sunday School and was a teacher of the Men's Bible class. In politics he was a Democrat but of liberal views. Personally he was slightly above medium height but of spare build and most charming manners, although never ostentatious. He was twice married and left a family of grown up children. He had a most promising son, who had adopted the fathers' profession and who was killed in the World War. This was one of the saddest events in the life of Mr. Gaither.

After being in active practice for nearly fifty-five years, and making as clean a record as was ever made by a Pennsylvania lawyer, Paul H. Gaither departed this life August 7, 1926, and was buried at Greensburg.

James Wallace Allison, Esq.

James W. Allison, son of William and Harriet H. (Carson) Allison, was born at Lake Pleasant, Erie County, Penna., October 15, 1847. Both parents were of highly respected pioneer families, the father having been born on the same farm in 1808 and the mother's parents having settled in that neighborhood in 1797. My impression is Mr. and Mrs. William Allison were of Scotch-Irish lineage. The father was a gentleman of the old school. I well remember how efficiently he presided over a Republican political meeting, at Lake Pleasant, some forty years ago. James grew up on the farm, was educated at the public schools, the Waterford Academy and the Michigan University Law School, graduating from the latter in 1874 with the L. L. B. degree. He was admitted to the Erie Bar June 1, 1875. In the course of his career he was admitted to the Supreme Court of Pennsylvania, the Supreme Court of Michigan, the Supreme Court of Ohio and the Supreme Court of Utah. From 1875 to 1881 inclusive, he was in active practice at Erie, then, because of ill heath, he returned to the farm at Lake Pleasant, where he remained for fifteen years. His health being greatly improved by the out-door life, he was the successful candidate for Clerk of Courts of Erie County in 1896, and thereupon took up his home in the city. Probably one object in seeking that office was to afford his growing family better educational advantages. Another object probably was to renew his touch with the law and with his numerous city and county friends. He made so admirable a clerk, being ever efficient, patient and polite, that he was reelected without opposition in 1899. My memory is that he reentered upon the practice here in 1903, after the close of his second term, but in 1906 he located in Cleveland, Ohio, became a member of the bar of that state and practiced his profession there until his last sickness. During recent years he had offices in the Engineer's Building in that city. He was an industrious painstaking lawyer of good ability and strict integrity. During the early years of his practice, he was often chosen as legal arbitrator, master or auditor and uniformly discharged his duties as such with impartiality and efficiency. He was a clear thinker and could express himself well, but ill health during his early years, deprived him of the higher professional honors to which his ability entitled him. Whatever he undertook he did well and continued faithfully in the profession to the end. He was an intense man and active in any cause he espoused. For example, his support of Hon. William A. Galbraith for judge in 1876 was so pronounced as to cause serious personal enmities. Mr. Allison was a courageous man of positive convictions and never left any doubt as to his position. He was remarkable in the matter of personal friendships. Some men may have had more friends, none in my acquaintance had those who were more loyal. For instance, between him and D. A. Sawdey and between him and C. L. Baker there existed a bond of friendship rarely equalled among men. When he was a candidate for clerk of courts they made his cause their own. He had many other friends equally devoted. The ties of friendship between Mr. Allison and those who knew him best were wonderfully strong. During his services as clerk, I was judge and our relations became very close and so continued to the end of his life. We had many enjoyable visits. I deeply regret I will be deprived of the pleasure of sending him a copy of these sketches. Many herein referred to were his friends. In one of his last letters he referred to the fact that Mr. Baker's death left him and me the only survivors of the thirteen whose photographs appear in the third row of the group bar picture made in 1900.

Personally, Mr. Allison was tall, but not of stout build, was generally smooth shaven, except a moustache, discarded in recent years, had a fine face, indicating a strong mental temperament, was in all respects a thorough gentleman and looked the part. He was a thirty-second degree Mason, active and popular in the fraternity. He was a Presbyterian and a member of the Central Church. Politically he was a Republican both by inheritance and conviction. He loved to discuss important subjects and was a delightful companion.

On October 15, 1874, he was united in marriage with Miss Clarissa Adele Fritts, the daughter of Jacob Fritts of Wattsburg; the ceremony being performed by a former pastor, Dr. William Grassee. They have four children, Miss Ruth S., Gertrude, now Mrs. R. R. Alexander, of Cleveland, Thomas C., of Columbus and Robert C., of Erie. Three of the children were graduates of Central High School at Erie, and the daughters later graduated at Western Reserve University in Cleveland. On October 15, 1924, Mr. and Mrs. Allison celebrated their golden wedding at their Cleveland home, which was a wonderfully happy occasion. To my letter of congratulations on that occasion, I received a reply as follows:

"November 18th, 1924.

My dear Judge Walling:—

It was a real pleasure to see your familiar hand, and to read your very kindly expressions of congratulation and good wishes, coming to us on the 50th anniversary of our marriage.

The day was, indeed, a RED letter day in our lives,—and although both of us gave a very reluctant consent to the "Show" being pulled off, we are now both very glad that the children overruled us;—for there was surely a GOLDEN atmosphere of loving friendships bestowed and maintained that gave us LASTING JOY and SATISFACTION. Mrs. Allison joins me in grateful acknowledgment and all good wishes.

Very sincerely yours,
JAMES W. ALLISON."

He died July 25, 1927, in the eightieth year of his age, survived by his widow* and four children, and was buried in Cleveland.

Note: *Mrs. Allison has since died.

Herman Jerome Curtze, Esq.

Herman J. Curtze, son of Frederick and Mary Ann (Beckman) Curtze, was born in Erie City, November 30, 1847. He was exceedingly well born, for when I came to Erie fifty years ago, there was no man here who stood higher than his father, who served thirty years as justice of the peace and alderman. Herman was one of eight children, all of whom became well known and highly respected citizens. After securing what education the Erie schools afforded, Herman studied at the Universities of Leipzic and Heidelberg, Germany, where he obtained the degree of L. L. D. In Erie he studied law in the office of Col. Benjamin Grant and was admitted to the Erie Bar, January 4, 1875. For a brief time he practiced with James C. and Frank F. Marshall, then opened an office for himself on State street, where he continued for many years. He soon had a large business to which he gave unremitting attention. No lawyer at the bar was more thorough and painstaking. He could speak the German language fluently, which was a great asset to him, as a considerable percentage of our population then was and yet is of that nationality. He gave great attention to the settlement of estates, conveyancing, passing of titles, etc., but rarely appeared in the trial of causes. In fact, he regarded himself too nervous to bear the strain of trial work; but when he settled an estate it was done right and every paper he presented to the court was carefully drawn. He was probably the most particular member of the bar in passing titles. No one questioned what he approved; sometimes he was even thought too exacting, but if he erred, it was on the side of safety.

Some thirty odd years ago he showed me his book of cash receipts, which for that time was a very substantial income. Some time later he spent the better part of a year abroad and near the same period was not in good health, after which he was compelled to lighten his work but continued in practice until his last illness. He was a man of sterling integrity and always enjoyed the full confidence of the court and the bar. He was popular with his fellow members and served at one time as president of the local Bar Association. At the end of his term he tendered the bar a notable banquet at the Erie Club, where there was an unusual exhibition of good fellowship. At the plate of each guest was a quart bottle of Rhein wine and more such graced the table. Col. Thompson presided. At the proper time the Colonel arose and on behalf of the bar presented Mr. Curtze with a beautiful loving cup. The host properly responded and the cup went round the festive board. Soon after, the Colonel observing the cup standing idle, arose and to add to the festivities, with due solemnity again presented the loving cup; which was again graciously accepted and passed around the board. Many toasts were happily responded to, but when Mr. Peter Henrichs, a most estimable citizen and a friend of both the host and the toastmaster, attempted to speak; the objection that he was not a member of the bar was sustained and he was not permitted to do so. It was certainly an occasion where good cheer drove the skeleton from the feast. Everyone so inclined drank plenty yet no one became seriously intoxicated. Col. Thompson came into court in a day or two later and told me it was like a trip to Germany. That

Rhein wine looked and tasted innocent, but had a kick entirely inconsistent with the Volstead Act, which, however had not been thought of at that time. The banquet, taken as a whole, was one of the happiest occasions in my experience and inaugurated the custom, since generally observed of the retiring president entertaining the Bar Association.

For many years, Mr. Curtze was a member and frequent attendant of the State Bar Association and never shirked a duty belonging to him as an honored member of the profession.

On June 4, 1878, he married Henrietta Goehling, of Brooklyn, N. Y., who survives him. They had no children. He was fond of art and surrounded himself with some of the works of the old masters. After a painful illness, extending over approximately a year, Herman J. Curtze died, January 1, 1926, and was buried in the Erie Cemetery. He met death as he met the work of his life with serene courage.

C. George Olmstead, Esq.

C. George Olmstead, son of Zalmon and Sarah Vam Freidenburg Olmstead, was born in Ulster County, New York, September 29, 1851, and came to Corry with his parents when a boy. He attended Corry High School and Albany Law School. He also studied law in the office of Hon. C. O. Bowman at Corry and was admitted to the Erie Bar September 7, 1875, and later to the higher state and federal courts. He located at Corry and soon acquired a large practice and was an active and successful lawyer for about thirty-three years. He was an all round lawyer, had a fine office business and devoted much time to advocacy. He became a strong trial lawyer and appeared often in the local courts as well as in federal and appellate courts. He had a phenominally quick wit, a good knowledge of law, a retentive memory and always tried his cases in an interesting and forceful manner. Having heard him try very many cases, I recall no occasion where he was overmatched at repartee. I do recall however an answer Judge Barker gave him when being cross examined in a railroad damage case, on which the judge had been called by the defense to prove proper signals were given, and when asked "How long was the whistle?" replied, "Mr. Olmstead I do not know the length of the whistle, but the blast was about four seconds."

He was a very popular lawyer and enjoyed the respect of court and bar. He was five feet ten inches in height, well but not heavily built, well dressed, had engaging manners, and was very companionable. His ready wit and innocent fun rendered him generally popular. His humor was spontaneous and never left a sting. Olmstead and Sproul were bosom friends but sometimes perpetrated practical jokes on each other. Both keen as razors, it was a delight to hear them exchange witticisms at a banquet. They often went hunting and fishing together, which recreations each greatly enjoyed.

Olmstead suffered a nervous and mental breakdown in 1908, from which he never fully recovered. Sproul's death in 1907 was a great shock and grief to Olmstead and I believe tended to hasten his collapse. On various occasions he was city solicitor for Corry but never held any political office although an active Republican. He was a life long member of the Methodist church and a member of the Erie Club.

December 25, 1878, he was united in marriage with Lillian Dawson, who survived him. They had children, one of whom is Major Dawson Olmstead of the U. S. Army. C. George Olmstead died June 22, 1913, as the result of being struck by an automobile and was buried at Corry. The terrible affliction which darkened the closing years of his life was another tragedy in the annals of our bar.

Colonel Edward Powell Gould

Col. E. P. Gould, son of Nathan and Margaret (Nicholas) Gould, was born in Springfield township, Erie County, Pa., March 6, 1834. His parents were born in this country, the father being of English and the mother of Welsh lineage. The Gould family was prominent in the western end of this county from an early day. The Colonel's uncle was at one time a member of the State Legislature. The Colonel attended the West Springfield Academy, also that at Kingsville, Ohio, was later a student and graduate of the University of Rochester, New York, where he was a member of the Psi Upsilon fraternity. He studied law in Rochester, N. Y., and later was a student and graduate of the Albany Law School. Becoming a member of the New York State Bar, he practiced for a time in Albany, but when the civil war started joined the army as a private and was immediately commissioned a Lieutenant and soon became Captain of Company "E," 27th N. Y. Infantry. He had served with such distinction, including a reenlistment, that at the close of the war he was the senior Captain in his regiment and mustered out with the rank of Colonel. Among his other activities subsequent to the war he was Chief Clerk to the Secretary of State of New York, at Albany. Returning to this county, he was admitted to the Erie Bar, May 31, 1875, and was ever after a resident practitioner here. Being a good speaker and enjoying the contests of the forum, he at once took rank as a trial lawyer, especially in criminal cases. He had good self control and nothing pleased him more than to get the opposing counsel angry. He had many hot contests with A. B. Force, Esq., who was then the efficient district attorney. Gould's methods were unique. On one occasion he secured the acquittal of a young man charged with stealing and wearing away a suit of clothes by demonstrating in court that the suit was so small his client could not possibly get it on. He also had a fair general practice, to which he gave careful attention. He was usually by himself, but for a time in partnership with S. L. Gilson, Sr., as Gould & Gilson.

His personal popularity led to his election and reelection to the State Legislature, where he was a very useful and popular member. Col. Gould was for many years solicitor for the Erie County Poor Board, which brought him in close touch with the State Board of Charities. The work of this organization greatly appealed to him and he became a state leader therein and so continued until his death, being then and for some years prior thereto president of the state organization. When about seventy years of age, the Colonel had a very severe sickness, so that his life was despaired of, but he recovered and for many years continued his work. In his younger days he was fond of hunting and even when advanced in years he indulged in long walks through the country.

A surprise party was tendered the Colonel on his eightieth birthday, which was a most charming affair and largely attended by members of the bar and others. We had arranged to present him with a gold headed cane, which, holding out of sight, I was about to do, when the Colonel, in response to some one's suggestion that he looked fine, said, in effect, he had never felt better, that although eighty years of age, he had never carried a cane and never intended to. Then addressing the Colonel, I told him that lawyers, while well meaning, were frequently impractical, that his friends of the bar then assembled in good faith and as a token of their affection had delegated me to present him with something utterly useless to him and for which he had no desire, nevertheless, it was my duty on their behalf to present him with the cane accompanied by their congratulations to him on the years that were past and best wishes for those to come, and handed it to him. I do not know to this day whether the joke was on me, on the bar, or on the Colonel. He however, rose to the occasion and made a fitting response, which I cannot recall. He greatly appreciated the gift as a token of affection from the friends who knew him best. He then fully expected to live for some years, as we all thought and hoped he would, but the future is a sealed book. In about four months (on July 31, 1914), while seemingly in good health, he dropped dead upon the street; a painless death at a ripe old age—"a consummation devoutly to be wished." He was buried in the Erie Cemetery.

On June 24, 1868, he was united in marriage with Miss Mary Ensign, the only child of D. P. Ensign, one of Erie's most highly respected citizens. The Goulds had one child, a daughter, Edwena, the wife of Arthur L. Stone, formerly of Erie, but now in business at Tampa, Florida. The surviving widow, after a few years, departed to join her husband in the great beyond. Colonel Gould was a Republican, a member of St. Paul's Episcopal Church, and for many years an active and highly regarded member of the Erie Lodge of Elks. He was above medium height, wore a heavy moustache and had a military bearing, but ever kindly and approachable.

Clark Olds, Esq.

Clark Olds, son of Lewis Wilson and Louisa E. (Ackerly) Olds, was born in Millcreek township, near Erie, on July 14, 1850. When about four years of age he came with the family to this city, which was his home ever after. His father was a direct descendant of Robert Olds of Sherborne, Dorset county, England. The first of the name to come to this country was Robert Olds, who was a resident of Windsor, Connecticut, in 1667, and in 1669 married Susannah Hanford. Lewis W. Olds, a most remarkable man, was born July 21, 1822, in Millcreek township, where his father, Asa Gilbert Olds, who came from Vermont, had located in 1816. Lewis W. amassed a fortune in the manufacture and commercial sale of wooden pumps, in which he was the pioneer. He became a large land owner, both in Erie and elsewhere. He erected many buildings in Erie, one of the most notable being the Olds Block on State street, now occupied by the Boston Store. As a Director of the Poor he had charge of building the alms house, west of the city, which has stood well for over fifty years. Mr. and Mrs. Lewis W. Olds lived to celebrate their golden wedding in 1898; she died in 1901 and he in 1908. His maternal grandfather, John Church, served with distinction in the war of the Revolution. Lewis W. Olds was probably the only layman in honor of whose memory the Erie County Court ever adjourned. His portrait, a most excellent one, appears in Reed's History of Erie County, vol. 2 page 888.

Clark Olds was educated at the Erie Academy and Michigan University, from which he graduated with the degree of B. S. in 1870; and two years later he received that of M. S. His fondness for out-door life, caused him to take up civil engineering and during his college vacations and for two years thereafter (1870-1871) he helped make a comprehensive survey of the great lakes. Deciding to take up law, he studied for two years (1872-1874) at the University of Leipzic, Germany, where he became familiar with the Roman and international law. Returning to Erie in 1874 he pursued his legal studies with his father's life long firend, William Benson, Esq., and was admitted to the Erie Bar on April 26, 1876, and from that time until his death, practiced law in the state and federal courts. His office for many years was at 722 State street. By fine ability and close attention to business, he became prominent at the bar, represented many important interests and engaged in the trial of numerous cases. He was an exceptionally agreeable associate, but intensely earnest and not always the most agreeable antagonist. He said to me on one occasion that he acquired his earnest and aggressive manner somewhat from Hon. S. A. Davenport, who never went after anything half hearted. While legal battles are fought hard now, there is far less bitterness of strife among lawyers than there was in days gone by.

Olds was the only local attorney who paid special attention to Admiralty practice. In addition to his regular practice he was trustee of many estates and handled large sums of money. When the vacancy occurred in the city's Board of Water Commissioners, by the resignation of Conrad Brown, who had been elected county treasurer, at the request of the remaining commissioners, Judge Gunnison suggested the name of Clark Olds to fill the vacancy and he was chosen. Thereafter the court repeatedly reappointed him until he served as a water commissioner for sixteen years, the longest service in the history of the board. As such he rendered wonderfully efficient service. He came in close touch with every officer and employee of the department and mastered all its details. During his long service, the plant was greatly enlarged and improved. To meet the needs of a growing city, new and larger engines and machinery were installed, miles of service pipe laid and to secure better water the intake was extended into the open lake and settling basins erected on the peninsula; also a filtration plant was installed at the pumping station. All was done harmoniously and in good order. Had the water works been his private property he could not have given it better attention. He was ever an agreeable associate and, notwithstanding his long service, never sought to dominate the board.

Clark Olds was intensely public spirited and took an active part in whatever tended to the city's welfare. No citizen of Erie probably did more in the development of our harbor and its environs. He was chairman of the Harbor Commission and assisted largely in securing legislation and funds for needed water front improvement and especially the construction of the public dock at the foot of State street, which was built for less than the appropriation. He was also active in raising Perry's flag ship, the Niagara, for the Centenary of the Battle of Lake Erie. He was a pioneer in the conversion of the peninsula into a public park, also director and president of the Erie Chamber of Commerce, and of the Erie County Mutual Fire Insurance Company. He was a director of the Erie Trust Company and of the L. W. Olds Real

Estate Company, also president of the Erie and Lakeside Cemeteries. He was an active Republican and a delegate to the National Convention at Chicago that nominated Theodore Roosevelt for President in 1904. For many years he was a delegate to the annual International Peace Conference at Lake Mahouk. He was active during the World War and served as Chairman of the Draft Board and was on the local Liberty Loan Committee. His last public service was as chairman of the committee that effected a revision of the rules of practice of the Orphans' Court. He frequently visited Harrisburg and Washington, alone, or as one of a delegation, representing Erie in matters of civic importance. I enjoyed a somewhat intimate acquaintance with Clark Olds, dating back to my law student days, and believe he possessed as great a fund of general information as any person in Erie. While he was a strong partisan he was a man of strict integrity, broad sympathies and high ideals. He was an accomplished gentleman of excellent appearance; stood six feet tall; was of athletic build and weighed about two hundred pounds. He enjoyed the companionship of his friends and was a typical host. He kept trotting or pacing horses at his farm near the city and his principal recreation was driving them, especially in early mornings.

On December 13, 1876, he was united in marriage with Livina Elizabeth Keator, of Cortland, New York. To this union three children were born, two of whom, Romeyn and Marguerite, died under distressing circumstances before reaching their majority, and Irving Sands Olds, Esq., a prosperous attorney in New York City. Irving's rapid rise in the profession was a matter of great comfort to his father. Mr. Olds, although apparently robust, repeatedly had typhoid fever and on one occasion, an operation for appendicitis saved his life when gravely threatened. He had previously suffered with a bladder trouble which necessitated a serious surgical operation. Mrs. Olds suffered more or less from ill health for some years and died December 18, 1919. Early in the year 1922 Clark's health became visibly affected and gradually grew worse so that in the summer he was confined to his home and after a protracted and painful illness, died August 16, 1922, aged seventy-two years. They were buried in the Erie Cemetery. In life they were devoted companions and in death they were not long separated. Mr. and Mrs. Clark Olds resided in their beautiful home at 216 West Seventh street for nearly forty years. He was an associate member of the American Society of Civil Engineers and from his memoirs there published I have been greatly helped in preparing this sketch.

Craig J. Reid, Esq.

Craig Reid, I believe a grandson of Rev. Robert Reid, who founded the first United Presbyterian Church in this city, was born, reared and educated in Erie, attended Albany Law School and graduated therefrom when twenty-one years of age. For a few years thereafter he practiced law at St. Louis. Returning home he was admitted to the Erie Bar September 11, 1876, and entered upon a brilliant professional career. He often appeared in the trial of causes and uniformly acquitted himself with credit. He was ever alert and active and probably the most fluent and forceful speaker among the younger members of the bar. That he would become a lawyer of the first rank was freely predicted. But as his future seemed assured his eyes began to fail and he was soon overwhelmed by blindness. He struggled on for some time but his general health failed and he was compelled to give up his profession. I think he thereafter did some work along other lines, but his career was blighted. He was a strikingly handsome young man of slight build, medium height and gracious manners.

On September 11, 1884, he was united in marriage with Miss Hattie A. Landon, a member of one of Erie's best families. They had no children. Mr. Reid was a Republican and a member of St. Paul's Episcopal Church. He died November 18, 1896, and was buried in the Erie Cemetery. The dreadful affliction which he suffered while yet a young man was one of the most regrettable in the history of the Erie Bar. He was survived by his widow, who is now a resident of Southern California.

John Proudfit, Esq.

John Proudfit, a son of Andrew and Isabella Smith Proudfit, was born at Friendship, New York, February 9, 1831. He came with his parents to Edinboro when a boy and was educated at Waterford Academy and Michigan University, at Ann Arbor. Later he taught school and for four years followed that calling in Texas, where he was when a break between the North and South became imminent in the winter of 1861. Being of strong union sentiments and finding himself in a hostile country, where a law was about to be enacted forbidding all persons from leaving the state, he decided to go north. The attempt, even then, was hazardous, but on February 7, he set out on horseback. He had about four hundred miles to travel before coming to the state of Arkansas and then several hundred more before reaching the north. He was often stopped and interrogated, but by a claim that he was from or going to nearby localities, was suffered to proceed. He endured many hardships and did not stop at a hotel until he reached Little Rock. When he came to the Ohio river he, with his horse, took passage for Pittsburgh and then finished his journey on horseback, getting home on April 9. He and his brothers soon joined the Union Army and did such gallant service, two of whom were killed, that the Edinboro G. A. R. Post was named for them. He enlisted in the 145 Pa. Volunteers and participated in numerous battles, including that of The Wilderness and Cold Harbor. In the siege before Petersburg he, with four hundred comrades, was taken prisoner on June 16, 1864, and sent to Andersonville where for many months he endured all the horrors of that awful prison and came home greatly emaciated. John Proudfit, notwithstanding his nearly four years of service and long imprisonment which greatly impaired his health, for the balance of his life, would never apply for a pension and never accepted one until granted to every veteran of the war. After the war he resided in Edinboro and for some years served as justice of the peace. Deciding to study law he entered the office of William Benson, Esq., at Erie and was admitted to the bar in 1876. At that time Mr. Benson had two other students, Captain E. L. Whittelsey (later judge) and Clark Olds. I followed them in the same office and Mr. Benson told me that at first he had the three come in and examined them at the same time and that Proudfit's answers were so masterful that he had to examine the others separately. Mr. Proudfit was admitted to the Erie Bar in 1876 and thence practiced law, with office at Edinboro, until his death. He served his clients well and did a nice local business, but so far as I recall, never tried cases in court, at least without assitance. He was an exceedingly high grade man and I have no doubt a peacemaker; and in the profession as elsewhere his record was spotless. He was an ardent Republican and always outspoken for the right as he saw it. I recall when he fought desperately, but in vain at a county convention, to save his party from committing a blunder. He never held public office, outside of his own borough, but at one time, about 1875, was a candidate for the Republican nomination for county treasurer.

April 29, 1869, he married Miss Emily H. Culbertson of Edinboro. They had no children. He was a staunch member of the Presbyterian Church at Edinboro. He was of good substantial appearance, tall but not heavy, and died April 15, 1911, at the age of eighty years. He was buried at Edinboro, where for half a century he had been a leading citizen.

Judge Edward Lyman Whittelsey

Captain E. L. Whittlesey, so called for more than half a century, son of Henry R. and Mary A. (Parmelee) Whittelsey, was born October 5, 1841, in Litchfield County, Connecticut, and when eight years of age removed with the family to Waterford township, this county, where he grew to manhood on a farm. He was of English extraction and his father became one of Erie county's substantial citizens. The future captain and judge obtained his education in the public schools, at Waterford Academy and at a Philadelphia business college. Probably the latter accounts for his exceptional fluency with a pen, a facility he retained to the end of his career. At the breaking out of the Civil War, he enlisted as a private in Company "E" Eighty-Third Regiment Pennsylvania Volunteers and served until the close of the war. The ranks of that regiment were decimated in more than a score of great battles and its record was second to none in the entire Union army. With courage, fidelity and ability, Edward L. Whittelsey passed through it all, but did not escape unscathed. In one of the great battles he was seriously wounded and lay for many hours with the tide of battle passing over him to and fro. The next day, being found alive, he was removed to a hospital, where he recovered and rejoined the regiment. Among many thrilling experiences, he was with General Strong Vincent, when the latter was killed at the battle of Gettysburg. By long and heroic services, Whittelsey became Captain of his Company.

When Colonel Rogers became Prothonotary of Erie County in 1866 he appointed Captain Whittelsey, with whom he had served in the war, deputy. So efficient was the Captain's services therein that in 1869 the people elected him Prothonotary and reelected him without opposition. Before the end of his second term he became a law student with Benson and Brainerd and on May 15, 1877, was admitted to the Erie Bar, and in due course to the state appellate and federal courts. He at once began a legal practice at Erie which continued without interruption for nearly forty years. During all those years probably no member of the bar devoted himself more exclusively to the profession than he. He was a hard and steady worker and thereby gradually won a high place at the bar. His papers were drawn with scrupulous accuracy and no member of the bar was more familiar with the practice. Whatever he did he did at his best and never neglected or overlooked anything. He exhibited those sterling qualities of mind and heart which endeared him to the profession and no one at the bar was more often agreed upon or appointed master, auditor or legal arbitrator than he. His judicial bearing, clear grasp of legal quotations and painstaking care gave great satisfaction to his services in such cases. His career demonstrated that a member of the bar may at the same time be an excellent office lawyer and an excellent trial lawyer. He never sought to take snap judgment or an unfair advantage, but he would courteously call the opposing counsel's attention to his neglect in such a way that it would be promptly remedied. He was always prepared for trial and there was no member of the bar who would secure a trial upon the merits with less delay than he. He never fell down on the law of the case for lack of preparation. If authority existed in support of his position he had it.

While not a great orator his summing up to the jury was clear, forceful and convincing. He was a quiet, modest man and to know how really able a lawyer he was you must be associated with him or against him in the trial work, or act as judge in a case which he tried. His appearance of candor and high standing for probity added weight to whatever he said or did. His legal arguments both in the lower and in the higher courts were uniformly clear and able. He always had a good pratice and so far as I know, never lost the confidence or business of a client. Among other important interests he represented the Soldiers' and Sailors' Home Commission for over thirty years. He confined his attention to civil practice and very rarely appeared in the criminal courts. Although a well known and popular citizen, during the years of his practice, he never allowed his name to be used in connection with any public office. He treated the law as a jealous mistress and acted accordingly.

In January 1916, Captain Whittelsey became judge of Erie County, without any solicitation on his part, through appointment of Governor Brumbaugh. It was at least in part through the suggestion of Hon. John S. Rilling, a Public Service Commissioner and close friend of the Governor. The Captain was then seventy-four years of age and probably one of the last veterans of the Civil War to be so honored. When approached he said he would accept the appointment but would not expect to be a candidate for the elective term beginning two years later. However, his judicial services were of such a high character that his election for the full term followed by an overwhelming majority. He carried onto the bench the same qualities that had distinguished his career at the bar and during his four years of judicial service, made a record of which any judge in the state might well be proud.

For very many years he was an active member of the Central Presbyterian Church. He was of medium size, wore a moustache, had a florid face, looked young for his years, was always neatly dressed, of excellent appearance and of gentle, courteous manners. While well acquainted with him for over forty years, I never heard him speak a harsh or unkindly word.

On December 26, 1867, he was united in marriage with Miss Charlotte Hunt. Six children were born to them, two sons, who died in childhood, and four daughters, to-wit: Mrs. Robert L. Roberts, Mrs. J. Reid Craig, Mrs. Charles A. Nelson and Miss Mary E. Whittelsey, all well known and highly respected residents of Erie. Mrs. Whittelsey died in 1899 and four years later the Captain was united in marriage with Miss Rebecca Belle Farley, a lady of the highest character and standing, who survives. His principal recreation was work, in addition to which he kept abreast of world news by reading a metropolitan daily paper. Judge Whittelsey ever enjoyed robust health and his death came suddenly and without prior sickness on January 20, 1920, at the age of seventy-eight years; he was buried in the Erie Cemtery.

Captain Charles LeRoy Pierce

Captain C. L. Pierce, son of George and Irena (Fisk) Pierce, was born at Brookfield, Madison County, N. Y., August 28, 1841. The father was a member of the old and prominent Pierce family of New Hampshire and the mother was a lineal descendant of Lord Symond Fisk of Suffolk County, England. Charles received his education at the district schools, the Ellington Academy and at the Waterford Academy. In 1861, when the civil war came he enlisted in the Ninth New York Cavalry and by reenlistment served therein continuously for approximately four years. He had a great war record and for faithful, efficient and heroic services, was gradually promoted to the rank of Captain. He lost his right leg in the last pitched battle of the war, that at Five Forks, Virginia, April 1, 1865.

He resided near Wattsburg and after the war was elected and by successive reelections served three terms as Clerk of the Erie County Courts and was one of the most popular and competent officials in the history of the county, being one of the first county officials to be honored by election to a third successive term. During his incumbency of the office he took up the study of law with Hon. S. A. Davenport and was admitted to the Erie Bar October 23, 1877. He at once formed a law partnership with Frank W. Grant, Esq., whose father had just died. This continued until the death of Captain Pierce. The firm, both well known and highly respected members of the bar, was doing a good business when Captain Pierce died suddenly, as the result of an accident, on January 11, 1880, in the thirty-ninth year of his age, and was buried in the Erie Cemetery. He was a large, fine looking gentleman, with a host of friends.

On October 17, 1867, he was united in marriage with Miss Garetta Hatch of Ellington, New York. They had three daughters, Gertrude, Bertha and Lucy, also two sons, Samuel H., now deputy district attorney at Portland, Oregon, and Charles Roy, a prominent attorney at Miami, Florida. The widow, who survived her husband forty-seven years, was entitled to great credit, for by returning to her occupation of teaching and by other efforts kept the children together and educated them so all became useful and prominent citizens. Not long ago I received a letter from her written at Portland, Oregon, about the Captain, in response to my inquiries, and I am saddened by the report that she has since died.

Captain Pierce was an active Republican, a member of the Methodist Church, a Grand Army man and an Odd Fellow. The family residence for many years was the brick dwelling at the southeast corner of Seventh and Walnut streets.

Frank M. McClintock, Esq.

Frank M. McClintock, son of James and Mary Hayes McClintock, was born at Beaverdam, Erie County, July 16, 1853, and grew to manhood on a farm a few miles from Union City. He was educated at public school, select school and Edinboro State Normal, thereafter taught for three years in Crawford County, then studied law in the office of James W. Sproul, Esq., at Union City, where he made rapid progress and was admitted to the Erie Bar May 11, 1878, and later was admitted to all state and federal courts, including the United States Supreme Court. He had his home and office in Union City and was in active practice from May 1878 until his death. At first his practice was local, but soon extended into Crawford, Warren and other counties, where he tried many cases. While he did much office business, his principal reputation was that of a trial lawyer. In fact, he loved the forum and was never happier than when engaged in some stubbornly contested case, civil or criminal. He tried hundreds of cases and won many notable victories. Years ago I was associated with him in several cases and found him a most agreeable and able colleague. He was a tireless worker and although never physically strong had great energy and undaunted courage. He continued to improve as an advocate until the closing years of his career. In his early practice, it seemed to me he was sometimes too protracted in cross examination, a fault common to young advocates. He was a fluent, earnest speaker and very persuasive with juries. A case Frank McClintock lost before a jury was generally hopeless. He was an upstanding lawyer, who enjoyed the full confidence of the court, his professional brethren and the public. He was an ardent Republican and in 1884 won the nomination of that party for district attorney. The congressional campaign that year, however, developed over two thousand voters, known as "Scott Republicans." With them McClintock had no sympathy and challenged their party loyalty to such an extent that they, in a body, supported Baker, the Democratic candidate for district attorney, causing his election. McClintock lost little by this defeat as he soon had a large practice. He continued an active Republican, but never again sought public office.

He was tall, slim and clean shaven, except he sometimes wore a moustache. He was a very companionable man and had many friends. Long years ago he joined the Presbyterian Church at Union City and continued steadfast to the end. He was also a member of the lodge of Masons at his home town. On one occasion, two waggish attorneys, Olmstead and Sproul, asked McClintock to go with them to luncheon at the Reed House and when the meal was over they suddenly and by prearrangement slipped out and left him to pay the bill for the three, which he did, but at his instance a mock order was issued committing them as paupers "without visible means of support." This was published and caused much merriment.

On January 6, 1882, he was united in marriage with Miss Adda C. Cross of Clintonville, Venango County. To them four children were born, all of whom are now (1927) living and one of whom, Francis F. McClintock,

Esq., is an attorney at Union City and was in partnership with his father during the last ten years of the latter's life. The death of Mrs. McClintock, in 1919, was a blow from which he never fully recovered and he died December 5, 1922, in the seventieth year of his age. They were buried in the Evergreen Cemetery at Union City.

Joseph May Force, Esq.

Joseph M. Force, better known as Joe Force, son of William J. and Nancy (Burwell) Force, was born on a farm in North East township, December 20, 1853. They were a fine family, the father, a leading citizen there for over fifty years, was of French Huguenot lineage and the mother of English and Dutch extraction. They were devout members of the Methodist Church and maintained an ideal Christian home. The father owned a small farm on the Side Hill road, which he tilled and in addition had a cooper shop. Joe attended district school and grew to manhood on the farm. He entered the Lake Shore Seminary at North East as a student in the fall of 1871, at first walking to and from the farm, a distance of three miles, but later the family moved into the borough. Joe was diligent, took high rank as a scholar and graduated with Rev. Frank J. Nash and others in the class of 1874. He was genial, generally popular and it is my memory, taught for a time in the seminary from which he had graduated. He soon entered Ives Seminary at Theresa, New York, as a teacher, and also continued his studies there, so it conferred upon him the A. M. degree. Returning home he entered the law offices of Force & Parmlee, at Erie, and was admitted to the Erie Bar, November 28, 1879. For about forty-three years thereafter he practiced law with offices in this city, for many years being in partnership with Henry C. Yard, as Force & Yard. He long and with great satisfaction served as a Referee in Bankruptcy for the Western District of Pennsylvania. As a practitioner he was industrious, painstaking and efficient. His papers were always carefully and neatly drawn and, while he made no specialty of court practice, he tried many cases and uniformly tried them with ability. He was a clear thinker, a logical reasoner and a good speaker, while his exceptionally high character gave him weight both with court and jury. He represented important and varied interests and had the full confidence of his clients. The T. M. Nagle interests were perhaps his best known clients. He was a consistent Republican but never sought public office, aside from his unsuccessful campaign in 1915 for judge against Judge Rossiter.

On May 28, 1885, Joseph M. Force was united in marriage with Miss Clara Gunnison, daughter of the late Hon. Jonas Gunnison and sister of Judge Frank Gunnison. They had one son, who died in infancy and an adopted daughter. When about sixty-five years of age Mr. Force suffered a paralytic stroke, from which he sufficiently recovered to continue at his professional work, but when he was in his sixty-ninth year he had a second stroke, from which he failed to recover and died in Monrovia, California, March 25, 1923, where he had gone in search of health. He was buried in the Erie Cemetery with Masonic honors.

Mr. Force was of medium size, usually wore a moustache, was fine appearing and a thorough gentleman on all occasions. He was eminently a public spirited citizen, always interested in what might promote the general welfare. He was a trustee of the Erie Academy, President of the Board of Trustees of the Erie Public Library, also a director and at one time President of the Erie Board of Trade. His principal recreation was agriculture and, as owner and manager of the Freeman Ellis farm in Harborcreek township, where he had a delightful summer home, was eminently successful. Raised a Methodist, in later years he transferred his membership, as did my friend T. W. Shacklett, to St. Paul's Episcopal Church, where both became prominent. He was a member of the Delta Tau Delta college fraternity and also of the Royal Arcanum. He was an active and prominent member of The Grange and so influential and popular in Masonry that the thirty-third degree was conferred upon him in 1918. It may well be said that in all the relations of life, as a son, as a brother, as a husband, as a father, as a citizen, as a neighbor, as a fraternal brother, as a lawyer and as a Christian gentleman, Joseph M. Force rang true. Since his death the widow and daughter have resided in California.

Henry C. Yard, Esq.

H. C. Yard, son of John Solomon and Catherine (Coonce) Yard, was born in Venango County, Penna., in 1846. When a young man he learned the trade of a harness maker and for a time carried on that business at Union City. About 1876 he accepted the position of deputy Clerk of Courts, his brother-in-law, F. H. Couse, being the Clerk. While so employed he took up the study of law with Force & Parmlee, and was admitted to the Erie Bar November 28, 1879. Joseph M. Force was admitted at the same time. They formed a partnership as Force & Yard, which continued for some twenty-five years, was well known and did a good business. Later he was associated in the practice with Hon. A. B. Osborne. Mr. Yard was a hard worker and intensely earnest in his professional work. He made every client's cause his own and fought each case to the limit of his ability. He was not as cultured as Force, but more aggressive, and was remarkably successful for one who took up the profession so late in life.

On one occasion he asked me to assist him in the trial of an important equity case, which he had brought to recover valuable real estate on the ground that the defendant held the same in trust for his client. The case at first did not look promising, but as the trial progressed, the merit of our client's claim became so apparent that no appeal was taken from the degree in our favor. The outcome of this case is an illustration of the fact that a lawyer should seldom pass adverse judgment on his client's case, especially in advance of the trial. Mr. Yard had the happy faculty of firm faith in the merits and importance of every cause in which he was engaged. He was of slight build, perhaps above medium height, wore a dark beard and, by force and manner, indicated the intense earnestness of his character. He practiced for seventeen years while I was on the local bench, and was so earnest that when unsuccessful he was prone to feel that the court had not been quite fair. He had also at times been inclined to feel the same toward my predecessor, Judge Gunnison. On one occasion, during the later years of his practice, however, I read from the bench, as was the custom in those days, an opinion reversing the auditor and deciding an important orphans' court case in Yard's favor. On leaving the court house he remarked to a brother lawyer, "What a growing man Walling is. That opinion in the Smith case sounded like an enunciation from Lord Mansfield." He was a steadfast Republican and his voice was not infrequently heard on its behalf.

He was a pillar in the First Methodist Church, active and influential in every department of church work. In this he was so intense that in his later years he became a licensed preacher of that denomination. He was twice married. His first wife died childless, before he came to Erie and about 1880 he was united in marriage with Miss Carrie Hagerty, a well known Erie lady. To them was born one child, Harry Yard, who has become well known in the theatrical world. Henry C. Yard died July 23, 1914, at the age of sixty-eight years and his widow died in 1924. They are buried in Lake Side Cemetery, at Erie.

Samuel Loren Gilson, Esq.

S. L. Gilson, one of the six children of Benjamin and Eliza Ann (Moore) Gilson, was born near Titusville, Crawford County, May 20, 1853, and came with the family to Greenfield township, this county, when about twelve years of age. He grew up on the farm, attended district school, Edinboro State Normal School and Michigan University Law School, at Ann Arbor. He paid for his education largely by teaching school and when about twenty-three years of age entered the law offices of Allen & Rosenzweig, at Erie, as a student. At the same time I was reading law with Benson & Brainerd, and the friendship we had formed in the home land continued. We were studying the same subjects and often met and discussed them. We came before the examining board at the same time and were admitted together on September 4, 1878. He located at Titusville and I at North East, both returning to Erie in a few years, he to enter the law firm of Gould and Gilson and I as district attorney. He did fairly well at Titusville, but probably never intended to remain there permanently. The firm was getting on all right, but when Grover Cleveland became President in 1885, probably at the instance of Congressman Scott, Gilson, who was a Democrat, both by inheritance and conviction, was tendered and accepted the position of Indian Agent in a far western district. This position he resigned after a short incumbency and returned to Erie. The firm having been dissolved, he took offices with Joseph P. O'Brien, Esq., and resumed practice. A few months later, on June 16, 1887, he was accidentally drowned while fishing in the bay, and sleeps in the Erie Cemetery.

On June 30, 1881, he was united in marriage with Miss Ella Clark, daughter of Joel Clark of Erie and a cousin of Judge Henry A. Clark. Mr. Gilson left a widow and two small children. The widow soon after bought the residence at 614 West Eighth street, where she reared the children and which has since been the family home. The elder child, a daughter, grew to womanhood, became a teacher, married a Mr. Howard of Rochester, N. Y., and at this writing resides at East Orange, New Jersey. The younger child, a son, Samuel L. Jr., grew to manhood, adopted his father's profession and is now a prominent member of the Erie Bar, and former City Solicitor and Postmaster. He also spends some time at Lock Haven, where he is engaged in legal practice with his wife's father.

By Mr. Gilson's death, the bar lost an able, industrious and conscientious member, who, had life and health been extended, would have made a fine record. He was a natural lawyer with exceptional ability to grasp and state legal propositions. He tried a number of important cases, one of the most notable being that of Perry v. Mill Creek Township, which he won both in the Common Pleas and in the Supreme Court. He was a large, fine looking gentleman, of good personality and commanding appearance, stood six feet four and weighed about two hundred and fifteen pounds and possessed great physical as well as mental strength. When practicing in Titusville, the town's fighting man, attempted to beat him up for something previously said or done in the trial of a cause, but Gilson disposed of his assailant so quickly and decisively as to leave no room for a referee's decision. His untimely death can only be accounted for on the ground that an all-wise and benevolent Providence doeth all things well.

David Adolphus Sawdey, Esq.

David A. Sawdey, son of Captain David and Eliza A. (Bond) Sawdey, was born in Conneaut township, Erie County, Penna., September 3, 1854. The father, a native of Providence, Rhode Island, removed to New Bedford, Mass., when sixteen years old and, as a sailor, became captain and owner of a sea going ship. Later, for some years, he was a merchant at Paris, New York, and in 1821 settled in Conneaut township, Erie County, Pa., where he acquired a farm of some six hundred acres, known for a century as the "Sawdey Farm." Captain Sawdey became one of Erie County's most substantial citizens; served with great credit as a member of the state legislature and also as a county commissioner. His first wife, having died, he was again married in 1849 and to this union two children were born, a daughter who died in childhood and the subject of this sketch. Smith D. Sawdey, for more than half a century one of Albion's first citizens, now (1927) in his eighty-fifth year, was a foster son of Captain Sawdey, but not a blood brother of David A. The latter was educated in the public schools, also at Fredonia, New York, and at the Michigan University, of which he was a graduate in the class of 1876. He studied law with Col. J. Ross Thompson at Erie and was admitted to our bar, December 1, 1881. Thenceforward he practiced his profession at Erie for over forty years. For a large part of that time he and C. L. Baker, Esq., occupied the same offices, first in the old Erie Trust Co. building and later in the Masonic Temple. He occasionally appeared in court in the trial of causes, but confined his attention largely to office and business practice. He always did a respectable amount of business and numbered among his regular clients many prominent people of the city and county. He was regarded as a very sound, conversative lawyer and enjoying to a high degree the full confidence of the profession and the public, was often entrusted with funds for investment. His business extended quite extensively into the orphans' court. In his human relationships he was steadfast and rarely lost a client or a friend.

He joined the Masonic fraternity in 1885 and gave thereto the best services of his life. For thirty years he was Deputy Grand Master for this district and by common consent the leading Mason in this section of the state. Largely through his efforts the Masonic Temple at Erie was erected about 1910. He passed through all the chairs of the local Masonic bodies, served on state boards, and came near being chosen to the highest state office in the gift of his brethren. He was for many years a thirty-third degree Mason and all he did for the fraternity will never be told. His will shows what his final intentions toward the fraternity were.

When he was five years old his father died, but he continued to make his home on the farm with his mother until her death in 1895. Even thereafter, while practicing law in Erie he retained his legal residence on his farm, which he greatly improved and enlarged by the purchase of some two hundred acres, making a farm of approximately eight hundred acres, and one of the finest in this part of the state. The management of this large property, to which he gave his personal attention, together with his multitudinous Masonic duties doubtless interfered somewhat with his professional work, as did ill health during the last year of his life. David A. Sawdey was of medium size, wore a sandy moustache, had an intelligent, kindly face, loved his friends and was a charming companion. He kept open house at his farm, was a typical host and fond of entertaining his legion of friends. While apparently very light hearted, he was sober minded and stood resolutely for that which was highest and best. His influence was uplifting upon the thousands of men with whom he came in touch. He was never married and in the fall of 1922 developed a malignant malady which, despite the highest surgical skill, ended in his death on April 10, 1923, in the sixty-ninth year of his age. His funeral, one of the largest ever held in that part of the county, took place on his farm and he was buried with Masonic honors in the beautiful cemetery at East Springfield.

He was a life long Democrat, as was his father, and a member of the Park Presbyterian Church. He was modest and undemonstrative, but many a worthy person and many a worthy cause were aided by his bounty.

Hon. John C. Brady

John C. Brady was born at Fort Dodge, Iowa, October 2, 1858, the son of John W. and Amanda Lott Brady, the former being a native of Connecticut and the latter a daughter of Deacon Lott, one of the best known and most highly respected citizens in the locality of North East. Soon after marriage Mr. and Mrs. Brady moved to Iowa where their two sons were born and where Mr. Brady was elected sheriff of Webster county. While the boys were young they were suddenly rendered homeless by the death of both parents and sent to North East where they lived around with relative and friends for some time. Meanwhile John, the older boy, worked at whatever he could find to do; and when a mere lad drove horses on the Erie Canal from Buffalo to Albany. About this time Harvey B. Pullman, Esq., one of North East borough's best citizens and a man of means, whose first wife was also a daughter of Deacon Lott, took the Brady boys into his own home, reared, educated and in effect became a father to them. He sent them to school and later to the Lake Shore Seminary at North East where John made fine progress and formed many intimate friendships, including that with the late Joseph M. Force, Esq., Hon. A. E. Sisson and the writer, which continued through life. John was then a large handsome boy (as he became a large handsome man) with a brilliant mind and ever cheerful.

Recognizing John's natural fitness for the law, Mr. Pullman secured for him a clerkship in the law offices of Davenport and Griffith at Erie, and about the same time he (Pullman) secured for me a like position in the law office of Benson and Brainerd. During a part of our clerkship General Sisson, Brady and I had rooms together on the third floor of 31 North Park Row. Brady was a good student, with special adaptability to the business end of the law. I will not attempt to relate the practical jokes we perpetrated on each other during that time; so how our clean linen was tranferred to Brady's bed, or how the wandering Indian came to appropriate Brady's favorite pipe may remain unsolved mysteries. We all smoked at that time but I quit soon after coming to the bar; Sisson, however, for many years had and perhaps still has the curious habit of smoking every alternate year.

Brady was admitted to the bar on or about his twenty-first birthday and at once began the practice at Erie, where he acquired a good practice and had, for a young lawyer, a fine income. He had no liking for mere oratory, but could express himself well and forcibly, and with his rare ability might have become eminent at the bar. He had, however, such remarkable business sense and unerring judgment as naturally led him into transactions aside from the law. Financially he could not afford to practice law; for example, he had a case on the list which he gave Mr. Allen one hundred dollars to try, while he went down in the lumber woods and made three thousand dollars in a business deal. He had the vision to see and the courage to grasp opportunities. In some of his early ventures Mr. Pullman gave him financial backing, but he soon needed none. Brady's sudden rise in the business world has probably never been equalled by any other member of our bar. He engaged extensively in the lumber business in Elk and Forest counties; also had large oil interests in Pennsylvania and Ohio. He was also interested in business projects in Mexico where he spent a winter. Mr. Brady was the organizer, principal stockholder and president of the Erie-Welsbach Gas Company.

He early saw the possibilities of electricity as a motive power and, perhaps as his crowning business achievement, established the Erie Electric Motor Company, the second electric motor company established in the United States. Under the magic of his genius the old unsightly horse cars were replaced by beautiful motor cars, and the extension of the system over the city and into surrounding country was the dawn of a new and greater day for Erie. He was probably the first to have a great vision of Erie's future, certainly no one did more than he to bring it about. In connection with the motor company he planned and developed Waldameer, that beautiful resort on the shore of the lake three miles west of the city which is still enjoyed by thousands of people.

His well known business ability led to his appointment as assignee of the German Savings Company and later as receiver of the Erie County Savings Bank; in both of which capacities he acquitted himself with great credit and in a highly satisfactory manner.

In politics Brady, probably following the example of his foster father, was a Democrat, but never sought public office. In 1887 a meeting was called to decide upon an independent candidate for Mayor; while the matter was being discussed, Mr. Brady casually entered the hall and before he could decline was unanimously chosen as the candidate. His triumphant election followed and he made one of the most efficient executives in the history of the city. In 1892 he was a delegate to the Democratic National Convention that gave Grover Cleveland his last nomination for the Presidency. Brady enjoyed a large personal acquaintance with leading Democrats throughout the state and was an intimate friend of Hon. William F. Harrity of Philadelphia, at one time chairman of the Democratic National Committee. Mr. Brady possessed fine social qualities and greatly enjoyed the companionship of his friends. He was one of the founders of the famous Cascade Club and at the meetings of that unique organization at its club house near West Lake road, frequently demonstrated his exceptional ability as a chef. He was a member and at one time president of the Erie Club also a very active member of the Kahkwa Club. He belonged to the Royal Arcanum, was a Mason, Knight Templar and Shriner.

On June 2, 1887, he married Harriet Helen, daughter of the late Hon. John W. Hammond, ex-Mayor of Erie. They had one child, a daughter, Lois, now married and living in Connecticut. When about forty-four years of age, Mr. Brady had a serious sickness, from which he never fully recovered, although he continued active to the last. He fought ill health in the same cheerful undaunted manner as he had fought the other battles of life, despite which he died in 1905, at the age of forty-seven years and was buried in Lake Side Cemetery, later removed to the Erie Cemetery. Thus prematurely ended the career of a doer of large things and probably the greatest financial genius who has appeared at our bar. In addition to his brilliant qualities he was a kindly man, ever thoughtful of his friends and his family, and never miserly or a hoarder of money. In writing the story of John C. Brady, the name of Harvey B. Pullman must stand out in gold letters.

Note: Several of the facts of this sketch have been taken from a copy of the Illustrated North American, published shortly after Mr. Brady's death.

Prof. Henry Adonijah Strong

Henry A. Strong was born at Portland, Connecticut, December 22, 1844, the son of Adonijah and Julia Chapman Strong. He attended Chase School, also Wesleyan University, where he graduated in 1866, second in his class, with the degree of "B. A." and later "M. A." In 1872 he graduated at Harvard Law School with the degree of L. L. B. He was that year admitted to the Connecticut Bar. He had a fondness for teaching, which from time to time interrupted his study and practice of law. He taught in Newburg Seminary in 1867, was principal of the Union Schools at Franklin, Pa., 1868 to 1870 and of the Erie Academy 1878 to 1881. He resided in Franklin from 1872 to 1878 and practiced law there, and I believe taught more or less during that time. He became a member of the Erie Bar in 1881 and thenceforth practiced law here until his death. He was a ready and forceful speaker and could try a case well, but confined his attention mostly to office practice, where he faithfully served a respectable clientage. He never was prominent at the bar, but as a leading and consistent temperance advocate appeared at every annual license court in opposition to the granting of liquor licenses and always forcibly presented his views. Prof. Strong was a prominent member of the First Methodist Church from his coming to Erie until his death, active in all its work and especially in the Sunday School, of which he was superintendent for many years. He contributed articles to Sunday School papers and in every way exhibited his deep interest in that department of church work. He would have made a fine minister of the gospel; in fact, I think his natural bent was more to that than to the law.

He was a medium sized man of florid complexion and, with his red moustache and side whiskers, presented rather a striking appearance. About 1873 he married a Mrs. Gordon of Franklin, who predeceased him by many years. They had no children, but his sister Miss Lillian Strong, who kept his home after Mrs. Strong's death, survives and is a well known resident of Erie. Prof. Strong died February 23, 1923, in the seventy-ninth year of his age and was buried at East Berlin, Conn. This closed a life devoted to high ideals and good deeds.

Charles Lafayette White, Esq.

Charles L. White was born at Lake Pleasant in this county, May 29, 1858, but removed with his parents to Corry, where he graduated at the High School of that city. He then entered the law office of Hon. Manley Crosby and was admitted to the Erie Bar October 2, 1882. For about two years thereafter he practiced at Carrington, North Dakota, then returned to Corry where he opened an office and practiced law continuously until his death. He was well known and well liked, had a good general practice but seldom engaged in the trial of causes in court. He had a saving sense of humor, was very genial and one whom it was ever a pleasure to meet. He lived in the neighborhood of the Berliner tannery, and when we called him as a witness to prove it was a nuisance he tersely characterized it, "the prince of stinks." He was a Republican, a member of the I. O. O. F. and of the Encampment. He served as school director in Corry but held no other office and was never married. He was of light complexion, medium height, slight build, never robust and gradually lost his health. He died June 13, 1894, and was buried at Corry. His death at the early age of thirty-six years was greatly regretted by a wide circle of friends.

Joseph Patrick O'Brien, Esq.

Joseph P. O'Brien (frequently called Joe O'Brien), son of Richard and Margaret (McCarthy) O'Brien, was born in Erie, March 18, 1860. His parents were Irish and his father, a man of remarkable ability and personality, was for many years one of Erie's leading citizens, being agent for the Pennsylvania Railroad, also engaged in lake transportation and in other lines. Joe, a brilliant boy, had the best of educational advantages, attending St. Patrick's Parochial School at Erie, and the Georgetown University. From the latter he received the A. B. and M. A. degrees, and, having completed a course in the Law Department of that university, the L. L. B. degree. In Erie he studied law with Allen & Rosenzweig and was admitted to our bar March 17, 1883. He at once began practice here and in a remarkably short time became a well known and prominent lawyer. No one in my time made more rapid progress at the bar. He was a strikingly handsome young man, with a magnetic personality and had probably as keen an intellect as ever came to our bar. He was a born orator and a logical reasoner. From the very start he was a dangerous opponent before a jury, and all predicted for him a brilliant career. Before he had been two years at the bar he was winning his way in the trial of causes. When he had been only three or four years at the bar he and I were attorneys for plaintiff in the case of Lacey v. The Lake Shore & Michigan Southern Railway Company, wherein he conducted himself like a veteran. He was then undoubtedly the most brilliant man of his age at the bar. In 1889 he became and for six years continued solicitor for Erie City, for which he conducted much important litigation and uniformly acquitted himself with credit.

He was an active Democrat and his reputation as a stump speaker took him far beyond the bounds of the county. He had a phenomenal memory and by one reading would master an ordinary work of fiction so he could state all its important contents, including names, dates, incidents, etc. Soon after coming to the bar he was united in marriage with Miss Mary Wynne, a daughter of the well known Wynne family of Lock Haven, her father having been mayor of that city. Mr. and Mrs. O'Brien had three sons, the two younger died in youth and the eldest son, Richard O'Brien, is a practicing attorney in Omaha, Nebraska.

Just when everything seemed to be coming his way and with the world under his feet, so to speak, Joseph P. O'Brien's health began to fail. In an effort to regain it he found employment as general counsel for a corporation which took him into a milder climate, but despite every effort and the best medical skill, he grew worse and as a last resort sought temporary sojourn in the Adirondack mountains, where he died June 7, 1904, at the age of forty-four years and was buried in Trinity Cemetery, at Erie. He was ever faithful to the Roman Catholic religion, as were his parents before him. He was also a prominent member of the Knights of Columbus and the Erie Lodge of Elks. Among his surviving relatives were his widow and his sisters, Miss Agnes O'Brien and Mrs. Charles H. English,* of Erie. Mr. O'Brien was a medium sized, well-built, smooth shaven young man of strikingly attractive personality and his untimely death was a sad tragedy. His widow now resides with her son at Omaha, Nebraska.

Note: Mrs. English died in October, 1928.

Hon. John Steven Rilling

John S. Rilling, son of Christopher and Elizabeth Ackerman Rilling, was born in Millcreek Township, Erie County, July 22, 1860; his parents were born in Germany. The father became prominent in the township and among other activities served as road commissioner. John was educated at the public schools and Edinboro State Normal school; studied law at Erie in the office of Davenport & Griffith and was admitted to the Erie Bar, February 19, 1885. In 1889 he was admitted to the State Supreme Court and in 1892 to the Supreme Court of the United States. He began active practice on coming to the Erie Bar and so continued for thirty years. He was possibly the best business getter at our bar and always had a large clientage. He practiced alone for some years, then in partnership with Henry E. Fish, Esq., and later in the firm of Gunnison, Rilling and Fish. He had great enthusiasm and tireless energy, was a hard worker and made fine progress. During his active years in Erie he was a large dealer in real estate. He had unusual executive ability and was a doer of things, and by far the best man at our bar to arrange annual banquets and other like gatherings. He was a unique individual in many respects, scarcely to be judged by ordinary standards. A good lawyer, but yet out-classed other lawyers seemingly of equal ability. His dynamic force of character gave him prestige. In other words, he had the punch, and was a leader, not a follower.

He was a very active Democrat and recognized as a leader in its state politics. He had the nomination of that party for lieutenant governor in 1894, and was a delegate at large to the Democratic national convention in 1896. For some years he was chairman of the Democratic State Committee. He was solicitor for the Erie City School District for years and thereby became thoroughly familiar with the state school laws. Hence, his appointment by Gov. Stuart as a member of the commission to frame the school code, which was finally enacted in 1911, was timely and fortunate. He was the only lawyer on the commission, and no one labored harder or more efficiently in that monumental work than he. The commission was composed of leading citizens and educators, among whom were David Oliver of Pittsburgh, Dr. Nathan C. Schaffer, Superintendent of Public Instruction, and Dr. Martin G. Brumbaugh, then Superintendent of Philadelphia city schools and now (1927) President of Juniata College. Between the other commissioners and Mr. Rilling there arose a life long friendship and admiration. He was later a member of the State Board of Education. Dr. Brumbaugh's admiration for Rilling was such that when he became Governor in 1915, he without solicitation appointed him a member of the Public Service Commission. This Mr. Rilling accepted, located in Harrisburg and became the resident and most active member of the commission. It was the crowning work of his life and he gave himself unsparingly to it. That he made a great commissioner was the general verdict of the legal profession and thousands of others throughout the commonwealth familiar with his work. He probably became personally known to more lawyers and judges in Pennsylvania than any other man. In fact, one time and another, he visited every county in the state but one.

In 1924, his term of office, and that of a recess appointment by Gov. Sproul having expired, Mr. Rilling resumed his residence in Erie, where he opened a law office and with his old time courage, started to pick up the broken threads of his practice. Long years of constant work and responsibility, however, had undermined his naturally robust constitution and, although he struggled valiantly, and at times seemed his former self, he was fatally and hopelessly stricken in the summer of 1926 and passed away on September 6. He was a Mason and member of St. Paul's Lutheran Church and for many years active in the civic organizations of the city and at one time president of the Board of Trade. He was one of the founders of St. Vincent's Hospital and ever active for its welfare. He served many years as a trustee of the Erie Cemetery. No man in his day gave more of his time and energy to the public or served it more efficiently than he. His last work being a movement to secure the abolition of grade crossings in Nineteenth street.

On October 20, 1887, he was united in marriage with Miss Stella Armstrong, of Erie. To them two daughters were born, the elder, Marion, is now Mrs. Capt. John R. Metcalf, of Erie, and the younger, Ruth, is Mrs. Chester Lang, of Schenectady, New York. Mr. Rilling was a kind and loving husband and devoted father. I have never known a better man in his family. He was also intensely loyal to his friends and eager to serve them. I shall never forget the effectiveness with which he urged my appointment as successor to Judge Elkin. John S. Rilling sleeps in the Erie Cemetery, but the great work he did abides and he must ever be remembered as a master of achievement.

Albert Burwell Force, Esq.

A. B. Force, son of William J. and Nancy Burwell Force, was born at North East, Erie County, Pa., October 29, 1845. They were an old North East family, the father, a leading citizen there for over fifty years, was of French Huguenot lineage and the mother of English and Dutch extraction. When the subject of this sketch was young, the family moved onto a farm in North East township, where he and his brother Joseph M. and two sisters grew to manhood and womanhood. The parents were devout members of the Methodist church and maintained an ideal Christian home. Albert was an ambitious boy, availed himself of the local schools and entered Allegheny College, where he graduated with the "B. A." degree. While in school and studying law he did odd jobs to help pay expenses, among which was taking the 1870 United States census of North East township and Boro and Greenfield township. While in college he formed the acquaintance of Colonel James O. Parmlee, of Warren, and when admitted to the Erie Bar on August 22, 1871, formed a law partnership with that gentleman under the name of Force & Parmlee, with offices at 31 North Park Row, Erie. They did fairly well for beginners and in 1875 Mr. Force was elected district attorney. As such he prepared all cases carefully, tried them with ability and was one of the most relentless prosecutors who has filled that office.

On October 12, 1878, he was united in marriage with Miss Louise Powers of Pittsburgh and soon after removed to that city, where he practiced law for some ten years, as a member of the law firm of Powers, Force and Powers;

the senior member being his wife's father and the junior, her brother. About 1890 he left Pittsburgh, went west and finally settled at Seattle, Wash. They had three children, a son, with whom the father resided in Seattle and two daughters, who remained with the mother in Pittsburgh. Mr. Force died at Seattle, September 24, 1928, and was buried in that city. Thus ended at the age of eighty-three years a life which never grew professionally to what it promised in early manhood. Mr. Force was a Methodist, a Republican and a member of the "Delta Tau Delta" college fraternity. When a young man he was tall, wore a sandy moustache, dressed neatly and looked well. He enlisted in the Union army shortly before the close of the war; I do not know that he saw active service.

Dr. Francis Newton Thorpe

Dr. Thorpe did so much of great value to our profession and the public, that, as a member of our bar, he deserves more than a passing notice, although he never entered upon the practice of law. The son of Judah W. and Rosanna (Porter) Thorpe, he was born at Swampscott, Massachusetts, April 16, 1857, and came with his family to North East when a boy. The only other child was a sister, Clara. The father, being a house carpenter, supported his family in comfortable circumstances. Dr. Thorpe became a student in the Lake Shore Seminary, a Methodist institution, located at North East, on its first opening in the fall of 1871 and so continued until his graduation in the class of 1875. George A. Hampson, Esq., of North East and I were the other male members of the class. Thorpe was a very diligent and exemplary student with a remarkably keen intellect and great capacity for acquiring education. The seminary continued as such for about ten years and he undoubtedly was the best student it ever had. There were many interesting incidents of our student days, one of which was a public declamation contest, in which he and I were entered. I recited "The Polish Boy"; I do not recall his subject. The judges awarded him first prize, but some of the audience, believing I should have had at least an even break, took advantage of a public occasion to present me a copy of Webster's Unabridged Dictionary. The book was of great practical use to me in those days and I have reverently treasured it ever since. This was my first intimation that judges' decisions are not always accepted as verity. I had on a previous occasion recited "Darius

Green and His Flying Machine" which was my initial appearance before a North East audience. Upon Dr. Thorpe's graduation in 1875 he became and for some years continued principal of the North East Academy. Continuing his studies, however, he received the Ph. D. degree from Syracuse University in 1883.

In 1885 he was admitted to the Erie Bar, having been registered as a law student with Hon. John P. Vincent. He also attended the Law Department of the University of Pennsylvania in 1885 and 1886. On my motion he was admitted to the bar of the state supreme court in 1887, as I recall the date. He was professor of American Constitutional History in the University of Pennsylvania from 1885 to 1898, inclusive, and was professor of political science and constitutional law in the University of Pittsburgh for sixteen years, beginning in 1910. Wherever he taught he was popular and his unusual gifts in that direction were fully recognized.

His lasting fame, however, must rest largely on his authorship, he having written and published seventy-six volumes, an amount rarely, if ever, surpassed by any author. While he wrote one book of fiction, one on agriculture, some biographies, including the Life of Dr. William Pepper, for many years at the head of the University of Pennsylvania, also some text books on general history, yet the great bulk of his writings was on constitutional law, constitutional history and kindred subjects. A list of his publications may be found in "Who's Who in America" for 1926-1927, page 1886. He became so eminent in his chosen field that he was employed by the United States Government to prepare for it works of the highest authority. His books on constitutional questions are often cited by the Supreme Court of the United States. For example, Chief Justice White, in speaking for that court, sustaining the constitutionality of the draft act relating to the World War, repeatedly refers to the works of Dr. Thorpe. Moreover, his works are used as text books in many schools, colleges and universities throughout the country and in foreign lands. The reason he did not teach for ten or twelve years, beginning in 1898, was because of his literary work and not from lack of opportunity, for during that time he was tendered many positions, including the presidency of the Vermont University. He had a remarkable acquaintance with literary men everywhere, and was chosen by Gov. Sproul as one of the twenty-five distinguished Pennsylvanians appointed to revise the state constitution under the Act of 1819, and did notable service as a member of that body.

In 1895 he was united in marriage with Marion Haywood Shreve, of Mt. Holly, New Jersey. Their daughter, and only child, married Dr. Diller, of Pittsburgh, nephew of Dr. Theodore Diller, the noted nerve specialist. It was ever Dr. Thorpe's habit to spend his summers at North East where for many years he owned, occupied and managed a beautiful fruit farm, becoming an expert in horticulture, as he was in other lines. Some few years ago he developed a malignant throat trouble, relieved and checked by surgical skill, but seemingly from the effects of which Dr. Thorpe died in April 1926, at the age of sixty-nine years, and was buried in the North East Cemetery, where he rests with his old friends and neighbors in the land he loved best. Thus ended the life journey of one of America's foremost men of letters, who had been honored by degrees from many great institutions of learning, at home and abroad.

He was above medium height, not heavily built, with a smooth shaven attractive face and good figure. He was a charming companion, always thoughtful and kindly, with a brilliant intellect, scintillating both wit and wisdom. He was an accomplished speaker, frequently gave lectures, and but few years ago responded to a toast at the banquet of the State Bar meeting in a most delightful manner. He never forgot his old friends or the old school days and was one who called my name to Gov. Brumbaugh's attention just prior to my appointment as justice of the State Supreme Court in December, 1915. The Governor and he had been close friends in Philadelphia years before.

As the time of the fiftieth anniversary of our graduation approached, he arranged a class reunion or golden jubilee at his farm, June 20, 1925, at which Mr. and Mrs. Geo. A. Hampson, Rev. and Mrs. Frank J. Nash, General and Mrs. Sisson, Mrs. Walling and myself were present, Rev. Nash being a graduate of the Seminary and General Sisson a former student. We found Dr. Thorpe surrounded by his wife, his daughter and two charming young grandchildren, and had a royal evening. I met him occasionally during that summer and saw that years of incessant toil, also sickness, had made some inroads upon his former fine constitution, yet his death the following spring came as a great shock to his many friends. In addition to his other activities he was a great Bible student and Sunday school teacher and an accomplished musician, belonged to the Presbyterian church and was a Republican in politics, as was his father before him.

Dr. Thorpe was intensely practical, possessed great industry and a rare ability for the acquisition, retention and dissemination of knowledge. In addition to being a profound Latin and Greek scholar and keeping up his study of the classics (as he daily read a chapter in the New Testament in the original Greek) he mastered and could speak several modern languages. Above all he was a man of the highest ideals and of spotless character. The world is not only wiser but better because of his life.

The Lake Shore Seminary, above mentioned, ceased to function as such about 1880, for lack of adequate patronage. The building and grounds now form part of St. Mary's College, a prosperous Catholic school.

Eben Brewer, Esq.

Eben Brewer, son of Doctor Brewer, was born at Westfield, New York, in 1848. He came to Erie when a young man to engage in the newspaper business, and for some years was the editor and publisher of the Erie Morning Dispatch. While so engaged he studied law and was admitted to the Erie Bar June 30, 1885. He continued his newspaper work and never actively engaged in legal practice. He was a large, handsome man of florid complexion, a good public speaker and a very able writer. Being public spirited he took an active part in politics and other matters of public interest. He was the first mail agent of the United States in Cuba, where he contracted yellow fever and died July 14, 1898, aged fifty years. A statue of Mr. Brewer, erected by United States postal employees, stands in Perry square, opposite the Erie Post Office. He married the widow of Commodore Lowry. She was an accomplished lady and a daughter of the late Milton Courtright, in his day one of Erie's first citizens. Mr. Brewer was a man of high ideals and of many useful activities and his tragic death caused general regret.

Albert Truesdell, Esq.

Albert Truesdell, son of Samuel Wheaton and Lucy (Upson) Truesdell, was born at Lawsville, Susquehanna County, Penna., August 3, 1831. He was of a pioneer New England family and his parents were born in Connecticut. He was educated in the common schools and at the Hartford Academy, also at the Windsor Academy, where he graduated and in 1861 was admitted to the Susquehannna County Bar. The same year he was appointed postmaster of Lawsville and served three years, when he was made United States revenue assessor, and served as such for four years. In 1872 he moved to Corry and entered the office of the United States Express Company where he served for two years. In 1877 he served as clerk in the State Senate at Harrisburg, and in 1878 he was appointed an alderman for the city of Corry, which office he held by successive elections for about thirty-five years, a length of continuous service equalled by few in this part of the state. He was an ideal magistrate, learned, dignified, honest, industrious, kind, wise and patient, with a world of common sense and broad knowledge of human affairs. He was admitted to the Erie Bar December 14, 1886, and, while he at times assisted in the preparation of important cases he never took an active part in the court trials. He was counsel in the settlement of estates and other office business, but seldom appeared in court. In many respects he was an exceptional man, but is best remembered by his extraordinary services as magistrate. He was popular with all classes and probably performed more marriage ceremonies than any other alderman or justice of the peace in the county. He was an expert penman and very often called upon to take testimony in cases pending in court. He also acted as coroner in many cases.

Esquire Truesdell was a tall, light complexioned fine looking gentleman, usually wore a beard, was of most agreeable manners and pleasing personality. He was a life long Republican and in early life took an active part in politics, in 1860 being chairman of the Republican County Committee and a delegate to the state convention that nominated Andrew G. Curtin for Governor. He had an unusual faculty of making and retaining personal friends, numbering among them many persons of distinction, including former Chief Justice J. Brester McCullom of the state supreme court.

On October 30, 1856, he was united in marriage with Miss Francis A. Warner. They had five children of whom only one, Mrs. Gertrude Truesdell Gilpin, of Corry, is now living. There are, however, three grandchildren, children of their deceased son, LeRoy Truesdell. Esquire Truesdell sustained a severe and painful personal injury near the close of his life from which he never fully recovered. He died January 9, 1913, in the eighty-second year of his age and was buried in the Pine Grove Cemetery at Corry. He was a member of the Presbyterian Church and all his life a student of history.

Professor James R. Burns

Professor James R. Burns was born at Edinburgh, Scotland, August 26, 1848, and came to this country with his parents when a small boy. The family settled in western Crawford County, where he grew to manhood. He graduated at the Edinboro State Normal School in the class of 1872. Soon thereafter he became a member of the faculty of the Erie High School, where he remained as teacher and vice-principal for approximately thirty-five years. Meantime, he studied law with Allen & Rosenzweig and was admitted to the Erie Bar May 10, 1886. He represented Erie City in the legislature in the sessions of 1885 and 1887, during which time he was granted leave of absence from the High School. On coming to the bar he formed a law partnership with Corwin Mallory, but never engaged actively in practice. His fame rests largely on his record as a teacher, wherein he was unexcelled in the city's history. Thousands of our boys and girls became wiser and better through the instruction of Prof. Burns, and to this day as they look back over the years mention his name with reverence and gratitude. What other member of our bar has done more for the uplift of the city? As a legislator he performed every duty with excellent judgment and painstaking care. He was was probably the best speaker in that body and always listened to with marked attention. I was in the senate at that time and well recall the high regard in which he was held and the great influence he exerted. As an orator the Professor was at his best and probably never had a superior in Erie County. He was practically blind as a child and suffered through life with very defective eyesight, yet he rose above this misfortune and his life was one of achievement. This drawback may account for the fact that he never abandoned the profession of teaching for that of law. He was a man of fine sentiment and in his contact with other men formed strong friendships. Probably he and George A. Allen were as devoted friends as any two men in Erie.

Professor Burns was of commanding appearance, over six feet in height, well proportioned and stood erect. He was of florid complexion and wore a full beard and was a man of splendid courage and strong convictions. A life long Democrat, his voice was often heard in support of his party. He was a devout Catholic and a daily worshipper at the altar of the church. He was never married and died on the first day of August 1910, at the age of sixty-two years. He was buried in the family lot of the cemetery at Crossingville, Crawford County, beside his father and mother. James R. Burns is gone, but the inspiration of his life abides.

Corwin H. Mallory, Esq.

Corwin H. Mallory, son of M. B. and Julia Mallory, was born at Conneaut, Ohio, May 29, 1863, and came with his family to Erie when seven years of age. He attended the public school and Erie High School from which he graduated about 1883, and for a time was an instructor in Clark's Business College. Having studied law in the office of Allen & Rosenzweig and also, I believe, with L. S. Norton, he was admitted to the Erie Bar July 8, 1886, and formed a law partnership with Prof. James R. Burns. The latter, declining to enter active practice, Mr. Mallory became associated with T. A. Lamb, Esq. On Monday, February 6, 1887, he was named assistant district attorney and as such appeared before the grand jury that afternoon, but during that evening he was taken violently ill and died the next day at one o'clock with paralysis of the heart.

He was slightly under medium size, had a handsome, clean shaven face and a captivating personality. Being an excellent speaker, he was chosen class orator at the High School and his oration on "Money in Politics", exhibiting a depth of thought far beyond his years, was widely read and favorably commented upon. He had a brilliant intellect and was thorough in whatever he undertook. A more promising young man has rarely come to our bar and his untimely death caused universal sorrow. The meeting, called to take action upon his death, was largely attended and remarks expressing the general feeling, were made by many of the leaders of the bar, including ex-Judges Vincent and Galbraith, also

Judge Gunnison, Col. Thompson, George A. Allen and others. He was buried in the Erie Cemetery. Thus ended a professional career, which in half a year had made a deep impression upon the profession and the public.

Charles Sealon Burchfield, Esq.

Charles S. Burchfield, son of Robert and Emaline (Austin) Burchfield, was born at Edinboro, February 11, 1858, and, after graduating at the State Normal School there, was elected and served as justice of the peace of that borough. Meantime, he studied law in the office of Hon. S. M. Brainerd and was admitted to the Erie Bar September 6, 1886. From that time until his death he resided in and practiced law in Erie. He had great native ability, was expert in the examination of law questions, especially those involving the state or federal constitution. One of his briefs, attacking the validity of a pure food law, not only won his case in the local court, but was used in cases involving a like question in several other counties. About the time of his admission to the bar he prepared a brief for the defense in the Rosenzweig case, which was highly praised by counsel. He had one of the most discriminating law minds at our bar; the cases he cited were uniformly pertinent. Mr. Burchfield came of a good family and as a young man was tall, well built and strikingly handsome. I first met him when making my canvass for district attorney in 1881 and he seemed to me then the most promising young man in the county. As a lawyer he was honest, bold and aggressive, had perfect health and should have been a leader of the bar, but he never quite gained that distinction. He had, however, a fairly good practice and was recognized as an able lawyer.

Mr. Burchfield was a man's man, honest, fearless, outspoken and had many friends. He was an active, popular and influential Elk and in politics a Republican, although he never sought public office. In his later years his health and strength declined and on December 5, 1911, when completing his fifty-fourth year, he died. The high regard in which he was held was attested by the fact that a special extra car was chartered to convey those who desired to escort his remains to Edinboro where he was buried. He was never married. Like many others, I was fond of Mr. Burchfield and regret he did not fully attain the eminence in the profession, which seemed to be within his grasp.

Hon. Albert Buell Osborne

A. B. Osborne, son of Judge Osborne, of Mayville, New York, was born in that village April 30, 1866. He received his education in the schools at Mayville and, having decided to adopt the legal profession, attended the Albany Law School, was admitted to the Erie Bar, May 31, 1887, and located at Corry, where he was soon well established. He was fine appearing, had a genial and attractive personality, was a brilliant young man and soon had a good practice. His popularity is attested by the fact that when twenty-five years of age he was elected Mayor of Corry and served with distinction, as he also later did as solicitor of that city. His practice took him into adjoining counties and before appellate courts. After being in Corry some ten or twelve years he came to Erie where he continued in practice, with some interruptions, until his death. While here he practiced with or at least had offices successively with George P. Griffith, Esq., Henry C. Yard, Esq., and Hon. M. W. Shreve. He often appeared in court, was a hard worker and tried his cases with ability. He was referred to as the most fluent speaker at the bar. He often appeared on the stump for the Democratic party of which he was an ardent member.

During his residence here he was the candidate of his party for congress, but, although he made a remarkable contest, was defeated by the sitting member, Hon. Arthur L. Bates. He had a literary turn of mind and served for a number of years as president of the Erie Library Board. From his youth he was fond of travel and after he became about forty years of age began devoting his time quite extensively thereto. He repeatedly visited Europe and elsewhere. In fact, it became almost an occupation. He wrote three books on European travel, which were intensely interesting and gained wide circulation. During his last four or five years he wrote extensively for travel magazines. He delivered numerous lectures largely for Pond's Lyceum Bureau, and attained eminence in that field.

While residing in Corry he was united in marriage with Miss Blanche Gifford, a teacher and the daughter of Dr. Gifford of that city. They have one son, Lieutenant Jack Gifford Osborne, who won distinction in the World War and is now engaged in the real estate business in this city. A. B. Osborne, as above stated, enjoyed traveling, also reading and camping. One blustering February day he sent out invitations for a picnic at Waldameer beach on the nineteenth of the following May, which were accepted and the occasion proved most enjoyable. The Osbornes enjoyed entertaining their friends and were socially most delightful people. He was a member of the Masonic fraternity and a vestryman in St. Paul's Episcopal Church. While traveling in Austria, he died suddenly at Prague, on July 21, 1913, age forty-seven years, and was buried at Mayville, New York, the home of his forebears. His father, of English ancestry, was a practicing attorney and served as judge of Chautauqua county. I recall seeing him in Mayville, when I was a boy and know he was held in the highest esteem. Mrs. A. B. Osborne took her husband's sudden death as philosophically as possible, and resides in this city, where she has numerous friends and is highly regarded.

Charles Heydrick, Esq.

Charles Heydrick, son of Peter C. and Margaret A. (Doughty) Heydrick, was born in Crawford County in 1864 and when a boy removed with his family to Erie. His father became prominent here in political and civic affairs and served as a member of the city council. Charles' uncle, Hon. Christopher Heydrick, of Venango county, was one of the leaders of the bar in this part of the state and served by appointment as a justice of the state supreme court. Charles was educated in the public schools and city high school, and, after serving an apprenticeship in the offices of J. C. & F. F. Marshall, was admitted to the Erie Bar, June 28, 1887. He at once took up practice here which was continued without interruption until his death. He soon became the champion of organized labor in the state and at one time was its candidate for judge of the superior court. He was a medium sized, smooth faced young man of pleasing personality and, but for his untimely death, doubtless would have had a successful legal career.

In politics he was known as a Democrat, to which party his father was a life long adherent. He was a member of the Modern Woodman of the World. He was a descendant of Balthasar Heydrick, who came from Germany and settled in Pennsylvania in 1734. Charles Heydrick was united in marriage with a well known Erie lady who survived him. He was stricken with typhoid fever and died January 1, 1905, at the age of forty years, and was buried in Lake Side Cemetery at Erie.

Willard J. Young, Esq.

W. J. Young (familiarly known as Will Young), the son of John Brown and Phoebe Jane (Middleton) Young, was born in Amity township, Erie County, Pa., October 9, 1861. His father, of English and Irish descent, was born in Ireland and his mother of Scotch descent, was born in Amity township, this county. Will grew up on the farm, attended district school, and later, Westminster College at New Wilmington, Pa., of which he was a graduate. He studied law in the office of Captain, later Judge Edward L. Whittelsey, was admitted to the Erie Bar, February 23, 1888, and for thirty-six years was a practicing attorney. He was a sound lawyer and being well liked by the bar and public, gradually acquired a large office business. He occasionally appeared in the trial of causes, where he acquitted himself well, but never aspired to the honors of the forum. He was best known as a business lawyer and as representing business interests, numbering among his clients the R. G. Dun Company, the Mutual Building & Loan Company, the Erie County Milk Association, the Central Bank & Trust Company and others. He also looked after the financial affairs and loaned money for a good many clients. As trustee for the Masonic bodies he made many investments and after his death that business was all found in perfect order. He was a careful, painstaking lawyer with exceptionally good judgment and where possible, kept his clients out of court.

He was owner of several farms, near the city, the management of which was his principal recreation. He was a member of the Grange, kept in close touch with many farmers throughout the county, was a thoroughly posted, up to date farmer and fruit grower, also an excellent judge of thoroughbred cattle. Personally he was of medium size, light complexion, usually wore a moustache and was a most delightful and interesting companion. He was a Presbyterian, a Republican and a prominent and popular member of the Masonic fraternity. Will was never married, and shortly after passing his sixtieth birthday his health began gradually to fail and he died on June 13, 1924, in the sixty-third year of his age. He was buried in the Erie Cemetery, leaving to survive him his mother,* two sisters, Miss Annette Young, Clerk of the Courts of Erie County and Miss Leaf A., at home, also three brothers, S. M., now (1927) Collector of Taxes for the Third Ward of Erie City; R. G., a farmer in Mill Creek township, and E. J., in the gas business at Washington, Pa.

*Note: The mother died since the above was written.

Hon. Charles Addison Hitchcock

Charles A. Hitchcock, son of Myron D. and Sarah A. (Wright) Hitchcock, was born August 9, 1836, at New Haven, New York. He was a lineal descendant of Luke Hitchcock, who came from England and settled in Connecticut in 1644, and his son, Captain Luke Hitchcock, a prominent citizen and celebrated Indian fighter in the early days of New England. The mother of the subject of this sketch was a member of the prominent Wright family of northeastern New York. Her father being a first cousin of Hon. Silas Wright, who served two terms as Governor of New York and also was a United States Senator. Charles was one of ten children and when he was young the family came to Erie County and located in Harborcreek township. In 1859 he was united in marriage with Hannah M. Edwards. They had five children; all but one died in childhood. Shortly after the civil war he located in North East borough, where he engaged in various enterprises and served two terms as justice of the peace. In 1876 he was elected to the state legislature where he served with distinction.

Having a natural bent for law he was registered as a law student with William Benson, Esq., and was admitted to the Erie Bar, June 25, 1888. Before coming to the bar he frequently acted as counsel in magistrates' courts and was regarded as a man of legal ability. But even after coming to the bar he gave most of his attention to other matters and seldom engaged in court practice. He was interested in mining and spent much time in the west and, during his later years, in New York City.

He was a large, handsome man with fine ability and

a delightful personality, who never seemed to grow old. He was a Mason, a Republican and a member of the Methodist Church. He was a life long student of geology and mineralogy. He died in 1914, in the seventy-eighth year of his age, and was buried in the North East Cemetery. He sleeps among his old friends in the land he considered the finest in America.

Ora L. Flinn, Esq.

Ora L. Flinn, son of William and Dardana Jones Flinn, was born in Greene township, Erie County, September 30, 1866. After completing his course at the North East High School, he studied law in the office of Judge Gunnison, also that of Col. Thompson, and was admitted to the Erie Bar, January 27, 1890, entering at once upon the practice of law at Erie, which he continued actively until prevented by his last illness. He was a hard working, painstaking young lawyer, tried his cases with ability and gave every promise of a brilliant career. But after he had been at the bar seven or eight years, his left side gradually became disabled and finally he lost the use of that arm and leg and was unable to walk. Although so grievously stricken, his mind remained clear and he continued to transact legal business. He was tall and trim built, but became heavy on being confined by his affliction. In addition to his practice, he did some real estate business.

In 1896 he was united in marriage with Miss Clara Mayo, daughter of the late Henry Mayo, who was one of Erie's most highly respected citizens. They had one child, Miss Helen Louise Flinn, who is a highly educated and accomplished young woman, holding a responsible position as teacher in Detroit, where she and her mother reside. Mr. Flinn was a Democrat and a Presbyterian.

After an illness of several years, Ora L. Flinn died, January 13, 1904, at the age of thirty-seven years, and was buried in the Erie Cemetery. "He had not reached on life's highway the stone which marks the highest point, but being weary, he rested by the wayside and fell into that dreamless sleep that kisses down the eyelids still."

Daniel McMahon, Esq.

Daniel McMahon, Esq., son of Michael and Mary Lehan McMahon, was born at Jackson Station, this county, January 10, 1859. His parents were married in this country but born and raised in Ireland. Daniel attended the public schools and Erie Academy, and at the age of thirteen became cabin boy on a lake steamer and after three years shipped as a sailor and at twenty-one became a licensed pilot, which he followed until elected alderman of the Fourth Ward, Erie, about 1883, and served for many years with great satisfaction. Meantime he studied law with Hon. John P. Vincent and was admitted to the Erie Bar July 1, 1901. Thereafter he practiced law in Erie until his death. He seldom appeared in the trial of causes but confined his attention mostly to orphans' court and office practice, also did conveyancing and handled real estate. He was thoroughly honest and faithful to his clients. True to the religion of his parents, he was ever a devout Catholic. In politics he was a Democrat. He was of medium size, smooth face and had a pleasing personality. He and I were friends for many years; occasionally he piloted myself and family for a sail upon the bay and on one or more occasions visited us on our farm. On May 6, 1890 he was united in marriage with Mary J. Leyer. They had two daughters, Agnes and Marion. Daniel McMahon gradually lost his health and died December 1, 1915, and was buried in Trinity Cemetery. His widow and daughters resided in the family home at 318 E. Sixth street, Erie, until their recent removal to Philadelphia, where Agnes is a teacher and Marion is employed by the Bell Telephone Co., both having good positions.

Chauncey Porter Rogers, Jr., Esq.

Chauncey P. Rogers, Jr., son of Col. and Mrs. Chauncey P. Rogers, was born in Erie March 15, 1869, and was of English, Swiss and Scotch extraction. His grandfather, Dr. Channing Rogers, was an eminent surgeon. At the inception of the civil war, the father of the subject of this sketch, enlisted as a private and, for meritorious and heroic services, was gradually promoted until he became Colonel of the Eighty-Third Regiment, Pennsylvania Volunteers. After the war he was elected prothonotary of Erie County and during his service as such the son, Chauncey, was born. The latter received his education in the schools of Erie and Corry and in Lehigh University. After leaving the university, he studied law with Bowman & Bole at Corry and was admitted to the Erie County Bar September 5, 1890, when twenty-one years of age, and practiced law for about twenty-five years, with offices at Corry. He had a natural aptitude for law and tried his cases exceedingly well, although he never had what might be called a large trial practice. He was, however, equally at home in court and in his office. He had many clients and gave their business careful attention. Chauncey Rogers was endowed with a brilliant intellect, excellent practical judgment and a delightful personality. He was large, handsome, cordial, the soul of honor and universally popular. He was a Republican, but never sought public office, although he served Corry with distinction as city solicitor and school director.

In addition to his law practice he had some business interests, among others was a director in the Rogers S.

S. Co., of Corry, and, as I remember, was also interested in some matters with the late Henry Kepple. Chauncey was ever an active man and had a liking for business. On December 9, 1905, he was united in marriage with Miss Alberta Louise Bush, a well known and most highly respected resident of Corry. About 1910 Hon. A. E. Sisson, then Auditor General, chose Chauncey P. Rogers, Jr., as his deputy, a position he filled with universal satisfaction during that and subsequent administrations. Had his life been spared he undoubtedly would long ere this have been Auditor General of the state, a position he was eminently qualified to fill. While holding this office he resided a few miles out of Harrisburg in Cumberland county and on the morning of December 10, 1919, on leaving home for the city he was struck and killed by an automobile. His untimely death, when in the very prime of a highly useful and honorable life, was a loss to the entire state. He had no children, but was survived by his widow, his father and by brothers and sisters. He was buried in Pine Grove Cemetery at Corry. His funeral was very largely attended and each seemed to realize, as did the writer, that he had lost a friend. He was a member of the Masonic fraternity, also of the Corry Lodge of Elks. A great lover of nature, he enjoyed yachting, motoring and other open air recreations.

George H. Higgins, Esq.

George H. Higgins, son of Moses and Nancy (Fralick) Higgins, was born in Sparta township, Crawford County, Pa., August 5, 1852. Moses Higgins was a native of Connecticut, but spent most of his life in Crawford County where he was a farmer and served thirty years as justice of the peace. The mother was a native of the state of New York. George was educated in the common schools of Crawford County and at the Watertown (N. Y.) High School. He studied law with Samuel T. Allen, Esq., at Warren and was admitted to the Warren County Bar in 1880. He then practiced for two years at Aiken, McKean County, Pa. Returning to Warren he formed a partnership with Mr. Allen, his preceptor, which continued until the latter's death in 1885. He then formed a partnership with Hon. Orren C. Allen, under the firm name of Allen & Higgins, of which William H. Allen, Esq., later became a member. About 1890 Mr. Higgins received the Republican nomination for President Judge of the Warren district, but after a momentous contest, was defeated by Hon. Charles H. Noyes, by a small majority. In 1893, Mr. Higgins withdrew from the firm in Warren and removed to Erie, being then well known here and a member of our bar for ten years, and formed a partnership with Hon. S. M. Brainerd, as Brainerd & Higgins, which did an extensive general business until the death of the former in November 1898. Thereafter Higgins continued in active practice until his last sickness. In Warren he had a large practice, was associated with men of ability and high standing, and was known as a very able lawyer. On coming to Erie he took and maintained high rank at our bar. He was a sound lawyer, a tireless worker, a strong speaker and a skillful advocate. He had great force and energy which he put into his advocacy. During his resident practice here he probably tried as many personal injury cases as any member of our bar. I sometimes appeared with him, at other times against him, and, after I became judge, he practiced before me for about eight years, so I came to know him intimately, and always regarded him a lawyer of ability. He was a large gentleman of fine appearance. When young he did manual labor and, as a brick mason, helped build the Warren court house, where he later won distinction as a lawyer. While not a wealthy man he was always prompt and reliable in his personal business affairs.

Mr. Higgins was an active Republican, a good campaign speaker, and won his party's nomination for Congress in 1898, but, at the election, was defeated by Hon. Athelston Gaston, the Democratic candidate, by seventeen votes. Higgins was twice married; his first wife died in 1890, leaving one son, Weld H., who has since died, leaving a son, George H. Higgins, who is an oil refiner residing at Warren. In 1893, Mr. Higgins was united in marriage with Miss Nancy A. Starbird, of Corry, who survived him, but has since died. There were no children of this marriage. Mr. Higgins' principal recreation was wing shooting and while so engaged, sometime prior to 1890, accidentally shot off his left hand. Despite which he continued in vigorous health until 1905, when he was tricsken with a fatal malady, died on November 19, and was buried in Oakland Cemetery, at Warren. In addition to his law practice, Mr. Higgins was president of a fraternal insurance company. When stricken he had nearly finished writing an oil country romance, which his sister very kindly completed. The book was published and well spoken of.

Don Fuller Smith, Esq.

Don F. Smith, son of Nathaniel Stacy and Dauna A. (Fuller) Smith, was born at Columbus, Warren County, Penna., May 5, 1875, was educated at the public schools and Corry High School. After studying law in the office of Hon. Albert B. Osborne, at Corry, he was admitted to the Erie Bar July 3, 1899. For a few years Mr. Smith practiced law at Corry, then for eight or ten years at Omaha, Nebraska. Returning to Corry in 1911, he resumed practice there and so continued until his death. He grew to be a strong lawyer and enjoyed a fine practice, which extended into adjoining counties. In the early years of his practice he was better known as an office and business lawyer, but in later years often appeared in court in the trial of causes and stood well in that branch of profession. I had a visit with Don late in August of this year (1928) and he spoke of being exceedingly busy. He never sought public office, but was City Solicitor for Corry.

He was a medium sized, clean shaven, fine looking gentleman, ever genial and with a personality, which inspired confidence. To know Don well was to be his friend. He was a member of the Kiwanis, a 32° Mason and an Elk. He was a loyal friend and very companionable. During the recent Sept. Term of Court he engaged in several trials and, traveling back and forth caught a severe cold, which resulted in pneumonia, causing his death on Oct. 8, 1928, at the age of fifty-three years. He was buried in Pine Grove Cemetery at Corry, the final resting place of many of our deceased brothers. He was united in marriage with Elizabeth Baker, who, with a brother, Dr. A. Louis Smith, survive. His principal recreation was making violins, of which he produced some very fine specimens; one made about twenty years ago has a value of five hundred dollars.

George Washington Barker, Esq.

George W. Barker, the descendant of a family who came to America in 1635, was born at Lansing, Iowa, March 29, 1860. He was well educated and a graduate of the Law Department of the University of Michigan, with the LL. B. degree, and was admitted to the Michigan Bar, also was admitted to the Nebraska, the Pennsylvania and the Illinois Bars and practiced in each of those states. Locating in Erie, he was admitted to our bar September 3, 1894, and practiced his profession here for some years. He was capable, industrious and gave careful attention to the business intrusted to him. He acquitted himself well whenever he appeared in court.

In 1894 he was united in marriage with Miss Jessie G. Smith, daughter of W. Barry Smith, one of Erie's best known and most substantial citizens. I knew Mr. Barker well as we were neighbors. In 1900 he located in Chicago where the family had extensive property interests and where he continued the practice of law, until his death, May 25, 1922, in the sixty-third year of his age. They had no children, but after his death, the widow returned to Erie and resides in the Smith home on West Ninth street. Mr. Barker was a tall, fine looking gentleman of excellent manners, most agreeable personality and high standing. He was fond of music, travel, the theatre and reading, which were his principal recreations. He belonged to the Episcopal Church and was a Republican. Mr. Barker and I had one thing in common; our homes were burglarized the same night by the same thief. As might have been expected his loss was greater than mine.

George E. Gibson, Esq.

George E. Gibson, son of F. W. and Tabitha (Kennedy) Gibson, was born in Perry County, Penna., October 31, 1860, and when young became a resident of Ohio and a graduate of the National Normal University at Lebanon, in that state. He also became a member of the Ohio Bar; but in 1894 returned to his native state and entered the law offices of Hon. A. E. Sisson and was admitted to the Erie Bar in the fall of 1895. He then took up legal practice here as an office associate with Clark Olds. Notwithstanding some drawback, being physically very lame, he soon won recognition as a good lawyer, an intensely earnest advocate and a man of sterling character.

On one occasion, while arguing a case before the state supreme court, his name attracted the attention of members of the court, who, upon inquiry, finding he was a great grand nephew of the late Chief Justice Gibson, invited him into the consultation room. At their request he stood underneath the portrait of that most eminent of Pennsylvania judges and they discovered a facial resemblance between them. Mr. Gibson was never physically strong and died, unmarried, on January 28, 1916. As a mark of respect and affection, a committee of his brethren of the Erie Bar accompanied his remains to their last resting place in Perry County.

Robert Henry Chinnock, Esq.

Robert H. Chinnock, son of Mr. and Mrs. Robert H. Chinnock, was born in Erie, February 22, 1872. His father came from England, when young, and became one of Erie's substantial citizens and a leading member of the Masonic fraternity. Robert was educated in the public schools and Erie High School, studied law with Hon. Samuel M. Brainerd and was admitted to the Erie Bar March 1, 1897. He at once entered upon the practice of law at Erie and so continued until his last sickness. He was a fluent speaker, enjoyed the contests of the forum and tried many cases. He was optimistic and always spoke enthusiastically about his professional work. So far as the writer knows, he never complained about anything. For a considerable time he served satisfactorily as deputy United States Marshal.

He was above medium size, had a smooth face, was a fine looking gentleman, apparently in robust health, but in the early winter of 1924, he became sick and, after a lingering illness, died March 28, 1924, at the age of fifty-two years, and was buried at Erie in Lake Side Cemetery.

On September 21, 1909, he was united in marriage with Eleanor F. Sawdey. They had five children, four sons and one daughter, who, with their mother, survive and reside in this city.

Albert Perry Howard, Esq.

A. P. Howard, of English and Scotch ancestry, was born at Franklin Centers, Erie County, Pa., August 18, 1866. The Howard family to which he belonged, was numerous and of high standing in that locality. He was educated at the Girard Academy and Edinboro State Normal School. He taught school, studied law with Hon. S. M. Brainerd and was admitted to the Erie Bar March 1, 1897. From that time until his death, he practiced law at Erie. He was a large man with an imposing genial personality and enjoyed the gift of making a good impression on his clients and the public. He soon acquired and retained a large general practice. He was lawyer for very many people from his own locality. Being admitted about the time I became judge he thereafter represented a number of people in his part of the county who had formerly been my clients. He successfully tried a number of cases against railroad companies, in one of which (Cook v. The Erie Electric Motor Company, 225 Pa. 91) he nearly "spilled the beans", so to speak, by referring to the defendant as "a great millionaire company." He practiced alone, except for about three years when he was in partnership with Leslie G. Peck, Esq. He was occasionally associated with Hon. S. A. Davenport in the trial of important cases. I especially recall that of Kuntz v. N. Y. C. & St. L. Ry., 206 Pa. 162, where they recovered and sustained a large verdict. I believe he was also associated with Judge Rossiter on one or more occasions. In addition to his trial work he did quite a large amount of general law business.

He was emphatically a man's man, greatly enjoyed

hunting, fishing and other out-door sports. He also kept an assortment of dogs and game fowls. He was a distant cousin of Commodore Perry. On December 1, 1897, he was united in marriage with Miss Lizzie Pieper, daughter of Christoph and Hannah Pieper, well known and substantial residents of Franklin Center. Mr. and Mrs. Howard have two children, George C., a graduate of Georgetown University, now an attorney in Washington, D. C., and a daughter Nellie Grace, who graduated at the Edinboro State Normal School and is a teacher in the Erie city schools. Mr. Howard was a vigorous young man but in later years his health declined and he died on April 25, 1920, at Yampa, Colorado, where he had gone in search of health. He was buried in the Girard Cemetery, the final resting place of many of his old friends and neighbors.

George Mills Titus, Esq.

George M. Titus, son of Chancey and Maria Titus, was born November 23, 1857, at Olean, New York; he was educated at the public schools and studied law with C. George Olmstead, Esq., of Corry. He was admitted to the Erie Bar, July 3, 1899, and practiced law at Corry. He was an expert bookkeeper and public accountant, and served three terms as city controller of Corry. He was an exceedingly fine gentleman of good ability and popular, but never sufficiently robust to engage strenuously in the practice of law. September 28, 1882, he married Sarah J. Crasper of Corry. They have two children, Douglas B. Titus, of Corry and a daughter, now Mrs. F. L. Elblie, of Erie. Mr. Titus was a member of the Episcopal Church, also of the Royal Arcanum and a Maccabee. He never seemed physically strong and died August 14, 1909, in the fifty-second year of his age, and was buried at Corry. He was a man of very high character, of whom his professional brethren always had a kind word and, had his health permitted, doubtless would have made good as a lawyer.

Gerry T. Kincaid, Esq.

Gerry T. Kincaid, son of Honorable Samuel E. and Dora Wilkinson Kincaid, was born June 10, 1876, in Wayne township, Erie County, Pa. After receiving a public school and Corry High School education he entered Allegheny College, from which he graduated in 1897 with the degree of "A. B." He studied law in the office of C. George Olmstead, Esq., at Corry for two and a half years and was admitted to the Erie Bar, June 25, 1900. He was later admitted to the state appellate courts, also to the federal courts including the United States Supreme Court. On his admission he at once entered upon the practice of law, with home and office at Corry where he continued actively and successfully until his death. His practice extended into Warren, Crawford and other counties. Upon the failure of Mr. Olmstead's health in 1908, Kincaid became the recognized leader of the Corry Bar and so continued while he lived. He was a tireless worker, resourceful and ever zealous for his clients and won many notable victories. One of his most brilliant early successes was saving the life of Howard, who was tried at Erie for murder and robbery. He enjoyed a large and remunerative practice, accumulated property and became interested in banking. His high standing at home is evidenced by the fact that for the last eleven years of his life he was solicitor for the city of Corry. He was an active Republican and his name was repeatedly mentioned for congress but he never embarked in politics. He was a Mason, an Elk, a member of the Rotary Club and of the Corry Country Club, also a member of the First Presbyterian Church at Corry.

On August 1, 1908, he married Miss Bess Beardsley, a teacher, who survives him. They had no children. In the domestic relations of life he was a model of thoughtful kindness. Personally he was five feet eleven inches tall, weighed about one hundred and forty-five pounds, was dark complexioned, smooth shaven, stood erect and presented a fine apeparance. He was interested in diverse recreations, but made a special hobby of none. In the fall of 1921 he was stricken with typhoid fever and died on October 2. He was buried at Corry, the city he loved. Thus ended, before fairly reaching its prime, a life remarkable for its actvity and achievements. Gerry Kincaid accomplished more in his twenty-one years at the bar than a large percentage of lawyers do in twice that time.

Louis Bear Jones, Esq.

Louis B. Jones, son of Charles and Amanda Yost Jones, was born on his father's farm in Greenfield township and was educated in the public schools and Edinboro State Normal School, from which he graduated in 1887. He taught shool before his graduation and thereafter for some time was principal of the High School at North Girard. In his work as a teacher he was energetic, faithful, painstaking and successful. He quit teaching, however, to enter the employ of the Wagner Palace Car Company at Buffalo, where he remained for some time and then entered the office of Bliley and Torry as a law student and was admitted to the Erie County Bar, July 21, 1902. Thereafter he was in active practice in Erie until his death. He was a thoroughly honest, reliable, hard working lawyer, had an unusually large acquaintance and a good practice. He enjoyed the full confidence of the court, his fellow members of the bar and the public. He did a large general office business and was very successful, although he but seldom appeared in court in the trial of causes. He was of medium size had a delightful personality and was popular with all classes. Few members of the local bar had more friends than "Lou Jones." His father was of Welsh extraction and the families of both his father and mother were among the early settlers of that part of the county. Miss Bertha Adkins, whose forbears were also early settlers at or near North East, was united in marriage with Louis B. Jones November 2, 1910. They had three children, the youngest, a daughter, born a few weeks after the death of Mr. Jones, which occurred August 4, 1915. He was buried at North East. He was an active and very useful member of the First Methodist Church at Erie. Mr. and Mrs. Jones had their home on East Sixth street in the valley of Millcreek, and in an heroic effort to save his family and property from the terrible flood of August 1, which swept through his home, he fatally injured his heart and died in four days. He was one of the thirty-four victims of that appalling calamity. His funeral, held at the home of his parents at North East, one of the largest I ever attended, was a mute evidence of the esteem in which he was held by those who knew him best. His death was peculiarly distressing to me for I had known his father and other members of the Jones family intimately since I was a small boy.

Prof. Robert J. Osborne

Robert J. Osborne, son of Robert John and Caroline Newton Osborne, was born at Beaverdam, Erie County, June 14, 1870. He graduated at the Corry High School in 1889 and at Buchtel College of Liberal Arts at Akron, Ohio, in 1893, with the Ph. B. degree. He received a scholarship and the Law Essay Prize for excellent work in college. After graduation from college he taught school for eight years in Corry and one year in Wilmington, Delaware, also did tutoring. Taking up the study of law, he entered the office of C. George Olmstead, Esq., at Corry, completed the course and was admitted to the Erie Bar June 22, 1903. He entered at once upon the practice of law at Corry and continued actively therein until his death. He enjoyed a good office and general practice, mostly of a business nature and the settlement of estates and seldom appeared in the trial of causes. He was in every respect a thorough gentleman of the highest character and greatly esteemed by the profession and the public. He was painstaking and the papers he presented to the court were uniformly prepared with care and accuracy. He was intensely interested in the World War and assisted over two hundred young men and families during its continuance.

He was tall, light complexioned, athletic, and of fine appearance. He made a host of loyal friends in college and as a teacher. He joined freely with his pupils in their athletic sports and yet maintained their entire respect. He was an amateur photographer, enjoyed the bicycle, was an enthusiastic motorist, a great admirer of football, was fond of music and played the violin. He was a Methodist by inheritance and a Democrat in politics. He had a saving sense of humor, was a charming companion and greatly enjoyed the visits of his college chums.

On October 14, 1895, he was united in marriage with Miss Clara M. Auer, of Corry. They had one child, a son, Joseph Crosby Osborne. Prof. Robert J. Osborne died Feb. 24, 1919, and was buried in Pine Grove Cemetery at Corry. He was survived by his wife and son, but sad to relate, the son has since died.

Joseph Crosby Osborne, Esq.

Joseph C. Osborne, son of Prof. Robert J. and Clara M. Auer Osborne, was born in Corry, February 1, 1898, He graduated as high honor pupil at the Corry High School, attended, as his father had done, the Buchtel College of Liberal Arts of the University of Akron, where he graduated with the degree of "Ph. B.," then took the course at the Western Reserve University Law School at Cleveland. He was a "Phi Beta Kappa" at college and obtained the "Order of the Coif" at Law School. He was a member of the Lone Star Fraternity at the University of Akron, was in the War Training Camp at the University and volunteered as nurse during the influenza. He was a Mason, a Democrat and a regular attendant of the Presbyterian Church. He was admitted to the Superior Court of Ohio in July, 1924, and to the Supreme Court of Pennsylvania and to the Erie Bar in October of the same year. He immediately entered upon the practice of his chosen profession in Corry, but before his life's work was fairly started, death overtook him on May 9, 1925, and he rests in Pine Grove Cemetery, beside his father, the man he loved best. It has been said "Death loves a shining mark." Certainly the decrees of Providence are sometimes shrouded in mystery.

He was six feet tall, not so strongly built as his father, but fond of college sports, bowling, basket ball, etc.; he was also fond of out-door sports, including swimming, hunting, fishing, motoring, etc. As indicating the true type of young man he was, it may be mentioned that on one occasion in college some of his fellow students were called up for reprimand for some misconduct, and he was not, but voluntarily stepped forward and said he was as guilty as the rest and deserved a like reprimand.

Leslie Gardner Peck, Esq.

Leslie G. Peck, son of Gardner E. and Sarah A. (Shadduck) Peck, was born in Harborcreek township, Erie County, Pa., February 1, 1877. He graduated from the Edinboro State Normal School in June, 1895. Later he attended State College (1897-8) one year. Then entered the law department of the University of Michigan, from which he graduated in 1902, with the L. L. B. degree. He did teaching to assist in defraying his college expenses. Returning home he entered the law office of Thomas C. Miller, Esq., was admitted to the Erie Bar, January 12, 1903, and immediately entered upon the practice with offices in Erie. He was a young lawyer of exceptional ability, industry and high ideals and soon became known as such to the court and bar. His ability as an advocate was also soon recognized and in a few years he assisted other young lawyers and sometimes older lawyers in the trial of causes. He was clear and concise in the statement of legal principles and fair, moderate and strong in his discussion of the facts. His frankness and candor enhanced the value of his advocacy. What Leslie Peck said always received respectful attention. While modest, there was not a lawyer at our bar with better moral courage. He continued in active practice here until 1912, being for about three years in company with A. P. Howard, Esq. Meantime his health became precarious and required him to spend some time in the west. Finally he was compelled to retire from active practice and he moved with his family to Wesleyville. Soon as his health permitted he engaged in house building there and also in the real estate business and then opened a law office in Wesleyville, and attended to some practice, became boro solicitor and justice of the peace. Although living in Wesleyville, he was in the automobile business with a man named Watson in Erie for about three years, ending in 1925.

Notwithstanding his long continued ill health and being compelled to abandon the work of his life, he remained serene and never uttered a complaint or an impatient word. He was a consistent member of the Central Presbyterian Church at Erie for twenty-three years, also belonged to Perry Lodge, F. & A. M. and the Royal Arcanum. He was fond of baseball and hunting.

On September 5, 1900, he was united in marriage with Miss Jane Edith Bole of Venango, Crawford Co., Pa. They have two sons, Leslie E., born in 1903, and Donald Bole, born in 1908. Mr. Peck's health continued frail until he died on April 19, 1926, and was buried in the North East Cemetery. Few have come to our bar in whom I felt a greater interest than Leslie Peck. I was acquainted with his parents before he was born and knew Gardner Peck well as a citizen and road commissioner of Harborcreek township. I knew his grandfather Peck sixty years ago, and I taught school in Venango township in the district where his mother's parents, Mr. and Mrs. George Shadduck resided over fifty years ago and was a frequent guest at their home. Both families came originally from Connecticut and were among the first settlers in that part of the county, in fact, Leslie's great uncle, Ira Shadduck, was the first white child born in Greenfield township. Leslie G. Peck's physical breakdown and premature death was a decided loss to our bar.

Edward A. Solomon, Esq.

Edward A. Solomon, son of Rudolph and Frances Solomon, was born in Erie, February 17, 1876. He was of German parentage and was educated in the public schools and after graduating from the Erie Central High School in 1895, entered the University of Buffalo and graduated from the law department thereof in 1901, with the L. L. B. degree. Thereupon he was admitted to the New York State Bar, where he practiced for a time, being connected with a Buffalo law firm. Later, locating in this city, he was admitted to the Erie Bar, October 19, 1903. Three years thereafter he engaged in mercantile business and so continued successfully for some nine years. Returning to Erie he resumed the practice of law, which he continued until his death. He had a considerable practice and seemed to be well established in his profession when he died on July 30, 1926, at the age of fifty years. He was buried in the Jewish Cemetery.

Mr. Solomon was under medium height, of gentle manners and good appearance. He was a Republican, an Elk, a Knight of Pythias, a member of the Protected Home Circle, of the B'nai Brith and of the Men's Club of the Jewish Temple. He married Miss Lillian Klein of Cleveland, and left a daughter and five sisters. His untimely death was not only a great loss to his family, but a shock to his numerous friends in Erie and elsewhere.

It may be noteworthy that I am writing memoirs of so many of my juniors at the bar.

Gustave H. Brevillier, Esq.

Gustave H. Brevillier, son of Henry L. and Elise Eichorn Brevillier, was born in Erie, September 9, 1882, and graduated at Erie High School in 1899, as president of the class. He studied law in the office of Allen and Rosenzweig and was admitted to the bar in 1904. After a brief practice in Erie he located in New York City, where he soon became known as an able lawyer and was phenomenally successful. He was tall, well built and apparently in good health, but he died August 20, 1923, and was buried in Washington, D. C. In 1918 he was married to Miss Eugenia Klein of that city, who survives him. They had no children. Gustave Brevillier was a member of one of Erie's best families and had a host of friends here, who were delighted at his success and greatly shocked at his early death.

Harry Knapp Blake, Esq.

Harry K. Blake, son of Captain Henry Thomas (U. S. N.) and Margaret (Dalton) Blake, was born in Detroit, September 7, 1871. His parents were of Irish lineage, but born in this country. He graduated from the Erie High School in the class of 1890 and, after spending some time in the University of Pennsylvania, became a law student in the Philadelphia offices of Judge F. Carroll Brewster, one of the state's leading lawyers and jurists and an outstanding legal author. In 1894, on motion of Judge Brewster, Mr. Blake was admitted to the several courts of Philadelphia and later to the U. S. Circuit and District Courts and to the Supreme Court of Pennsylvania. He was a brilliant young lawyer and, with offices in Philadelphia, soon enjoyed a practice extending into adjoining states.

On June 28, 1898, he was united in marriage with Miss Katharine Brown, of Erie, daughter of Conrad J. Brown, formerly Water Commissioner of Erie City and also Treasurer of Erie County. Mr. and Mrs. Blake resided in Philadelphia until they returned to Erie in 1907 when Mr. Blake was admitted to our bar and for the balance of his life practiced his profession here. During that time he also practiced in the U. S. District and Circuit Courts. He was a brilliant man of charming personality and popular with his brethren of the bar, but, because of ill health in his later years, never attained the position at our bar to which his fine abilities entitled him. He was above medium height, clean shaven and of fine appearance. He was of athletic build and never lost his ability to play baseball. He died February 24, 1917, and was buried in Erie. He left a widow and a son, James Campbell Blake, a naval officer, who graduated from the United States Naval Academy at Annapolis in 1922; also a daughter, now Mrs. Donald T. Brebner, of this city. While located in Philadelphia, Mr. Blake was for a time in partnership with William Gorman & Sons. In religion he was a Catholic and a member of the society known as the "Friendly Sons of St. Patrick," also member of the Philadelphia Law Association, of the Society of the Students of Judge Brewster, and of the Erie Lodge of Elks.

Lytle Flower Perry, Esq.

Lytle F. Perry, son of Rev. David E. S. and Maud (Townley) Perry, was born at Albion, Erie County, Pa., May 18, 1888. His father is a Protestant Episcopal clergyman. Lytle was educated at Allegheny College and, after studying law in the offices of Lewis, Jones and Lewis at Coudersport, was admitted to the Potter County Bar in June 1911. For some years he practiced in that county with his preceptors, then located in Erie and was admitted to our bar March 14, 1914, where he continued in active practice until his death. In 1919 he established the Erie County Law Journal, now in its ninth year, and remained its sole proprietor as long as he lived. This publication proved a great benefit to the profession.

On January 5, 1909, he was united in marriage with Miss Eugenia C. Benson, granddaughter of the late Hon. Isaac Benson of Coudersport, in his day, one of the foremost citizens of Potter County. It was to him that his brother, the late William Benson, of our bar, said in his will, "Isaac has plenty." Mr. Perry enjoyed in a high degree the confidence of his professional brethren and the public, and his untimely death, on November 30, 1927, resulting from an automobile accident while on a hunting trip to Warren County, was greatly deplored. He was buried at Coudersport and left surviving, his widow and three children. He was a member of the Episcopal Church.

Lee Griswold, Esq.

Lee Griswold, son of Senator Marvin E. and Leila (Lee) Griswold, was born in Erie, February 15, 1899. He attended public school until he was stricken with infantile paralysis when fourteen years of age. Despite this great handicap he traveled extensively with his family and later took full courses at Yale, both in the literary and law departments, where he won high honors. Returning home he was admitted to the Erie Bar, April 19, 1926, and began practice, being for a time associated with Brooks, English and Quinn. The affliction, however, against which he had made such an heroic struggle for fifteen years, gradually destroyed his vitality and he died January 16, 1928, and was buried at the old family home of the Griswolds in Connecticut. With high ideals, with a brilliant intellect, with a family name second to none in the city, Lee Griswold departed this life at the age of twenty-nine years. He was an only child and is survived by his mother, his father, Senator Griswold, having died a year previously.

Other Members

I have been constrained to omit from separate mention the names of some of our deceased brothers, not from lack of merit on their part but from lack of information. In February 1905, Judge John P. Vincent, then in his eighty-eighth year, read an article concerning the Early Bench and Bar before the Erie County Historical Society in which after speaking of Hon. Thomas H. Sill, he says:

"The next member of the bar to open an office in Erie was GEORGE A. ELLIOT, Esq. He was a college graduate. He practiced law successfully for many years, and then retired from practice. He was a cultivated and most agreeable gentleman. I had the honor of his friendship and enjoyed with him many a pleasant and instructive hour, and the recollection of them is still a pleasant memory.....

"JOHN S. RIDDLE opened an office here about the same time that Mr. Walker did (1824). He, too, was a college man. He was one of the ablest lawyers in Western Pennsylvania. He was never very robust in health, and died in the prime of life. He was a thorough lawyer, and a successful one, so far as his health permitted. He represented the county in the legislature for two terms.—

"WILLIAM KELLEY came here about the same time. He was a good lawyer, and had a large practice at one time, but his health was frail and he soon gave up the active practice of the law for other pursuits. He was largely instrumental in procuring the incorporation of the Erie Canal company, and also in the construction of the Erie & North East railroad. He was prothonotary for two years.....

"The HON. JOHN GALBRAITH came here from Venango County in 1839. He formed a partnership with Carson Graham, Esq., who had been admitted to the bar in 1837. The firm soon had a large practice. Mr. Graham subsequently removed to Wisconsin, where he became judge of the courts......

"WILLIAM M. WATTS was admitted to the bar in 1839. His father and two of his brothers were able and distinguished lawyers in the eastern part of the state. Mr. Watts represented the county for two terms in the legislature. He was one of the most companionable of men and had hosts of friends wherever he was known. He was more inclined to politics than law.....

"MATTHEW TAYLOR was admitted in 1845. He was a man of great ability and had acquired a high reputation as a clear-headed, able lawyer. But his health was poor and he died a comparatively young man.....

"SAMUEL A. LAW was admitted to the bar in 1841. He had a fine, clear, legal mind, and would have risen to distinction as a lawyer. I knew him well and intimately. We were room-mates for a long time. A few years after his admission to the bar he went back to his native town in the state of New York, and became prominent in the politics of the state. He, too, died in the prime of life."...

Judge Vincent's article speaks of many other members of the bar of which we have written more at large in these sketches. Speaking of Carson Graham, some thirty years ago, a large, handsome gentleman of middle age called on me and introduced himself as Prosper Graham, son of Carson Graham. Aside from the facts stated by Judge Vincent, Carson Graham served as district attorney, and I am aware that he was an exceptionally able lawyer.

HON. MURRAY WHALLON, born in 1816, was admitted to the Erie Bar, October 19, 1839, and was in active practice for many years. He was the second Mayor of Erie after it became a city. I do not see his name mentioned among Judge Vincent's sketches; if not, the omission was accidental, for I know the judge had a high opinion of Mr. Whallon, both as to ability and character.

HORACE M. HAWES practiced law here for some years and served as district attorney in 1846. (Of course prior to 1853 each district attorney was appointed as deputy attorney general). Later, removing to California, he acquired great wealth.

C. S. GZOWSKI, who was admitted to the Erie Bar in 1839, removed to Canada, where he acquired such fame that a monument was erected to his memory at or near Niagara Falls.

M. D. CHRISTY, who was admitted to the Erie Bar in 1885, came highly recommended from the Warren, Pa., Bar, and engaged in practice here for several years. He was a lawyer of good ability, but soon became the victim of declining health and died many years ago.

EDWARD GRAZER was admitted to the Erie Bar in 1876, but remained here only a short time. He was then of middle age and of kindly bearing, but where located or what the years brought him, I know not.

EARL N. SACKETT, a large, young gentleman of excellent appearance, was admitted to the Erie Bar in 1875, and for some five years practiced his profession with offices at Union City. Later he located at or near Buffalo. I cannot write his obituary for as far as I know he may still be living. I started to write a sketch of Albert B. Force, Esq., who was district attorney of this county from 1875 to 1878 and then discovered he was still living and a resident of the state of Washington.* Both Danford R. Cushman, residing at North East, and Thomas S. Woodruff, residing at Girard, came to the bar ahead of Mr. Sackett.

DON CHARLES BARRETT was admitted to the Erie Bar in 1826 and was in active practice here for some years, and served as district attorney in 1835. At one time he was a law partner of James C. Marshall.

WILLIAM BRIGDEN came here from Crawford County and was admitted to the Erie Bar in 1849. He lived here for many years, but was never in very active practice.

JUDGE C. C. CONVERSE, who resided for some years on West Sixth street, was admitted to the Erie Bar in 1874, but never engaged in active practice here.

JOHN F. DUNCOMBE, formerly of this county, was admitted to the Erie Bar in 1854 and located at Fort Dodge, Iowa, where he engaged in practice for many years and became one of the leading lawyers of that state.

Note: *Mr. Force died Sept. 24, 1928.

CHARLES HORTON, Esq., who had been a prominent pioneer resident of Elk County, removed to North East about the close of the Civil War and was admitted to the Erie Bar, January 29, 1866. He was in every respect a high type citizen, but I believe never took up the practice in this county.

DR. F. H. ABELL, a prominent Erie dentist, studied law while practicing his profession, and was admitted to the Erie Bar in 1877, but continued in active practice as a dentist and never entered upon the legal profession.

The last two side judges in Erie County, Hon. William Benson and Hon. Allen A. Craig, were admitted to the bar near the close of their official terms, but so far as I know never became active at the bar.

DONNELL WILSON MARSH, member of a prominent Erie County family and nephew of Ritchie T. Marsh, Esq., was admitted to the Erie Bar, September 20, 1926. He began practice with Marsh & Eaton, but was killed in an automobile accident, June 21, 1928. He was an exemplary young man of great promise and his untimely death caused universal regret. He was buried at Waterford.

*

THOMAS J. WELLS, a brother of the late Capt. John L. Wells, of this city, studied law with Hon. S. A. Davenport and was admitted to the Erie Bar, August 4, 1864. He located in the west and died many years ago. So far as I am informed he never entered upon the practice in this county.

INDEX

	Page
Dedication	5
Forword	7
Abell, Dr. F. H.	360
Allen, Hon. George Ambrose	181
Allison, James Wallace	253
Babbitt, Hon. Elijah	21
Baker, Cassius Leland	171
Baker, Hiram Abiff	169
Barker, George Washington	336
Barrett, Don Charles	359
Battles, Rush S.	140
Benson, Judge Paul Allen	102
Benson, William	93
Benson, Hon. William	360
Blake, Harry Knapp	352
Blakeslee, Henry W.	219
Blickensderfer, Ulrich	241
Bole, Hon. Andrew Fayette	247
Bowman, Hon. Charles Ordean	158
Brady, Hon. John C.	293
Brainerd, Hon. Samuel Myron	195
Brevillier, Gustave H.	352
Brewer, Eben	312
Brigden, William	359
Brooks, Samuel B.	212
Brown, Major Isaac Brownell	205
Brown, Colonel William Wallace	202
Burchfield, Charles Sealon	319
Burnham, Charles	157
Burns, Prof. James R.	315
Butterfield, Hon. Henry	179

	Page
Camphausen, Hon. Edward	164
Caughey, Rev. Andrew Harvey	121
Cessna, Judge Johnathan Boone	237
Chapman, Captain William Brooks	234
Chinnock, Robert Henry	338
Christy, M. D.	358
Converse, Judge C. C.	359
Covell, Alphonso William	214
Covell, Clarence Lewis	215
Craig, Hon. Allen A.	360
Crosby, Hon. Manly	190
Curtis, Colonel Carlton B.	43
Curtze, Herman Jerome	257
Cutler, Hon. George H.	52
Davenport, Hon. Samuel A.	131
De Camp, Hon. George W.	150
Downing, Hon. Jerome Francis	143
Duncombe, John F.	359
Dunlap, Hon. James Darwin	48
Dunlap, Captain Myron Erastus	239
Elliot, George A.	356
Flinn, Ora L.	328
Force, Albert Burwell	305
Force, Joseph May	283
Foster, Alburn J.	162
Gaither, Hon. Paul Hugus	251
Galbraith, Davenport	40
Galbraith, Judge John	31
Galbraith, Hon. John	357
Galbraith, John William	39
Galbraith, Judge William Ayres	33
Gibson, George E.	337
Gilson, Samuel Loren	288
Gould, Colonel Edward Powell	262

	Page
Grant, Colonel Benjamin	86
Grant, Frank Wilder	88
Grazer, Edward	358
Griffith, George Perry	137
Griffith, William	141
Griswold, Lee	355
Gunnison, Judge Frank	106
Gunnison, Hon. Jonas	104
Gzowski, C. S.	358
Hallock, John Keese	209
Hawes, Horace M	358
Heydrick, Charles	323
Higgins, George H.	332
Hinds, Calvin J.	54
Hitchcock, Hon. Charles Addison	326
Horton, Charles	360
Howard, Albert Perry	339
Hutchinson, Captain David Wells	147
Hyner, John L.	211
Johnson, Hon. John Barnette	68
Jones, Louis Bear	344
Kelley, William	356
Kelso, Hon. Chas. W.	42
Kelso, William C.	41
Kincaid, Gerry T.	342
Laird, Hon. Wilson	112
Lamb, Theodore Albert	224
Lane, William S.	73
Lathy, George William	217
Lathy, William Edward	219
Law, Samuel A.	357
Longstreet, Francis Price	194
Longstreet, Rev. Samuel Price	192
Lovett, Charles E.	248
Lynch, Col. Charles M.	167

	Page
Mallory, Corwin H.	317
Marsh, Donnell Wilson	360
Marshall, Francis F.	29
Marshall, James C.	26
Marvin, Judge Selden	128
McClintock, Frank M.	280
McCreary, General David B.	115
McMahon, Daniel	329
Norton, Lysander Sterrett	45
O'Brien, Joseph Patrick	300
Olds, Clark	265
Olmstead, C. George	260
Osborne, Hon. Albert Buell	321
Osborne, Joseph Crosby	348
Osborne, Prof. Robert J.	346
Parmlee, Colonel James Oliver	221
Peck, Leslie Gardner	349
Perry, Lytle Flower	354
Phelps, Mortimer	121
Pierce, Captain Charles Le Roy	278
Proudfit, John	271
Rambo, David W.	154
Reed, Gen. Charles Manning	14
Reid, Major Bernard J.	231
Reid, Craig J.	270
Riblet, Henry Michael	177
Riddle, John S.	356
Rilling, Hon. John Steven	302
Rogers, Chauncey Porter, Jr.	330
Rosenzweig, Louis	186
Sackett, Earl N.	359
Sawdey, David Adolphus	290
Sill, Hon. James	11
Sill, Hon. Thomas Hale	9

	Page
Smith, Don Fuller	335
Solomon, Edward A.	351
Southern, Judge Henry	228
Spencer, Samuel Selden	124
Sproul, James W.	243
Sterrett, David Brice Innis	155
Strong, Prof. Henry Adonijah	297
Sturgeon, John Calvin	174
Taylor, Matthew	357
Terry, Dr. Henry R.	123
Thompson, Chief Justice James	74
Thompson, Colonel James Ross	78
Thompson, William L. Scott	84
Thorpe, Dr. Francis Newton	307
Titus, George Mills	341
Truesdell, Albert	313
Vincent, Judge John Pericles	57
Vincent, General Strong	64
Walker, Hon. John H.	15
Walker, Major John William	19
Wallace, William	149
Watts, William M.	357
Wells, Thomas J.	360
Wetmore, Jerome W.	111
Whallon, Hon. Murray	358
White, Charles Lafayette	299
Whittelsey, Judge Edward Lyman	274
Woodruff, Hon. Samuel Ebenezer	90
Yard, Henry C.	286
Young, Willard J.	324

www.ingramcontent.com/pod-product-compliance
Lightning Source LLC
Chambersburg PA
CBHW071952220426
43662CB00009B/1101